Among the favorite hunting spots of King Henry IV of France was a forest on the side of a hill topped by an old feudal castle, a modest church, and a few houses and inns. The name of this isolated village without a history was Versailles.

Jacques Levron describes the growth of Versailles from a sleepy country town into a royal court renowned for its elegance and splendor with the insight of one who understands the unique personalities of the monarchs responsible for its history. Henry IV hunted in the forests of Versailles, but it was Louis XIII, tired of long trips back to Paris after pleasant recreation, who decided to establish a manor house there. It was his château, gradually embellished and transformed, that was to remain the heart and soul of the huge palace constructed over a period of thirty years by the Sun King— Louis XIV. This magnificent palace was to house the court through the reigns of Louis XV and Louis XVI, until the French Revolution put an end to its particular little world.

Against the historical background of the palace and the kings, M. Levron paints a fascinating picture of the daily activities of all those who participated in court life. He describes the way in which the king spent his day, from the moment he rose in the morning, ceremonially attended by his highest-ranking noblemen, to the moment he went to bed at night. Each move he made during his waking hours was prescribed by etiquette, and the same was true for all who

asts,
nes,
l by

n of
the
l to
for
tful
ign
rts
ce,

er-
ev-     ief of
rld     ailles.
An-     Uni-
nts     ionale
ich     e ap-
tly     *Deux*
        , and
        wards

ANY
.Y. 10022

DAILY LIFE AT VERSAILLES IN
THE SEVENTEENTH AND EIGHTEENTH CENTURIES

JACQUES LEVRON

# DAILY LIFE
# AT VERSAILLES
## IN THE SEVENTEENTH
## AND EIGHTEENTH CENTURIES

*Translated by Claire Eliane Engel*

THE MACMILLAN COMPANY
New York

Library of Congress Catalog Card Number: 68-31604

FIRST AMERICAN EDITION 1968

Translated from the French *La Vie Quotidienne à la Cour de Versailles*

© Hachette, Paris, 1965

The Macmillan Company, New York
Collier-Macmillan Canada Ltd., Toronto, Ontario

*Printed in the United States of America*

# CONTENTS

# CONTENTS

# ILLUSTRATIONS

# LIFE AT COURT
# BEFORE VERSAILLES

The Kings of France were always itinerant. They actually enjoyed travelling from the palace in the city to the fortress of Vincennes, from Chinon to Fontainebleau, from the Louvre to St Germain-en-Laye, and this vagrant life was one of the most characteristic features of court life. It also lends some difficulty to describing the court's everyday life, for the scene was constantly shifting. The courtier—there is nothing invidious about the word—was fulfilling a domestic function in relation to his master; he had no definite daily task and he retained some freedom of speech and movement.

### THE VALOIS COURT

The emergence of etiquette under François I, and the permanent presence of women, which was much appreciated by the son of Louise of Savoy, modified the court image. The role of every participant was fixed. From dawn till dark, courtiers followed one another as in a well-planned ballet: it was the most eminent of the princes who handed the King his shirt, and the first gentleman of the bedchamber supervised his dressing. 'Here,' remarked Brântome, 'is fine, grand and honourable employment.' This chronicler of the activities of gay ladies had been familiar with the great noblemen for so long that he knew all the gossip about them. Hunting, dining, walking, supping, dancing and attending upon the Queen were pastimes which left nothing to chance or fancy. And yet the number of people who surrounded the King increased continuously during the sixteenth century. All the people who crowded into the palace tended to form a screen between him and his subjects, to separate him from the nation. It was a fault which worsened under the Bourbons.

As the influence of foreign courts increased—especially that of

Spain—etiquette became stricter and more finicky. Everyone had to comply with it on pain of losing the master's favour. Catherine de Medici, who had not forgotten the example of the Italian princes, used to remind her son, Charles IX, of the principles that her late husband had put into practise. Even entertainments were regulated, and gaming was allowed only in accordance with precise regulations.

Luckily, gentlemen had various distractions which required less discretion: equestrian games, jousts and tilts which provided them with opportunities to display a physical energy that pleased the ladies who usually attended such spectacles. When the games became lively, they could indulge in a certain freedom of gesture and speech, but etiquette resumed its sway as soon as the games were over.

A whole population of suppliers made their living out of the court. Some of them followed the King on his journeys, and were known as the 'purveyors of the retinue', taking part in its everyday life. They did not always make a fortune, for the nobles—as we shall see later—paid them badly or not at all. Yet the title of 'royal purveyor' provided them with a less exalted but richer clientele that was proud to patronize the same merchants as the King. They were actually part of the court décor. They were welcome at the Louvre as well as at Blois; they were summoned to attend the King and always endeavoured to please him. But they could only approach him under escort of royal guards.

As was the case at the Italian courts, the King was surrounded, protected and difficult of access. At the end of the century civil wars disrupted for a time the recent and well-planned court regulations. Superficially, etiquette had not been changed, yet a wind of discord and disfavour often passed over the court. People had to be very careful about their speech, or they risked exile. It was better to follow the advice of the poet, Jean Dupuis:

> 'Vous qui avez le vent à gré
> Et qui savez flatter la cour,
> Gardez-vous bien que le degré
> A descendre ne vois soit court.'[1]

[1] 'Oh, you who know whence the wind bloweth, and how to flatter the court, beware, lest the step you descend be not a quick one.'

The ladder of honour was easier to descend than to ascend, as many noblemen knew from bitter experience.

Before ascending the throne, Henri III had gathered round him a retinue of magistrates and soldiers. Catherine de Medici had warned him against these favourites but in vain. The quarrels that broke out between the King's followers and those who sided with his enemies were often settled by duels. Even the ladies took sides: 'We are always ready to cut each other's throats', wrote Henri of Navarre, who was not altogether displeased by such excitements. 'We carry daggers, mail shirts and often breast-plates under our cloaks.'

A few weeks later, Henri III was murdered at St Cloud and the court dispersed. The King of Navarre, out to conquer his kingdom, was not likely to yield to an etiquette which did not fit in with a campaigning life.

## HENRI IV'S REIGN

So the normal order of things changed profoundly during Henri IV's reign. Henri loved simplicity. Obviously, the *Vert Galant* was able, when he thought fit and when circumstances required, to display himself as the grandest of monarchs and to arrange solemn festivities carefully.

He was the only southerner ever to reign over France and he was quite able to display regal grandeur when necessary. Otherwise, the court looked like a gay pageant in which Valois formality, that had seen better days, had to go hand in hand with lively familiarity. The guard was still there, but they had to allow entry to the King's friends, his innumerable compatriots from Béarn or Navarre. The King mixed with them all, chatted and joked with everyone. It was a merry sight. Henri IV would call to one and greet another; he had an unbelievable visual memory and was never wrong; 'Your servant, Bellegarde, your faithful servant!'

He had the same easy-going attitude at audiences. The time would come when to see the King at Versailles would involve passing almost insuperable obstacles, but Henri IV liberally granted audience to all who asked. Contemporary witnesses were positive about this: 'As for those who came to discuss business with him, he greeted them with endless caresses, met them and often kissed them.' (Legrain). 'He loved to chat with those who came from the provinces to see him, to make them talk about their business and about what was happening in the country, and to this or that man.' (Villeegontier).

Meals were equally simple. The formality of the Valois had been abandoned. Everyone came and went freely. The King loved to chat with those around him, and their table manners were not always very pleasant. One whose duty it was to taste the wine— that is, to drink a few drops, poured into the cover of the glass to make sure it contained no poison—actually drained the whole glass. He may have been thirsty, or just absent-minded. Under Henri III he would have been ignominiously dismissed from court and deprived of his office; but Henri IV merely said: 'At least you might have drunk my health.'

The afternoon was given over to walking, gambling or hunting. Henri himself loved to roam through Paris. He showed his usual familiarity to all he met. As Philippe Erlanger remarks, his familiarity spread from him to others, not from them to him. There is a whole collection of anecdotes about the King and the people he met on his way, and of dialogues between them, for Henri did not always use his coach. He rode on horseback or even walked. He loved the spectacle of the street, chatted or joked and never failed to take off his hat to the ladies who looked at him from their windows as he passed.

When he returned from his walk, the King indulged almost daily in his favourite pastime: gambling. Again, he preferred people of 'small substance' to respectful courtiers, and they were sometimes of doubtful origin. They played for very high stakes and the parties went on very late into the night. Henri often lost and Rosny used to grumble that he had to disburse very large sums of money. The minister used to lecture his master about this and was always quite outspoken. Henri would answer him and the following celebrated remark throws a clear light on the King's temper:

'Some blame me for caring too much for new buildings and rich display, others for hunting and dogs and falcons, others for cards and dice and other such games; others blame me for my liking for the ladies and for the delights of life; others for feasts, banquets and junkettings; others for assemblies, comedies, balls, dancing and ring-tilting . . . yet would I say that, so long as they go not too far, such pastimes should rather be praised than blamed.'

And he added:

'Besides, I will make those people see that I would give up mistresses, love-making, dogs, hawking, games, cards, building, feasts, banquets and all other pleasures and pastimes rather than lose the slightest opportunity to achieve honour and glory.'

In fact, Henri spent some part of his evenings working. He received his ministers, talked with them and wrote letters. He never neglected the affairs of state.

Could he really give up love-making and hunting, as he claimed? He used to hunt every day, for several hours, and he passed this enthusiasm on to all his descendants. Henri's hunts became legendary. He hunted in all the forests that surrounded his capital, at St Germain-en-Laye, St Cloud, Vincennes and Grosbois.

He also hunted in a forested region of ponds and sandy soil on the side of a hill topped by an old feudal castle, partly repaired during the Renaissance, a modest church, a few houses and some inns.

The name of this village without a history was Versailles.

# CHAPTER ONE

# LOUIS XIII AND VERSAILLES

To judge Louis XIII impartially and lucidly is particularly difficult. He was long regarded as a secretive, melancholy and mysterious prince; but the impression was false, for Louis XIII was the victim of the memoir writers and of Alexandre Dumas, and a fairer assessment of a king with whom Richelieu incessantly worked to the greater glory of France is long overdue.

Was Louis XIII secretive? He had his intimates—some of them rather too intimate—and he relied on Cardinal de Richelieu, though sometimes their tempers clashed. Was he melancholy? No prince was more gay or fonder of pageants, dancing and music. An excellent musician himself—his son was to inherit his taste—he actually wrote ballets which he took great pleasure in staging and performing, a foretaste of the entertainments of the Grand Siècle.

The truth was that the King preferred a small gathering to a big audience. He could make a sacrifice to pomp and ceremony, but he delighted in more intimate settings. Fontainebleau, St Germain-en-Laye, the Louvre, all those majestic palaces in which he mainly lived, were too big for his own taste. He had always to be on show.

That is why he tried to retire into a closed and obscure place, still unnoticed by the bulk of his subjects. Versailles was exactly what he needed.

Saint-Simon's well-known lines, in which he mercilessly castigated the region, have been quoted frequently: 'A thankless, dreary place, without a view, without woods, without water, without soil, for there is nothing there but shifting sands and marshes, without air, which can not be good.'

This was a gross exaggeration, although it is true that Versailles is surrounded by hillocks and forests, several brooks had carved valleys at the foot of low hills: on the side of one of them clung the old castle and the church; on another was a windmill. The third rose in the north towards St Germain: this was the hill of St

Antoine. The configuration of the land was strange: the road crept up slowly from Sèvres to Versailles and yet, when looking at the view from Cour de Marbre or the heights of Satory, one feels as if Versailles were at the bottom of a basin. It is enough to go to the second floor of the palace or to its roofs to discover westward a huge expanse of land, the plain of St Cyr which, at the time of Louis XIII, stretched out open and empty mostly, except for the belfries of villages standing out in the distance—St Cyr, Villepreux, Fontenay, Bailly—and the dark groves that merged into the forests of Marly and St Germain. 'Without woods, without water, without soil' wrote Saint-Simon; it would be difficult to be more mistaken.

On one point alone was Saint-Simon right: marshes were numerous and scattered through the region. From the 'Stinking Pool' to the Clagny marsh those stretches of water were far from pleasant. They were filled up gradually. Besides, the village was difficult of access. There was only one road, the one from Sèvres to Villepreux. Bad tracks connected these hamlets to the mill.

But it was, perhaps, the very isolation of this lost village which attracted Louis XIII. And to attract him to this 'thankless, dreary place' there were his childhood recollections. He had hunted there on August 24, 1607, when he was six years old. His doctor, Héroard, has recorded the scene: 'Tetay', said Louis to Ventelay, the master of his household, 'have the coach ready, I want to hunt'. At four-thirty he got into the coach to go hawking; he was taken towards the stone mill near Versailles and he came back with a levret, five or six quail and two partridges. He gave his orders with heat and passion. Louis XIII never forgot Versailles. After 1621 he often went back there to hunt. When he hunted at the end of the afternoon, he decided not to go back to the Louvre, and had himself invited to supper in the old castle which now belonged to the Gondis, and spent the night at St Germain-en-Laye, barely three leagues away. So it was on March 15, 1621, on March 6, 1624, and on June 28th of the same year. On that day he had left Paris very late and only reached Versailles at five in the evening. He hunted a fox and returned to the Louvre at eight. This compulsory ride home to St Germain or Paris irritated Louis. That is why in 1624 he made up his mind to have a hunting-box at Versailles, a simple little house where he could retire with friends to spend the night. From sixteen different owners he bought for less than 10,000

18

*livres* an estate which already totalled 117 *arpents*.[1] Most of it was on the hillock facing the village, on the plateau and among the woods.

It was just a rabbit warren. It was soon completed by a very simple building, a 'manor-house'—a hunting-box as the Marquis de Sourches later described it; a *piccola casa*, according to the Venetian Ambassador, a 'card castle', according to Saint-Simon. But the latter has been misunderstood; he was alluding less to the modesty of the construction (a central building with two lower wings) than to the multi-coloured materials—red bricks, white stone, blueish slates and lead.

The King came more and more often in 1625 and 1626. Louis XIII usually came with a few gentlemen. So far, women had not been admitted to the King's *piccola casa*, which probably explains the unpleasant rumours about the King's habits. At last, in 1626, he decided to invite at the same time Marie de Medici and Anne of Austria, his mother and his wife, and he had a supper prepared for them: 'The King personally carried the first dish to the princesses and then sat at the Queen's feet. After dinner, he treated the ladies to the delights of hunting.'

But he did not keep them for the night. There was no Queen's bedroom in this first chateau at Versailles. If the King entertained the court ladies and treated them to a meal—a very modest one—he did not allow them to stay, and he candidly confessed that 'a large number of women would spoil everything'. He would gladly have made an exception for Mlle de la Fayette and he tried several times to draw her to his far-away manor, but she never visited Versailles.

The park was taking shape. A large number of young trees were planted in 1627. The Comptroller-General of the Gardens of all the royal houses of France, Jacques Boyceau, planned the first alleys and the first basins. Louis XIII came more and more frequently. Here, for instance, is his time-table for August 24th: 'The King arrived at 11.15. He was cold and sat near the fire which had been kindled to warm him, then on his bed and had his furred gown wrapped round his legs'—a picturesque detail! People today are always complaining about the disappearance of seasons. In 1627 they were already stiff with cold at Versailles on August 24th!

[1] Roughly, one *arpent* = one acre.

An hour later the King felt warm again. He then walked out and went to see the soldiers around the guard-room. He spent a few moments with them, chatting familiarly, then got into his coach—a small one, drawn by a single horse—and spent the rest of the day visiting his plantations. On the 25th he heard mass at St Julien, returned, lay on his bed and had dinner served in his closet.[1] In the afternoon, he hunted and rode back to Paris.

## LOUIS XIII'S CHATEAU

Under the Old Régime the *concierge* of a chateau was no mean officer. He was not there to watch the visitors, which was the task of the guards of the gate. In a way, the *concierge* was a kind of jack-of-all-trades. Primarily he had to look after the furniture; a highly responsible job which was not entrusted to just any one.

The first *concierge* of the chateau was François de Montjay. He flourished the impressive titles of 'squire, archer of the King's Life Guards, *concierge* and furniture-keeper to His Majesty in his chateau at Versailles.' François de Montjay died early in 1630 and his devoted wife followed him to his grave a few months later. Steps had to be taken to replace them. According to a custom that has continued to this day, a very full inventory of the furniture of the chateau was drawn up for the use of the next keeper to assume Montjay's responsibilities. This is a highly important document[2] which enables us to reconstruct the full daily décor of Versailles when the King was in residence.

There were twenty-six habitable rooms. The King's suite, the finest and the best, was on the first floor. It consisted of a closet, a bedroom, a presence chamber in which he received visitors and a dressing-room, all of them connected by a gallery. In the latter had been hung a large and very recent painting which displayed a memorable event, the siege of La Rochelle, which had taken place as recently as 1628.

In each room of the King's suite the walls were hung with tapestries. The closet tapestry represented goddesses, that of the bedroom, woven in Flanders, displayed the history of Mark

---

[1] Let it be well understood that dinner, in the seventeenth century, was what is now called lunch.

[2] This document, in the Seine-et-Oise archives, was published by E. Cuard in the *Revue de l'Histoire de Versailles*, 1906.

Anthony in seven pieces of twenty-six *ells*. The eighth—for which there was no space—had been relegated to the furniture room. The inventory does not describe the six tapestries in the presence chamber.

The furniture was extremely simple. The bed of green damask had three fustian mattresses, with curtains to match the damask. Two *tenaille* chairs (rather uncomfortable contraptions), six stools to match, covered with fringed damask, a *tenaille* table and a leather carpet on the floor completed the furnishing.

In the closet were a locked chest, upholstered in leather, two trunks, a table on which were two silver candlesticks with large candles and a writing desk in Eastern leather. In this closet were kept the King's garments—at least those he used to leave at Versailles: a gown of green velvet, lined with squirrel, with buttons; a green damask gown, lined with taffetas, and dressing gowns of various kinds. There were also his games, backgammon, *trou-madame*, chess, *tourniquet*, *oie*, *renarde*, *moine* and spillikins. Versailles was for relaxation, where one could stay for a few days to hunt and rest.

It is clear that no council was ever held in the king's closet, the main ornament of which was a brand new billiard table with its cover, twelve balls, six cues and two four-pillared tables, a plain one and one which could be slung open. In the King's dressing-room were the inevitable commode, a cupboard in which were hidden the green velvet dressing table and another table covered with green taffetas.

The other rooms were allotted to the Comte de Nogent, M de Souvré, the Duc d'Angoulème, MM de l'Ile-Rouet, de Chape and Praslin, the Duc de Montbazon (Hercule de Rohan, peer of France and Governor of Paris). They occupied the whole first floor, both in front and on the wings, and they were not much better furnished. The Marquis de Mortemart had been allowed three Bergamo tapestries with a green background, two arm-chairs and a table, but his bed was lined only with a worn-out grey taffeta. The captains of the guard were only given a wardrobe, a cupboard and a *chaise-percée*. The other occupants did not have even these conveniences.

On the ground floor was the lumber-room in which were piled mostly the pallet beds for extra guests; then the armoury with twenty-three pikes and forty-two half-pikes. Further on were the apothecary's store, the kitchen with its impressive array of saucepans, and finally the *concierge's* room, which was not the worst furnished, as the *concierge* was the only one never to leave the castle.

There were no rooms arranged for ladies. The chateau of Versailles, which was to see the passing of so many Queens, legitimate or illegitimate, was first of all a man's castle. Apart from the *concierge's* wife, there were not even chambermaids.

Louis XIII came mainly to hunt. Yet he sometimes stayed on when the weather was bad. Then the games were produced, backgammon or chess; billiards were played, too.

Life gradually became organized. Sometimes, moreover, the King used to seek refuge at Versailles to meditate and to flee from court intrigues. There was nothing more convenient than this quiet manor, so close to a peaceful village.

### LOUIS XIII's NEW CHATEAU

In 1632 the King acquired the manor of Versailles, which until then had been the property of the Archbishop of Paris, François de Gondi. A few weeks later, in the presence of the vicar and the villagers, the judicial pole with the Archbishop's coat-of-arms was taken up and the King's arms were nailed to the elm tree at the cross-roads. Henceforth, Louis XIII was at home. He bought more and more land to enlarge the park and the hunting terrain.

As early as 1631 he decided that the first chateau was too small. He entrusted a little-known architect, Philibert Le Roy, with the task of enlarging the building and altering its appearance. Philibert brought the façade forward, lengthened it and at each extremity added a detached pavilion. He also altered the courtyard façade and closed the fourth side with a portico of arcades decorated with railings. The structure was completed by four small pavilions at the outer angles. Everything was ready for the Feast of Our Lady of 1636.

The park was also the object of embellishment. The Superintendent of Royal Buildings, Sublet des Niyers, fitted out the Rondeau des Cygnes, which later became the Bassin d'Apollon. Jaques de Menours, nephew of the architect Jacques Boyceau, designed the beds that blazed with many-coloured flowers. The inside remained extremely simple, with plaster-work for the fireplaces and earthenware tiles for the floors. The furniture was a little less primitive. There were a few elegant pieces given to the King by his sister Christine of France, Duchess of Savoy. The King himself was easily satisfied. Being very thrifty, he spent ridiculously little on Versailles. According to the accounts of the Royal Buildings, this second chateau cost little more than 213,000 *livres*, and the gardens 42,000. The upkeep did not amount to more than 40,000 *livres* in five years. As for furnishing and decoration, it was not even mentioned.

Versailles was only a secondary residence, 'a chateau where the King went often to divert himself with hunting', according to the caption of one of Israel Silvestre's engravings. On Gomboult's map of the royal houses, it is only shown in the little side vignettes surrounding the Chateau de Vincennes: 'It is only a small house for a gentleman with an income of ten to twelve thousand *livres*', wrote a contemporary.

And yet one reason for writing at some length about this second Chateau de Versailles is—and it cannot be said too often—that it provided the framework for Louis XIV's daily life for nearly a quarter of a century. The big works did not begin until 1661, when the King was twenty-three. They lasted for ten years. Louis XIII's chateau, gradually embellished and transformed, was to remain the heart and soul of the huge palace. It seems that Louis XIV's bedroom was built exactly at the site of his father's.[1]

It would be a mistake to ignore this first décor built by Louis XIII to frame the life at Versailles.

[1] There may be some doubt about this. Louis XIV's room may have been built on the site of the King's closet.

# CHAPTER TWO

# VERSAILLES: THE BACKGROUND OF LOUIS XIV'S REIGN

For twenty years the chateau at Versailles remained empty and no one could have guessed that this humble manor, hidden in the Val de Gallie, would become one of the main concerns and one of the least contestable glories of Louis XIV's reign.

The years between 1638 and 1660 were not propitious for building. The Fronde of rebellious noblemen, the discontent which rumbled through a country crushed by heavy and clumsy taxation, the blunders of Mazarin and Anne of Austria, all were instrumental in drawing the young King away from his already keen interest in the arts and in architecture.

He was not unaware of Versailles. He hunted there from time to time. But he was thirteen when he went there for the first time, on April 13, 1651. He inspected the countryside surrounding his little estate and heard the names with which he was soon to become so familiar, St Cyr, Noisy, Marly, Trianon. He had no ambitious plans yet, but he felt a deep affection for this piece of land which his father had cherished. He was to remain faithful to his father's memory by requiring his architects to retain the card castle, which did not fail to restrict their plans.

In proportion as the rebellion died away and France settled down, Louis XIV's designs grew more definite. He had travelled much and seen many chateaux. Those which he had inherited, St Germain, the Louvre, Fontainebleau, he found far from displeasing. He had been overwhelmed by the beauty and the grandeur of the Palais Cardinal in which Mazarin had amassed his treasure. In 1659 he had admired the city Richelieu had created in Touraine, and understood during his visit how a town can support and extend a chateau: the lesson would not be forgotten. He had been enchanted by Chambord and by Vaux, where Fouquet had organized for him an ill-timed display. So in 1661 the King made up his mind: he had his own ideas about architecture and meant to have them complied with. He wanted to have a palace with the stamp of his own genius, and he chose Versailles.

## WHY VERSAILLES?

The reasons for his choice have often been debated. Why not accept contemporary opinion? In an addition to Dangeau's *Diary*, we have the following comment by Saint-Simon:

'When the King first fell in love of Mme de la Vallière and kept the matter secret no longer, the court was at Saint Germain-en-Laye, and Versailles was in the state in which Louis XIII had left it, or very nearly so, which was nothing at all. The King used to go there once or twice a week, with a very small entourage, to spend part of the day with Mme de la Vallière, and he devised a coat with a special kind of embroidery which he bestowed on a dozen of noblemen he allowed to escort him during those little private rides to Versailles.'

In her memoirs, written in 1666, the Grande Mademoiselle noted: 'We often went to Versailles. No one was allowed to follow the King there without his order. This sort of distinction intrigued the whole court.' One reason was that Versailles was convenient for quiet love-making. The King preferred it to any other chateau. Like his father he liked this rather wild place. Did he plan something magnificent for the chateau itself? Early in his reign, in 1661, this was not certain. He observed only that the land extended as far as the eye could reach around the palace, so that he could create an immense park. As early as 1660 he ordered a general survey: he wanted to know exactly the area he had for planning these developments. Like Louis XIII, he continued to buy land, immensely enlarged the circumference, absorbing the villages of Trianon and Choisy-aux-Bœufs, the estates of Vivier and La Boisière. The Ménagerie was to be built where they once stood.

The building of the gardens, under Le Nôtre, had in a way preceded the building of the palace. For a few more years, Louis XIV made do with his father's house. In the park he could sometimes entertain the whole court and proudly, joyfully display his amours and his youth. But he refused to be bothered with courtiers for long, and although a few far-seeing people already thought of building their own homes in Versailles, to be near their master, the majority drove home in the evenings. Sometimes, when festivities went on too long, they had to sleep in their coaches!

The main work really began only in 1666. Until then the King was content with indoor embellishments, done mostly by Charles Evrard and Noêl Coypel. But Louis XIV's passion for building suddenly focused on Versailles. And yet, in 1667, his love for Louise de la Vallière was fading while he was falling in love with the dazzling Athénaïs de Rochechouart-Mortemart, Marquise de Montespan. How now could the King's choice of Versailles be explained? A wish to leave behind him a proof of his will and genius? A wish to create a palace even more magnificent than Vaux-le-Vicomte? The approximation of two dates may be illuminating and yet it may be mere coincidence. Fouquet was arrested in Nantes on September 5, 1661, and the master builders who had worked for him at Vaux, Le Vau and Charles le Brun, were immediately engaged at Versailles. Yet was it not merely because they were acknowledged as the best artists in their time? Louis XIV had no alternative but to employ them.

The King had decided to build a palace after his own ideas, something really new and original. He never became disinterested in the other royal buildings, and during his reign, work went on enthusiastically at Fontainebleau, St Germain and Compiègne. The Louvre had not been neglected. But all these palaces were there before Louis XIV; they were the continued work of his predecessors, and even of dynasties before his own. Though they had been on the throne for over half a century, the Bourbons had not yet built any chateau from the very foundations, with the exception of Versailles. What Richelieu, Mazarin and Fouquet had done with striking taste, majesty and grandeur, was surely not beyond the capacities of the King of France. And Louis XIII had bequeathed him a modest building, the very position of which enabled him to conceive the most magnificent developments. Why not go on with what had already been begun?

Such were the ideas Louis XIV was vaguely contemplating when, against the advice of his councillors, he ordered what was in their view a mediocre residence to be turned into one of the most beautiful palaces in the world. The King persevered in spite of Colbert's remonstrations. He had the ulterior motive of seeking to subdue

26

the rebellious nobility around him, who were constantly conspiring against his dynasty. Versailles fitted admirably into this scheme. The palace was to be huge, and princes and dukes were to regard it as a matter of honour to secure a garret therein. As for the rest, they would have to find lodgings around the royal residence. A whole city would be created to house them. Gradually, Paris would be abandoned. Court life would be centred upon the new palace, and Louis XIV would thus have carried out his great design: to mould the monarchy and the aristocracy into the framework of Versailles.

## THE STAGES OF CONSTRUCTION

This was to take about thirty years. It will suffice here to outline the main stages of the work. The execution of the plans drawn up by Le Vau began in 1668. After long hesitation, Louis XIV decided that his father's small chateau was to be preserved. Starting from that central building, the architect conceived its 'envelope'. Between two large pavilions he built a long terrace with a magnificent view over the shrubberies and flower-beds which were simultaneously created by Le Nôtre. Instead of the pointed slate roofs that were traditional during the Renaissance, terraced roofs were built. Above the cornice of the attics a balustrade, trophies and vases stood out against the sky. On either side of the wings, in front of the Marble Courtyard, Le Vau erected long parallel buildings, framing broad courtyards. He filled up the ditches, connected the outer buildings with the others and extended the whole scheme with colonnaded pavilions.

In this way the present layout of the palace was so arranged as to condition later enlargements. Le Vau died in 1670. One of his pupils, François Corbay, faithfully carried out his master's ideas. In 1671 the heavy work was done and the castle was practically completed by 1674. During those six years, Louis XIV very often lived at Versailles in the early chateau, in the midst of scaffolding, rubble and dust. Scaffolding and plaster surrounded him out-of-doors too. Following the measures taken to attract inhabitants to Versailles, the new town, north of the palace and along avenues that met in front of it, was quickly rising from the ground.

Four years later, after the signature of the Treaty of Nimegen, work began again, this time under Mansart, who directed it until

27

1708. Now the palace assumed its final aspect. To replace the terrace between the two pavilions that faced the park he built the Great Gallery, now known as the Galerie des Glaces. He then altered the outside of the Marble Courtyard (1679–1680), and of the pavilions of the front courtyard which, joined together, became the Ministers' Wings; later, he erected the long wings, the south wing (1678–1681) for the Princes of the Blood, the legitimated bastards and the court officials, and the north wing (1687–1689). Their disposition matched that of the façade: the same decorative elements were done by the same group of sculptors.

In 1682, Louis XIV brought the court and the government to Versailles once and for all. Nothing was finished yet and everyone had to settle somehow in narrow lodgings of two rooms or at the most three. This huge crowd had to be fed, as well as the 1500 people working in the kitchens, the pantry and the wine cellars for the King's sustenance. On the site of the old village of Versailles, whose inhabitants had been expropriated, and more precisely where the little church of St Julian had stood, Mansart built the Grand Commun, large, severe, harmonious buildings surrounding a rectangular courtyard.

This was not all; between Paris and Versailles the traffic of carriages and horses was endless. Stables in proportion to the needs of the palace had to be provided. Those which had been built in the Rue de la Pompe were too small. Between 1679 and 1681 Mansart undertook the building of the Great and Small Stables (the Grande and the Petite Écurie). The hotels of Lauzun and Chaumont-Quitry, which faced the palace at the end of the Avenue de Paris, were pulled down; several rows of trees were removed and there slowly appeared the two splendid buildings, the general layout of which had been cleverly devised as a horse-shoe. They were not high enough to spoil the view of the surrounding countryside. The stables stretched between the three avenues, rounding off perfectly the view of the Place d'Armes and its surroundings. In the centre of the Grande Écurie, supervised henceforth by Monsieur le Grand, the riding school was so big that it could be used for ceremonies, feasts, plays and big receptions. Almost a century was to elapse before a proper theatre was built within the palace.

Hardly were the stables completed than Mansart started work on the Orangery (1681–1686). To hold back the land, which sloped sharply southwards, he built a central gallery connected with side

28

galleries. Thus the Orangery, with its high bay windows, separated by pairs of columns, supported the terrace which was reached from the Pièce d'Eau des Suisses up the hundred steps.

As the years went by, Louis XIV sometimes felt the need to retire to a simpler building in order to lead a less pompous existence. Mansart completed the Trianon in 1687 with the help, perhaps, of his brother-in-law Robert de Corté, two years after the death of the master-mind of Versailles.

The palace had acquired its final form. From now on alterations mostly affected the interior. The park was animated and fountains started to throw up their rainbow waters to the changing sky, high above the multi-coloured flowerbeds. Although the work was slower, and the war of the Spanish Succession a heavy drain on the kingdom's finances, the architect crowned his masterpiece by the building of the chapel. The one which had been consecrated in 1682, where the Hercules Drawing-room now stands, was too small. In the centre of the north wing, the horizontal lines of which it ruins, the large building was completed in 1710, the work of Robert de Cotte.

1668–1710: it had taken forty-two years to build round Louis XIII's hunting box a palace whose fame soon became universal. Too seldom do we face up to the facts of chronology. The King was thirty when Le Vau began his work: it was an old man of seventy-two, immovably fixed in his grandeur, isolated from human sympathy by bereavements, tragedies and his own will, who was carried into the chapel that was finished at long last.

## THE INTERIOR OF THE PALACE AT THE TIME OF LOUIS XIV

Towards 1709, following the advice of the King's lieutenant in his province, a nobleman from Limousin came to Versailles to mix with the courtiers who crowded the halls and galleries. His sword at his side (which the palace *concierge* required of all visitors, though he could lend one to the absent-minded, or to those who did not possess one), he would cross the first courtyard where the Gardes-Françaises were in attendance, usually doing nothing. Not wasting time on the ground floor, he ascended the Ambassadors' Staircase (no longer there, having been pulled down by Gabriel in the eighteenth century). The first curve of the staircase took him to the Salon de Vénus, where he was greeted by a statue of Louis XIV in Roman draperies, the work of Jean Warin. Had he taken the second curve, he would have arrived at the Diana drawing-room. The goddess of hunting and of the night was depicted in three murals above the doorway, in scenes from her story. Here, too, stood a bust of the King when young, one of Bernini's masterpieces.

In the middle of this salon stood the King's billiard table. Louis loved the game and it was a great honour for a courtier to be challenged and defeated by him. When it was not in use, the table was covered by a crimson cloth fringed with gold. It was surrounded by a dozen stools, a few small tables and some larger ones with vases, perfume-pans and chandeliers. All this furniture in solid silver was less valuable for its substance than for its carving. The work of Claude Ballin, our visitor was just in time to admire it: it was soon to be minted to pay for the crushing costs of the war. It was replaced by less sumptuous sets of furniture in gilded wood.

Turning to the right, our provincial visitor entered the Salon de l'Abondance, and then the Salon d'Hercule, the last one before the Salon de la Chapelle, which opened upon the royal tribune. The first served as ante-chamber to the celebrated room where Louis XIV kept his medals and curios. But by that time, the next room, the Salon d'Hercule, was a complete shambles. Until 1708 it had served as the royal chapel. Then it was turned into a state apartment, one of the most impressive in the palace. Louis XIV did not see it finished. The work stopped at his death and was not resumed until 1729.

All these salons, like those that followed, formed what is known as the King's State Apartments. There were eight rooms and they ended in the Grande Galerie. Louis XIV lived there until 1684, when he was installed in a new suite with windows that opened upon the Marble Courtyard: it was none other than Louis XIII's former apartment completely renovated.

The Grand Appartement was only used for court ceremonies. One walked through it in procession to reach the chapel. Courtiers crowded there, in the hope of catching their master's eye. The crowd there was always very thick.

Three times a week those drawing-rooms had a more precise use: those evenings were called the *soirs d'appartement* or evening receptions. On Mondays, Wednesdays and Thursdays the Salon de l'Abondance was used for refreshments, with three buffets arranged in horse-shoe fashion. High silver vases served hot or cold drinks, fruit juice, lemonade, wines, chocolate and coffee, which was beginning to be seen, the fashion for which never ended, despite Mme de Sévigné's gloomy prophecies. Valets were constantly filling the vessels.

In the Salon de Vénus, other tables were piled with patisseries, fresh or candied fruit in pyramids, cleverly arranged in silver or crystal trays.

One would then pass into the Salon de Mars, the ceiling of which, painted by Audran, represented the god of War in a chariot drawn by wolves. On either side of the fireplace stood marble tribunes for the King's violinists. In fact, several times each week the King used to go there to listen to a concert or to indulge in his hereditary passion for card-games. Card tables had been set out, and valets in a blue livery with silver or gold buttons marked the score-cards or gave out counters. They remained standing behind the players. The King would join them and even take the place of one of them.

Next to the Salon de Mars was the Salon de Mercure, called the bedchamber. Right in the centre of the far wall, separated from the courtiers and visitors by a silver balustrade, stood a magnificent bed, covered with the same gold and silver brocade that lined the walls. After Louis XIV gave up his old apartment, it was only used twice: the Duc d'Anjou, the King's grandson, when proclaimed King of Spain, slept there before leaving for his new country and, after Louis XIV's death, during the week before his burial at St Denis the corpse, draped in his coronation robes, lay in state on this ceremonial bed.

Nothing survives today of this room's furniture. The large silver mirror and the balustrade were melted down, and the Titians which hung on its walls are now in the Louvre. Only the clock presented to the King by Antoine Morandin in 1706 remains and stands in a corner.

Dazzled by such splendour, our visitor entered the Salon d'Apollon at last, the grandeur of which surpassed even that of the preceding rooms. This was because of its very special use: it served as the throne room. Here the rarest marbles had been gathered, the best known paintings by Rubens or Van Dyck, with mural hangings of crimson velvet on gold and silver embroideries, which alternated with the seasons. The throne itself, a silver armchair eight feet high, occupied the back of the hall, standing under a canopied platform that was covered with a Persian carpet of a reddish colour. When Louis XIV sat here for solemn ceremonials or to receive ambassadors, he could look at his own portrait by Rigaud above the fireplace.

The Throne Room had another use. On the evenings when there was an *appartement*, the princesses and court ladies used to dance there before the King. And the courtier who was acting as guide to our provincial gentleman would add that one could sometimes see the King, unaffectedly sitting on the steps of the platform and looking happily at these amusements and sometimes even taking part in them.

Each of these rooms had been given the name of a planet: Venus, Mercury or Mars. 'As the Sun is the King's device,' wrote Félivien, 'the seven planets have been selected to suggest subjects for the decoration of the seven rooms of the State Rooms.' The building of the Great Gallery and the two drawing-rooms at either end involved the disappearance of the other rooms. Our Limousin visitor had already realized that the solar myth reigned over Versailles, both in the palace and in the gardens.

He respectfully entered the Salon de la Guerre. Jointly created by Mansart and Le Brun, its decorations celebrated the recent French victories. The ceiling depicted the three European powers, Germany, Holland and Spain in league against France. At the other end of the Great Gallery, the Salon de la Paix showed them defeated and gratefully accepting the peace offered them by a magnanimous conqueror. In the middle, the canopy of the Gallery depicted, with rare mastery, in which realism and allegory combined, the great deeds of the war and the reforms that were the main achievements of the first twenty years of the King's reign. It took all the painter's skill to avoid monotony in covering this huge area. Coysevox, with gilded bronze trophies, with sculpted bas-reliefs and stuccos, had beautifully completed the decoration of the Gallery, the most sumptuous in the palace.

This was where the courtiers were crowded together from morning till night, for the apartment in which the King had lived since 1684 opened onto the Gallery. The visitor knew well that he could not have access to it and that the guards would politely, but firmly, stop him. He was told that the King had some fifteen rooms there, which had been greatly reconstructed in 1701. Coming from the Salon de la Guerre one entered first the Cabinet des Termes where,

1. Versailles between 1664 and 1665, by Patel

2. Louis XIV, by Le Brun

every evening after supper, Louis XIV gathered the Royal family, who meekly answered his summons. Next was the royal cabinet where the council met every day. It was completely decorated with mirrors, to which were affixed little brackets of wood or bronze.

The next room had been for a long time the King's salon. After 1701 and following the considerable alterations devised by Louis, it became his presence chamber. Our visitor was informed that various ceremonies were performed there, the *lever*, certain audiences, the *coucher*, and the *petit couvert* every day at one o'clock. The alcove was closed by a balustrade and the Coustou bas-relief on the wall, symbolizing 'France watching over the King's sleep'. Several fine paintings by Van Dyck, Dominichino and Valentin, of religious subjects mostly, decorated the room. Besides the King's bed, the room was furnished with two armchairs, a dozen stools, a table and a screen.

The King's room occupied the exact centre of the palace and the view from the windows stretched beyond the Marble Courtyard and the Place d'Armes to the fine Avenue de Paris, on the axis of which it stood. To one side was the Salon de l'Oeil de Bœuf: at first there had been two rooms, a drawing-room with paintings by the Venetian painter Bassano, and the royal bed-chamber. In 1701, the two rooms were turned into one. Every morning the courtiers who were permitted to be present at the little, and afterwards at the great levee, according to the order of admittance strictly fixed by etiquette, waited until the Swiss guard allowed them in. The visitor was able to get a glimpse of the large hall and admire two paintings by Veronese that adorned it.

The Salon de l'Oeil de Bœuf was still called the second ante-chamber. In the first ante-chamber the King supped at ten every night with the royal family. The second ante-chamber was in the side wing above the Marble Courtyard, on the South. It was next to the guard room which opened upon the loggia above the Queen's staircase.

Thus the King had reserved the whole central part of the north wing for himself, leaving the Queen the south wing that stretched along the gardens. After 1710, the Salon de la Paix had been connected with it—though the Queen had long been dead—and a curtain, which could easily be pulled aside to uncover the view, separated it from the Great Gallery.

The Queen's suite consisted of five rooms where she lived and carried out her duties, and a number of small closets which, doubling the state rooms, enabled her to retire and rest with the ladies of her household.

This suite had been arranged for Maria-Theresa of Austria. She died there on July 30, 1683; the Dauphine, Maria-Christina of Bavaria, died there too in 1690. It was next occupied by the Duc de Bourgogne's wife, Marie-Adélaïde de Savoie, who had taken the title of Dauphine and died shortly before her husband on February 12, 1712. The rooms were then left empty until Louis XIV's own death.

The main room was the Queen's bedchamber. In it were born Philip V of Spain and Louis XV. In that room, after her toilet, the Queen used to entertain the duchesses who had the privilege of the *tabouret*. She also gave private audiences there.

Public audiences and presentations took place in the next room, the Salon des Nobles, with a ceiling painted by Michael Corneille and a fireplace of blue-grey marble. The walls were hung with green silk.[1]

The ceremonial supper took place in the Queen's ante-chamber. The fine ceiling, with its gilded bronze bas-reliefs, had lost its central painting by Vignon.

On the other side of the Queen's room, near the big staircase called the Queen's staircase, there was a special hall for the gentlemen of the King's household whose function it was to watch over the sovereign. The ceiling of this room had been painted by Antoine Coypel in 1680 and it was a strange mixture of mythology and contemporary episodes: to Jupiter's procession, escorted by Justice and Mercy, the artist had added a train of courtiers who seemed to be watching people coming up the Marble Staircase, which was the main access to the royal apartments.

Completely dazed by all he had seen in the salons or had been told by his guide, our Limousin visitor finally went down the staircase. He had a last look over the gallery that lay below the Great Gallery, which was long used as a theatre. It is true that plays were most often acted in the park, for Louis XIV had a passion for open-air performances. Unhappily, the weather was not always propitious. The lower gallery has few exits; usually, the plays were moved into the riding school of the Grande Écurie.

[1] Those silks are modern. They have been recently put there and the room opened to the public for the Le Brun exhibition of 1963.

The visitor wondered why those two buildings, strictly identical, were called the Grande and the Petite Écurie. Actually it was just a matter of organization. In the Grande Écurie were only war horses, saddle horses and show horses; the Petite Écurie was reserved for carriage and cart horses. The big riding school, with its tribunes, could seat several hundred persons. The King was greeted there by Monsieur Le Grand, who did all he could to please his master. In 1682, within a few hours, the whole setting of an opera by Lully, which should have been performed in the park, had been taken there: rain had prevented the original programme from taking place. The King was terribly disappointed. Yet, he did not know how very resourceful the *Grand Maître des Menus Plaisir* was. The trees from the orangery made a natural setting and *Persée* was performed with a success which was mainly due to the stage manager.

The visitor was easily convinced. Having admired the whole setting, he might eagerly have sought to spend a whole day with the King and his courtiers. Nothing could have been easier, for the King's everyday life was lived according to a changeless ritual. Etiquette and precedence were meticulously respected. From dawn to dusk, each courtier knew where the King was, what he was doing, and who were the high dignitaries around him.

But to approach him was quite another question. One could move freely about the Palace of Versailles, but only those favoured by birth or merit had access to the royal presence.

That should never be forgotten.

# CHAPTER THREE

# THE KING'S DAY

In 1682 Louis XIV had been on the throne for forty years. He had won the greatest victories over his enemies and France was the most powerful nation in Europe. Throughout the civilized world all eyes were focused on the palace which occupied a preponderant place in the King's mind and was his principal interest.

Until then the court had been itinerant. As the work proceeded the time spent at Versailles became longer. Yet Louis XIV also lived at Fontainebleau, Compiègne and St Germain, where he had spent the first twenty years of his life. Even after 1682 he still allowed people to believe that the Versailles establishment was not permanent, and that he had left St Germain simply because of the alterations which were being effected. Actually, his mind was made up: he would never return to the Louvre or to any other palace. As Versailles became the seat of government, the nobility must come to live there if they wanted to enjoy their master's presence.

What had made the King change the fundamental character of the French monarchy so profoundly? On that subject all historians are agreed. Louis XIV sought to tame the nobility in order to rid them of their taste for conspiracy. He had been deeply shocked by the rebellion of the Fronde and the humiliating episodes of 1649, and had not forgotten his mother's and Mazarin's struggles against the rebellious princes and their natural ally, the people of Paris. It was to isolate them from the capital, where the evil ferment could always turn them from their duty, that he forced on them the rural life of Versailles.

This is the usual explanation. But there are reasons to doubt it. Chronology does not support this over-simple idea. That the unhappy days of 1649—when he was not yet eleven—and the night during which he had to run away from the Louvre to St Germain in a derelict coach had left their mark on him may be accepted. But in 1682, thirty years after the Fronde, there were no longer any rebellious noblemen to fear.

There was another reason for the King's choice: his taste for grandeur and pomp, combined with his innate pride. What he wanted was a stable court, settled around him in the finest palace in the world, to form a background to his daily life. He was flattered to reflect that the attendants who were ready to assist him in the most intimate offices were the Ducs de la Rochefoucauld, d'Aumont, de Gesvres and de Beauvilliers—the greatest names in France.

Louis had created the myth of Versailles: it was probably the greatest miracle performed by the Sun King.

For these noblemen, these dukes, these descendants of old and authentic families, were far from being fools, undiscerning sycophants or mediocrities. If there were a few nonentities among them —who were roundly scourged in Saint-Simon's memoirs—the majority lacked neither intelligence nor culture. They were rich, owning magnificent estates and houses in Paris. They were often pre-eminent in their provinces.

Louis XIV's skill had been to convince them of the fact that all their intelligence should be put into the observation of etiquette, that all their wealth was not worth the most humble garret in Versailles, and that, away from the sovereign, life was not worth living.

Let us here remember M. de Vardes. After an intrigue against Mme de la Vallière and an unfortunate remark about the Duchesse d'Orléans, the King's sister-in-law, he had been imprisoned in the Bastille and then exiled to Montpellier, where he remained for twenty years. When he returned, the King, who had forgiven him, could not refrain from making fun of his attire. Vardes had the tact to abase himself cleverly: 'Sir,' he said, 'when one is wretched enough to live so far away from you, not only is one unhappy, but also ridiculous.'

Outside the court there was no salvation and Stendhal underlined the fact mercilessly: 'Louis XIV's masterpiece was to create the tedium of exile.'

### PROTOCOL, CEREMONIAL AND ETIQUETTE

Louis XIV's main design was to gather round him the most powerful representatives of the French nobility and to chain them to his triumphal chariot. This he had achieved in a few years. To those whom he was unable to house at the palace he gave such tremendous financial privileges that they thought of nothing but owning a house or even a mere apartment in Versailles. Yet it was not enough to gather people together and turn them into devoted courtiers; it was necessary to occupy them, so that they would not be aware of the passage of time. The King succeeded in making them slaves to the most stringent etiquette.

He did not create it, but he turned it into a dogma. He abandoned some diversions and some of his freedom to submit to it himself and become its principal slave.

When his reign began, the King was carefree. At St Germain-en-Laye he was found running over the roofs at night to join a mistress. It is very difficult to visualize the Sun King in such a situation, or allowing his arm (was it really his arm?) to be pinched by his mistress, Mme de la Motte-Houdancourt, who did so once with such strength that he screamed: 'The bitch!' The scene took place in the Queen's chamber.

Such lapses were unthinkable after 1682. Etiquette reigned supreme, even over the time devoted to his love affairs. Etiquette was an exacting mistress. And although the King gladly relied on Monsieur, his brother, to watch over ceremonial, he made it quite clear that he wanted to be informed of the slightest details. That poor Marquis de Vardes, back from exile, had bowed to the Dauphin, who had been summoned by the King just after he had kindly welcomed his former victim. Vardes was severely reprimanded: 'That was a blunder, Vardes. You should know that no one may be saluted before me.' And Vardes apologized: 'Ah, Sir, do forgive me! I know nothing; I have forgotten everything.'

The perfect courtier had to know his etiquette and study it like his catechism. Everyone trembled at the thought of committing a blunder, and one understands why all noise ceased as soon as the ushers had shouted from afar: 'Gentlemen, the King!' Then a religious silence weighed upon the assembly, so that one heard nothing but the tapping of the royal cane on the floor. 'One is puny at court, and however proud one may be, one has to realize it. But the complaint is general and even the great are small.'

Such attention to minute detail in the most commonplace activities required an application to which everyone submitted with good grace. The slightest mistake drew endless comments and was the subject of infinite discussion. Respect for the rules of precedence was another source of discussion. Courtiers—and not only courtiers but all Frenchmen—had always been sensible of the rights drawn from rank and prerogative. To usurp position led to the worst quarrels and in Versailles such rivalries were always very heated. The King personally worked out everyone's rank and created the rites surrounding his own person. To the very end of his reign he interested himself in these questions and issued new rules when he thought they were not precise enough. For example, in 1710 he decided which rank the Princesses of the Blood should take under certain circumstances and personally made his will known to those it concerned.

Saint-Simon, who was fascinated by such problems, never fails to inform us at great length: 'Princesses of the Blood should not eat at the Grand Couvert. After supper, they do not follow the King into his closet: such an honour is only for the sons, daughters, grandsons and grand-daughters of France. They are only invited on special occasions, wedding feasts in the royal family or other exceptional events.'

This rule was dated March 4, 1710. The Spanish War had brought France nothing but disappointment. The winter had been terrible, and the future was gloomy. At Versailles they froze in the galleries and the silver plate was sent to the mint. Meanwhile, the greatest of Kings was deciding the precedence of the Princesses of the Blood.

Louis XIV was well aware of the vanity of such details, but by enforcing them he was holding the attention of his courtiers. As he had no more money to give away, he put a heavy premium on his smallest favours. 'He was well aware', Saint-Simon wrote, 'that he had not favours enough to produce a lasting effect. Instead, he substituted jealousy for ideals, the tiny signs of preference which turned up every day and almost at any minute. No one was more ingenious at inventing the hopes to which these little marks of preference and these distinctions gave rise.'

## THE LEVER

As from 1684 the King abandoned his former apartment. The Queen's death had freed him from any connubial duty and if, in spite of his age, after the solemn ceremony of the *coucher*, he would go and bestow his affections on Mme de Maintenon, he always went back to his own bed.

The King slept. In the palace life seemed suspended. For a few hours the courtiers had recovered a fragile freedom. The only people awake were the guards on duty in the guard-room next to the King's bed-chamber. Also his first valet, who never left his master, even at night, and who slept near him.

At seven in the morning the valet got up. Whether his name was Blouin or Bontemps, he was a most reliable man. He alone had permanent access to Louis, though he always knew how to keep modestly in his place. A quarter of an hour later, fully dressed and apparelled, the first valet silently let in the *feutiers,* the men who lit the fire. Then another opened the shutters, while a third rolled away the bed on which the first valet had slept and what was left of the collation kept ready for the King, in case he woke in the night and felt hungry.

It was now 7.30. The first valet approached the royal bed and, without disturbing the curtains around it, murmured 'Sir, it is time.' He then let in the first doctor and the first surgeon. The former examined his patient and ordered some remedy, and took the opportunity of an interview alone to beg a favour or to recommend an applicant. Sometimes, he would tell the King some important news which had arrived during the night. He was assisted by the first surgeon.

At 8.15 it was the turn of the first gentleman of the bed-chamber whose year it was to be on duty to enter. Four noblemen shared this highly prized office, each of them for a year. The first gentleman opened the curtains of the bed: he was the only one entitled to do so. The King's private life was ended. He had now to live in public, facing his audience. As if touched by a magic wand, the palace of Versailles woke up and the courtiers, in hierarchical order, were filling the antechambers.

Now began the various entrances, first that of the great, then that of the second rank, and then the entrance of people merely of quality.

The only people entitled to *grandes entrées* were the members of the Royal Family, the Princes of the Blood and the high officers of the Crown, who had assumed for generations the main domestic duties: the Grand Chamberlain, the Grand Master and the Masters of the Robes, and the First Valet of the Robes on duty. The other three gentlemen of the bed-chamber and the three first valets were also allowed in.

The first valet approached the King and poured on his hands a few drops of spirits of wine; then the Grand Chamberlain produced the stoop, and the King made the sign of the cross. Everyone present then went up to the Council Room, the doors of which had been opened. A chaplain was waiting there. The service lasted barely a quarter of an hour, and the King followed it from his bed, usually adding a few personal prayers.

Then the main dignitaries poured back into the bed-chamber. The barber entered (Quentin, for a long time), together with the valet of the wig closet (next door to the wardrobe). The first valet supervised it. The King chose his wig out of a huge collection, made by the best wig-makers in the kingdom. In the Archives of Seine-et-Oise there is a curious contract, which had passed before a Versailles notary, between the first valet and a wig-maker of Lille, in Flanders, who undertook to 'procure a quantity of the best possible hair to be found, of the right length and colour, to provide the ornament of His Majesty's head and face', at a price of twenty *sous* an ounce, which was no small sum.

By now it was 8.30. The King got out of bed, put on his slippers and the dressing-gown which was held out to him by the first chamberlain. Then he went up to one of the armchairs on either side of the fireplace, sat down and the Grand Chamberlain removed his nightcap and the first barber or one of his assistants proceeded to comb him. The sovereign would gossip with the audience. This was the perfect opportunity for those who had something to tell, or to beg of him. Better do it at once: time was short. That was the end of the *petit lever*. At the door of the Oeil-de-Boef salon the Swiss was calling the second entrances, carefully checking the qualifications of the courtiers who were crowding to enter the King's chamber.

They were more numerous than those of the First Entrance, but they owed their privilege only to their very well-defined offices. Among them were the doctor and surgeon ordinary (of lesser rank than the first doctor), the four cabinet secretaries, the readers of the Chamber, the intendant and the comptroller of the silver plate, the first valets of the robes, besides the valet on duty, who was among the First Entrance. Finally, there were some highly favoured noblemen who had secured a *brevet d'affaires* by virtue of which it was permissible to enter the King's chamber when he was on his *chaise percée.*

This is a delicate subject! But we must remember that our ancestors were not so prudish about these matters as we are. They saw nothing strange in receiving visitors when in such a posture. In the Middle Ages people went in groups to the privy, which was sometimes arranged to receive several people at once. In monasteries latrines were a succession of holes made one beside the other. The *chaise percée*, in use in the seventeenth century, was an improvement on that secular custom, as some sort of privacy was possible as well as some concealment from onlookers.

In the most modern and comfortable house, the *chaise percée* was a regular piece of furniture. It was covered with fringed velvet, provided with an earthenware basin, and also with a folding table which enabled one to read or write while satisfying the laws of nature. But as it is difficult to throw off old habits, people often brought such chairs together (every room had its own) so as to gossip agreeably.

The King resumed his place in an ordinary armchair. The barber finished doing his hair and fixed on his head the wig he had selected. That was the morning wig, not so high as the one he was to be seen wearing later in the day.

Until then, apart from members of the Royal Family, no one other than high officers had come near the King. Now it was the turn of the 'persons of quality' to attend the *grand lever*. Their entrance was a matter of great ceremonial. Each gave his name to the Usher, who repeated it to the First Gentleman, who in turn repeated it to the King. Some of them remained by the door and, as they were so far away, chattered so loudly that they had to be silenced.

The King then asked for his breakfast. It was a few minutes past nine. The breakfast was rather light: usually, just two cups of herb tea or broth, but they were most solemnly served, after having been formally tasted.

The King would then complete his dressing. He was shaved by the barber only every other day. Then he was dressed. He himself removed his dressing-gown and his night-shirt, together with the relics he habitually wore. His shirt was brought and presented to him by the Dauphin if he was there. If not, it was handed by the Ducs de Bourgogne, de Berry or d'Orléans. Everything proceeded slowly; the dressing went on without the King leaving his arm-chair. But he was well used to it and did 'practically everything by himself, skilfully and gracefully'. Various noblemen crowded round him to help.

Neckties were produced, from which he selected one which he knotted himself. Three handkerchiefs were brought, from which he took two. Then his clock-maker, who had wound up the King's watch, handed it to him.

The King was ready. He went back to his bed-side, knelt on his prayer-stool and offered a few prayers, the second of the day. Louis XIV was pious and, however irregular his life, he never forgot that he was God's anointed, and God's representative at the head of a Most Christian Monarchy, and His first servant.

The King's piety, which became more fervent as the years went by, and as Mme de Maintenon's influence made itself more felt, was always deep and sincere. Moreover, he showed great care to obey all the laws of the Church. This heavy eater was determined to follow punctiliously the Church's fasts and abstentions, and the court had to conform. A few days before each Ash Wednesday, he never omitted to preach a little sermon to those who attended the *grand lever* to remind them of their duty. He went even further. He asked the provost of the household, the Marquis de Sourches, to report to him any infringement he might have observed, and he did not fail to show by his coldness his displeasure to forgetful courtiers. Were there any? According to La Bruyère, they were devout in order to please a devout King; they would have become atheist under an atheist King.

The King had finished praying. He stood up and, after having changed his wig, entered his study. He was followed by those whose presence was necessary, either because he wished to have them near him or because he had to give them orders for the day, 'so that everyone should know what the King had to do that day.'

Then the procession was formed again and in great pomp walked across the former Royal Apartments towards the chapel. During the whole second half of his life, after the Queen's death, Louis always heard mass at ten, then went back to his study to hold a council or audience until dinner time. On the other hand, before Maria-Thérèsa's death, he only went to mass at twelve. At least, that is what Primo Visconti wrote: 'The King remained with the council from ten till twelve, when he went off to mass, always with the Queen and their family'.

Daily attendance at mass was compulsory for all the members of the household, the officers and the courtiers. Preceded by ushers and the members of the bed-chamber, the King walked slowly, rosary in hand. He followed mass with great respect, demanding complete silence. The assistants had to kneel when the bell rang for the *Sanctus,* and remain kneeling until the priest's communion.

### THE KING AT WORK

For three hours Louis had been awake and had busied himself only with the ceremonies of the *lever* and with prayers. God having been served, he was now ready to attend to his regal business in his study.

It was the room he liked best in the palace, for as we know, there was in his view nothing more delightful than his daily work. The mornings were devoted to the meetings of the councils, of which the most important was the State Council, usually held on Sunday and sometimes continued into Monday when the business had not been completed. It sat again on Wednesday. The Finance Council sat on Tuesdays and Saturdays. The Councils Extraordinary, such as that of Despatches, sat once or twice a month, according to circumstances.

During the meetings of the councils ministers were allowed to sit in a row facing the King. However, it was usual for them to remain standing during the Council of Despatches.

There was no council meeting on Thursday. This day was reserved by the King for private audiences, mainly those with architects and gardeners. Officers of the bed-chamber were often summoned to settle household details. When the King was worried by any problem, he would ask for a sheet of paper and in his large and studied handwriting would write himself a note, eventually to be used as an *aide-mémoire.* For instance, in 1686, when the school of St Cyr was founded to please the woman who had such a profound influence upon his mind, he wrote down all the things that had to be done to be sure that the house would open on the given day.

'Letters patent properly drawn up.
Things required for the endowment.

Furniture of all kinds.
An agent to be chosen'.
Etc.

On some days there was neither councils nor audiences. On Fridays the King received his confessor. He kept him as long as he thought fit, sometimes until dinner-time.

Work did not occupy all his time. The King would rest and relax without leaving his study. He would summon musicians or writers, who were always at their master's disposition. One might wonder whether Lully or Delalande were very happy, conducting their works in such restricted space. But the King was content, and the watchful courtiers profited by these improvised concerts or poetry recitals.

In fact the doors were seldom closed during audiences. Saint-Simon noticed that courtiers were crowded into the next room while the King was sitting at the far end, talking with the lucky man.

When the audience was over, the King rose. It was one o'clock. He walked back to his room once more. That was the time to push forward so as to be noticed by the King. Many anecdotes reveal the importance of that moment in the view of all the noblemen who had been waiting for it since morning.

As a matter of fact, to be able to seize the opportunity one had first to secure the protection of some high person close to the King. They alone could procure such a favour. For instance, there was the Mayor of Angers, Grandet, who had been entrusted by his compatriots to seek the King's permission to establish in their city a literary academy after the fashion of the French Academy. Grandet sought the help of the governor of his province, who happened to be the first Equerry, the Prince d'Armagnac, whose zeal and intelligence were highly appreciated by the King. But the Prince was reluctant to bother the King. By mere chance Grandet met in the ante-chambers of the palace one of the gentle-man attendants, Chevais du Boulay, who promised to place him in an advantageous position. He got him into the front row when the King was passing. Grandet was a tall man and Louis noticed this newcomer and, by an astonishing feat of memory, remembered that he had already seen him a few years ago, and that he was from Anjou. He turned towards the Governor of Anjou, asking him

45

who was this man from his province. Grandet was at once presented and could put forward his request. He was granted a private audience, and pleaded his cause with an enthusiasm that did not displease the King. Shortly afterwards the letters patent, bearing on the foundation of the Academy, were duly granted.

All the petitioners did not enjoy such luck. After long and unsuccessful attempts, they could only put their letters on the petition table to attract the King's attention. The table was brought out into the guard's room each Monday; it was covered with a velvet gold-fringed cloth. During the first years of his reign, Louis liked to receive these requests personally, then he got bored by the tedious business and entrusted it to Louvois, and later Louvois' son, the Marquis de Courtanvaux. But he always insisted on being told about the most important petitions, and made sure they were all answered.

The King was back in his room. Dinner was served.

### DINNER

The King dined in his room and always alone. After the Queen's death, he was sometimes served in the ante-chamber of the Dauphine's suite. When she too died, he returned to the usual routine.

The dinner was always a *petit couvert* and even a *très petit couvert,* based upon the number of dishes and services prepared for His Majesty according to orders given in the morning during the *petit lever.* The King's table was brought in. Next, the principal courtiers and noblemen were admitted to the ceremony and remained standing at a certain distance from the table. Then the first gentleman went to call the King, who sat down.

Everyone knows that Louis XIV had a large appetite. According to the Palatine Princess—who does not always refrain from exaggeration and inaccuracy—he sometimes consumed four plates of soup, some game and salad, two slices of ham, a piece of mutton with garlic gravy, a full plate of pastries, fruit and a few hard-boiled eggs. But all those dishes were not taken away empty. Often, the King tasted only a small helping of each. Besides, it must be remembered that he had eaten nothing since the day before—apart from two cups of broth or herb tea for breakfast—and that he had worked for three hours.

Moreover, dinner was served with a slowness and a ritualistic pomp which would have exasperated all but the King. Each service was a truly theatrical display. This is how the King's meat was brought in:

'Two guards entered first. Then followed the usher of the room, the major-domo with his stick, the gentleman-in-waiting of the King's buttery, the Comptroller General, his office clerk, then the officers (that is, those of the food department) carrying the meat, the kitchen equerry and the keeper of the King's china. Behind them two more Royal Guards ended the procession.'

In all some fifteen persons had to make their way from the Grand Commun, where the victuals were cooked, to the King's chamber, through the courtiers who were present at the meal. Though all the dishes were covered—and this is the origin of the French word *couvert,* still used to designate the preparations for a meal—the King ran no risk of scalding his tongue, for the services followed one another without keeping him waiting, so that they were waiting at the door.

The ceremonial was just as rigorous when the King asked for a drink. The gentleman cup-bearer cried aloud: 'Drink for the King!' Then he bowed and went to the dresser, where the chief cup-bearer stood, who handed him a gold tray with a covered glass and two crystal decanters, one filled with wine and the other with water: Louis XIV never drank undiluted wine. He returned, escorted by the chief cup-bearer and his attendant. When the three had reached the table, they bowed low. The two cup-bearers both tasted the wine and water in silver-gilt cups; the gentleman cup-bearer bowed again, uncovered the glass and presented the carafes. The King helped himself to wine and water. Then the gentleman cup-bearer bowed once more and returned the tray to the chief cup-bearer, who took it and the glass back to the dresser. Thus three persons and some seven to eight minutes were required to provide the King with a glass of wine and water. Let us hope he was not too thirsty when he asked for it!

It is not surprising when describing this scene, which so closely resembles the mass (the bowing of the attendants when presenting the burettes to the priest) that the services of four hundred and ninety-eight persons were used in providing the King with a meal.

Louis XIV ate only with a knife and his fingers. The fork was first used in France in the reign of Henri IV. Louis XIV's grandson, the Duc de Bourgogne, had been taught how to use one. But his grandfather forbade him to use it when he was admitted to his table, and the Dauphin's son went back to old usages to please him.

No guest whatever was allowed to dine with the King; the rule was enforced all through the reign. Members of the Royal Family or Princes of the Blood could be present, but they never participated in it. On this point Saint-Simon was perfectly clear:

'Often enough did I see Monsieur, coming from St Cloud to see the King, or coming out of the Council of Despatches, the only council he attended. He gave the King his napkin and remained standing. A moment later, seeing that he was still there, the King asked him whether he would not like to sit down: he bowed and the King ordered a seat to be brought. A stool was put behind him. A moment later, the King said to him: "My brother, do sit down". Monsieur bowed again, and sat down until the meal was finished, and then he again handed the King a napkin.'

Thus, even the King's brother remained standing during a meal so long as the King had not asked him to be seated on a humble stool. One tends to think of courtiers at Versailles doubled up by perpetual bowing; but in fact their natural position was of perpetual standing.

### AFTERNOON

When dinner was over, the King went back at once to his study. Sometimes, he would take along some noblemen he wanted to see privately, Mostly, he took a short period of relaxation with his dogs. Then he would call for his robe attendants and change. There would be in attendance just a few distinguished persons, selected by the first gentleman of the bed-chamber.

As soon as the King was dressed, he left his study and went out either to hunt or for a walk. He would go down into the Marble Courtyard by the little inside staircase which got him away from the crowd of courtiers. Those who had succeeded in slipping in hoped to be able to talk to him during these few minutes; it was one of the rare opportunities during the day when it was possible

3. Madame de Montespan and the Duc d Maine, by Mignar

The Princess Palatine

4. Madame de Maintenon and her Niece, by Elle

to approach him. He could be handed a request or a petition as
he crossed the Courtyard and before entering his coach.

Everything was ready. The Life Guards were standing at attention at the back of the Marble Courtyard, along the palace railings.
The chosen few who were to accompany the King were already
in their coach or on horseback. It was a magnificent display that
no one tired of watching. 'Life Guards, courtiers, busy valets',
wrote Primi Visconti, 'all reminded me of a queen-bee coming out
into the fields with her swarm.'

At least once a week the King would hunt stags in the forest of
Marly or in the woods around Versailles; he would go out shooting
twice. On other days he would take out the court ladies. The
Palatine Princess claimed that Louis hardly ever walked in the
park. 'You are the only one who enjoys the beauties of Versailles',
he is reported to have said to her one day. On the other hand,
Saint-Simon recorded just the contrary. 'When the King does not
hunt, he walks in his gardens or has a look at the buildings.' It may
be that at the end of his life the King had had enough of his park,
but for many years he delighted in it. There are many stories
about his discussing the works in progress with his entourage. He
was very fond of his gardens, so much so that he busied himself in
writing a short guide to the park for the use of foreigners, in
which with a mixture of pride and good humour he described all
the beauties he had contrived.

The walk often ended at Little Venice, where the Grand Canal
flotilla was anchored. If the weather was fine and the master in a
playful mood, he offered a collation to the ladies. Tables were
brought and cakes and comfits produced, and the King was not
the last to do them justice. The return ended at any hour, but
seldom after five in the afternoon.

### THE END OF THE DAY

At the end of the day the King remained on show. Returning
after hunting, he changed again (for the third time since morning).
This time he assumed his most magnificent garb. Then he would
sit at his writing table, signing his 'friendship letters', the un-
official ones which his secretaries had written in accordance with
his instructions. When something serious occurred, he would
summon another council at the end of the afternoon.

49

Usually he did not spend more than an hour in his study and he would then visit Mme de Maintenon. Once or twice a week he would attend evening prayers in the chapel. Courtiers, especially the ladies of the court, crowded there, hoping to be noticed by the King and his sanctimonious attendant.

Prayers took place at five in winter, and at six in summer. There was no regulated procession to the chapel, and some people took advantage of the fact to approach him. In his memoirs the Marquis de Sourches tells of many favours obtained at this time.

After the service came the moment impatiently awaited by the crowd who had jostled since morning in ante-chambers and drawing-rooms: the *Appartement,* or reception. This was held three times a week. In this word actually coined by the King were implied all the pastimes that took place between seven and ten in the evening from October to Easter. Louis XIV insisted on this rite being observed. 'Madam,' he said to the Dauphine shortly after her wedding, 'I want you to hold an *appartement* and to dance at it. We are not like private people. We belong entirely to the public.'

The entertainments were varied: cards, billiards, dancing, concerts or sometimes plays. Buffets were set up, allowing spectators to eat cakes and ice-cream to their heart's content throughout the evening, and also to drink, since the heat, made worse by a huge quantity of candles, was overpowering. The King and the courtiers seemed not to mind it. Foreigners were less tolerant. The Countess of Osnabrück, who was at a reception in 1679, remarked that because of the 'crowds and the overwhelming heat the pleasures of the French court were mixed with much discomfort'.

Louis XIV was a friendly host. He would not allow people to rise at card tables when he came near them. He went from one to the other with perfect courtesy. Out of respect for him, guests did not raise their voices, so that only a subdued murmur could be heard which did not mar the elegance of the occasion.

The ball which brought the *appartement* to an end concluded at ten o'clock by a quadrille. After which came supper *en grand couvert.*

## THE GRAND COUVERT

Supper *en grand couvert* was something exceptional, though Louis XIV on the other hand maintained the habit of supping in public. He only abandoned it for sickness, mourning, or when he was eating meat on fast days. But he only transgressed for important reasons.

As long as the Queen lived the *grand couvert* took place in the ante-chamber. The tradition lasted during the Dauphine's lifetime. Only the Royal family sat at supper, and even the princesses of the blood were excluded. After the death of both the Queen and the Dauphine the King supped in the first ante-chamber, or footmen's ante-chamber, the windows of which overlooked the Marble Courtyard.

Thanks to the descriptions of Saint-Simon or the Marquis de Sourches it is easy to make out where the King sat: in the middle with his back to the fireplace. Behind him stood his first doctor and a few courtiers. Intoxicated with pride, the Duc de Saint-Simon does not hide the fact that he had often the honour to be among the elect. The other courtiers and the ladies, a little further off, remained standing. The King's armchair was of wood, painted red with gold lining-out, and covered with fringed crimson velvet.

Supper was less abundant than dinner. In order to sleep well, the King avoided too much food. During the ceremony, the King's little band played on a near-by dais. Supper was not prolonged beyond eleven o'clock.

### THE COUCHER

After supper the King went to his study for a few moments, but not for long. He bade goodnight to the mass of courtiers, who then retired. He returned to his bed-chamber, escorted only by those who in the morning had attended the great and the second entrances. In fact, they took part in the same ceremonial but in reverse. Louis first went to his bedside to say his evening prayers, which he recited with the chaplain on duty, who held a candle to light the King's prayer-book, 'even though the whole room was very well lit'.

Before the King sat in his armchair to be undressed, a little comedy took place, which shows the value placed by courtiers of high rank on the smallest favours bestowed by the King. Who was to hold the candlestick? The chaplain handed it to the first valet, Bontemps or Blouin, who took it to the King. Louis glanced at those who surrounded him and in a loud voice named him who was to hold it all through the ceremony. Saint-Simon wrote: 'It was a most valued distinction, and the King knew so well how to give importance to a trifle'. The lucky one removed his glove, stepped forward and held the candlestick throughout the *coucher*.

The King undressed with the aid of the first valet. He put on his nightshirt, his night jacket and his dressing-gown. He rose, went to the fireplace corner, bowing his head slightly. He gave his orders to the colonel of the French Guards. The people of quality then left, leaving behind the people of the first and second entrances and the bed-chamber attendants. Then began the *petit coucher*, which was short. After a few private matters, Louis removed his dressing-gown and got into bed. The lights were extinguished, with the exception of the night-lights. The only person to remain with the King was his valet, who had silently unfolded his camp bed.

It was past eleven. The King slept. The Life Guards were awake in their guard-room. The Swiss slumbered at the doors of the various suites. The palace seemed asleep. Tomorrow, the sun would rise upon a day exactly similar. Everyone would be back in his place. How easy to understand why even the King himself was bored by this endless performance! Happily, there were distractions which made some relaxation of this suffocating etiquette possible, and also a few unforeseen events.

# CHAPTER FOUR

# PLEASURES AND PASTIMES

To break the monotony of everyday routine, the King put aside a few hours each day for his favourite amusements, hunting or walking in the park in the afternoon along the Grand Canal or at Marly, and on his return, the pleasures of the *appartement*, cards, billiards, music and dancing.

### HUNTING

All the French Kings had a passion for hunting. The early ancestors of the Bourbons found in it not only an energetic and healthy sport, but by the pursuit of wild animals or mere game, of the kind that was harmful to crops, they performed a service to their subjects. Hunting, therefore, was both agreeable and useful.

It was quite different in Louis XIV's time. The Ile-de-France had been practically denuded of wild beasts and reservations had to be organized, so that the King could have his sport. The Parc-aux-Cerfs at Versailles, which acquired such bad repute because Louis XV owned there a small house where he kept his mistresses, had no other origin. But the park was too small. It had to be enlarged as early as 1678, and a pheasant farm was created, from which, wrote Dangeau, two thousand pheasants and five hundred partridges flew out at the same time on August 16, 1685. Breeding was organized in many well-provided places in this large area surrounded with walls (about 6,600 hectares) known at Versailles as the Grand Parc.

'Never give up business for pleasure's sake, but have a kind of rule which gives you some sort of freedom and entertainment. None is as innocent as hunting.' This advice, given by the King to the Duc d'Anjou, future King of Spain, had been his own rule throughout life.

He hunted at least three times a week. He soon gave up hawking, a form of hunting which his ancestors had followed constantly. The kite-breeding farm of Noisy-le-Roi was sold in 1685, but the office of captain or lieutenant of the King's hawks was carefully maintained. Louis had enough to do with riding to hounds and shooting. 'Nothing so far approached his packs in number and magnificence.' Soon after the Queen's death he broke his arm while riding at Fontainebleau. Also he had to contrive a light carriage drawn by four horses, which he used to drive at great speed, 'with a skill and a precision superior to that of the best coachmen, and with all his usual grace'.

Such compliments from the pen of Saint-Simon are of special significance, for on this subject the Duke was hard to please. He acknowledged the fact that the king's young postilions (pages of the Grande Écurie from twelve to fifteen years of age) were both clever and quick. The King had many dogs and bitches who knew him and were faithful to him, for he used to feed them every day after dinner. The Versailles kennel, built behind the Grande Écurie, where the Préfecture now stands, was a huge building and the Master of the Hounds, François, Duc de la Rochefoucauld, played a role at the palace almost as important as those of Monsieur le Grand or Monsieur le Premier. He was one of Louis' confidants.

The King was a fine shot. 'No one was so good a shot', wrote Saint-Simon, 'or so graceful'. His daily bag was always impressive. He was known to have killed more than 250 game in a day. When it was over, he would distribute what he had shot among the ladies of the court who had accompanied him. They tied them to their belts and drove back to the palace, proud to have been the object of such attention.

The hunting was magnificent. None but accomplished riders accompanied the King, who forced no one to follow him: 'He did not want anyone to go who did not enjoy it, or who found it ridiculous, and he took no offence at those who never came.' For him hunting was a pleasure and not an obligation.

Together with billiards, it was perhaps his favourite relaxation. When the hunt was over and he was back in his apartment, the King enjoyed recounting the day's activities. From his levee on, he talked about hunting, and in the evening it was practically the only topic of conversation. Amateurs are all alike. Together with the Dauphin and M de la Rochefoucauld he would shut himself up in his room to look at maps of the Great Park and discuss with them anything that could be done there to improve the hunting.

Although Saint-Simon claimed several times that the surroundings of Versailles were the worst possible, 'the dreariest and ugliest country in the world', Louis XIV was pleased with it. Once he actually transgressed one of the rules of his daily life, rules that he so rigorously enforced, when he gave up a council he had evolved in order to go hunting. It was on Tuesday, February 20, 1685, and it was so extraordinary an event that Dangeau mentioned it in his diary. The weather was glorious, one of those winter days that herald an early spring. The King was in an excellent mood. Turning to the Duc de la Rochefoucauld, he parodied a few lines of the prologue from Quinault's *Atys* and started singing:

> *Le conseil à ses yeux a beau se présenter*
> *Sitôt qu'il voit sa chienne, il quitte tout pour elle,*
> *Rien ne peut l'arrêter*
> *Quand le beau temps l'appelle.*[1]

Though he was forty-six, the King could still laugh and joke with friends.

### BILLIARDS AND CARDS

For years there was a billiard table in the Salon de Diane. It was a magnificent piece of furniture with delicately carved legs and gilded decorations. Later another billiard table was placed in one of the King's private apartments, which were decorated with silver orange-tree tubs. It became one of the favourite rooms for courtiers to approach their master.

Louis XIV went there almost every day between seven and eight. The Palatine Princess, his sister-in-law, did not like it at all. She used to complain: 'We go to the billiard table and lie flat on our stomachs without anyone uttering a word. We remain crouching until the King has played a game. Then we all get up and go off together to some music.'

[1] 'The weather was so marvellous that as soon as he'd seen his bitch, he dropped everything for her sake; nothing could stop him when a fine day called him.'

It is true that the King had an obsession for billiards. He was not a bad player, but he sometimes lost and the courtiers were terribly worried when there was an argument about a stroke. Who would be so daring and tactless as to oppose the King? Luckily, the King had a few real friends who did not hesitate to give their verdict. One day, the Duc de Gramont was obliged to be frank:

'Monsieur de Gramont,' said the King, 'you must judge the last stroke.'

'Unnecessary, Your Majesty. You have lost.'

'How can you decide against me before finding out what it's all about?'

'Sir, don't you see that, were the stroke even slightly doubtful, all these gentlemen would hasten to say that you had won?'

The King had his favourite partners. According to some contemporaries, Chamillard, who was Secretary of State for Finance, owed his office to his talent for giving the King points. This epitaph-like quatrain was written about him:

*Ci-git le fameux Chamillard*
*De son roi le protonotaire,*
*Qui fut un héros au billiard,*
*Un zéro dans le ministère.*[1]

When he had had enough of billiards, the King would settle down to cards. There was a tremendous lot of gambling at Louis XIV's court, and some of the courtiers acquired part of their income from their more or less legitimate winnings. Gambling was forbidden in Paris but not at the palace. The Marquise de Sévigné was deeply shocked. *Haca*—an Italian game, something like baccarat —was played at court, 'and 5,000 *pistoles* in a single evening were a mere nothing'.[2]

The Palatine Princess described the behaviour of the fortunate gamblers. 'One of them screams, another bangs the table so violently with his fist that the whole room resounds. A third shouts such blasphemies that one's hair stands on end.'

When the King was present, 'the courtiers behaved rather better,

[1] 'Here lies the famous Chamillard, the King's protonotary, who was a hero at the billiard table but a nonentity at the ministry.'
[2] The *pistole* was about twenty pre-1914 francs.

but they still played for very high stakes: 200,000 francs in ten days, 100,000 *écus* in a month, such were the gains or losses of some of them.'[1]

The Queen was often drawn in. Her favourite game was *hombre,* a Spanish game played by three with fifty-two cards. She was so artless, wrote Primo Visconti cruelly, that she continually lost. The Princesse d'Elbeuf (one of Turenne's nieces, who was quite poor) made her living out of the Queen's gambling. Louis XIV was no wiser and used to gamble for very high stakes. It has been suggested that he did so in the hope of ruining his courtiers, but it is by no means sure that he had such Machiavellian ideas. Cards can even betray Kings. 'It is true that a courtier', Dangeau wrote, 'must be able to play gallantly in the King's presence—that is to say, to lose.'

### CONCERTS AND PLAYS

It has been said that Louis XIV lived to music. The musicians of the King's chamber, the great and the small orchestras, violins and the chapel choir were constantly at his disposal. He liked his musicians. He wanted them with him, whether he was travelling, playing cards, taking supper, or in chapel. He was most generous to them: he gave letters of nobility to Lully and made Delalande so rich that he was able to buy several houses in Versailles.

The ordinary musicians of the King's music—the *Ordinaires de la Musique,* as they proudly termed themselves in legal deeds—were very numerous. To the thirty or so artists bequeathed to him by his father, Louis XIV, on the advice of Lully, added violins. One band of twenty-four great violins, and the other of sixteen small violins. This was a sort of revolution, for until that time the violin was regarded as an instrument suitable only for dancing. He also added trumpets, flutes, hautboys and female voices. The choirs were composed of ninety singers, male and female. They were conducted by sub-masters who were under Lully's and, later, Delalande's orders. This impressive ensemble performed almost every day in the chapel. They could deal equally well with Delalande's great motets and with operas and ballets. For seventeenth-century composers it was an incomparable instrument, either for religious, symphonic or dramatic music.

[1] The *écu* was worth about ten pre-1914 francs.

The King's music enjoyed a privileged position. Not enough note has been taken of the fact that most of the salons in the palace had platforms: they were meant for the chamber orchestras that were always ready to perform the King's favourite pieces. A late seventeenth-century tapestry shows Delalande, his baton in his hand and a score in the other, conducting a small ensemble of violins, 'cellos, flutes and hautboys, while young singers stand in the front row.

As usual, they were crowded together in an extraordinary fashion. Such crowding was the rule at Versailles. An engraving shows musicians accompanying the Duc de Chartres dancing a minuet in the presence of the Duc de Bourgogne. It looks as if the platform area had been cut out of the wall of the hall.

Louis XIV not only liked to listen to music, but he was quite a good performer himself. He played the lute, the harpsichord and above all the guitar. His favourite guitar player, whom he often summoned, especially in his old age, was Robert de Visée. The King also sang: his voice was not strong, but he had a sure ear and sang tastefully. He could read Lully's opera scores before they were performed in public. He carefully followed Delalande's work when he knew the composer was writing some minor piece for him and had him summoned several times a day to talk with him. Above all he liked the prologues of operas, with allegories that celebrated his own glory. He could memorise them with the greatest ease, which did not surprise Saint-Simon. 'In private he would sing extracts from these prologues, and even during public suppers would murmur this praise under his breath.' Early in his reign he was particularly fond of big concerts with full orchestra and choir, symphonies for *appartement* evenings and motets for the chapel. La Fontaine wrote:

> Ses concerts d'instruments sont le bruit du tonnerre
> Et ses concerts de voix ressemblent aux éclats
> Qu'en un jour de combat font les cris des soldats.[1]

The King's tastes grew quieter with age. He gave up the brass and timpani of the Grande Écurie Orchestra. To Mme de Main-

---

[1] 'His instruments made a noise like thunder and his choral concerts remind one of soldiers shouting during battle.'

tenon's apartment, where he retired after supper, he summoned his fiddlers or guitar players, or he listened to chamber music.

As the King was fond of music, everyone had to like it. The concert which followed billiards every day brought this complaint from the Palatine Princess: 'An air from some old opera, which has been heard scores of times, is sung.' Noblemen strove to emulate the King and gave concerts also. 'Court and town sing the Lully arias that have pleased the King, and they are hummed by every cook in France.' They were played on the Pont-Neuf and at every street corner. Music teachers were numerous at Versailles: several dozens in fact, and most of them belonged to the King's music.

Dangeau, who was not a particularly good musician, never failed, being a good courtier, to describe in detail the concerts and operas performed before the King; he is therefore a valuable source of information. His kindness towards the King's favourite composers was entirely relative. According to him, Lully claimed a certain sum from those of his fiddlers who gave concerts elsewhere than at Versailles ('doubtless to thank him for having taken them into his orchestra', commented Dangeau on February 9, 1685). He zealously recorded the pensions paid by the King to Delalande and the attentions bestowed upon him. One day a short opera, *Issé*, a pastorale composed by an obscure musketeer and song-writer, André Destouches, was performed before the English Pretender and his wife. Dangeau wrote: 'The King and courtiers agreed that Destouches' work was as good as Lully's, and that it had not been stolen'. Yet Destouches' daring and suggestive discords were far removed from Lully's canons. This had not occurred to Dangeau.

He courteously mentioned how successful the King's composers and their performers were. He appreciated singers of both sexes. Yet they were terribly cramped at Versailles. There was no regular theatre in the palace, and the State Apartments were scarcely intended for performances. Most of Lully's operas and Molière's ballet-comedies were performed in the park. One might rightly question what could be heard of some passages which the wind carried away or which were drowned by the noise. Was it not to enable the audience to get a better idea of works that were too often performed out-of-doors that Lully strengthened the brass and added violins?

When it rained the Galerie Basse provided shelter. As early as the autumn of 1663, Molière came to Versailles. His company trundled their sets along on a heavy cart. Trestles were erected in a recess of the Galerie Basse, and the musicians sat at the opposite end. The company played *L'École des Maris, Les Fâcheux* and *Le Dépit Amoureux*, and created *L'Impromptu de Versailles*. The King was delighted. The Grand Écurie was also occasionally used. The magnificent Riding School could easily be turned into a theatre as for a performance of *Roland* on January 8, 1685. Finally, comedies were acted at Trianon, but the auditorium could hardly seat more than thirty people. One can imagine the intrigues to secure an invitation. They were part of the daily life of Versailles.

Musicians had to be masters of all talent. They even turned themselves into actors. They acted *Georges Dandin* on February 10, 1713, 'before the King and the ladies'. They were praised and it was said that they acted as well as professionals. They did the same thing a few weeks later in *L'Avare*. As they were not forgetful of their own talents, they played symphonies during the intervals: a strange confusion of activities.

### WALKS IN THE PARK AND TRIPS ON THE WATER

When he was not hunting, Louis XIV took walks in the park. He liked to take his guests with him and to treat them to a collation in one of the bowers. When the weather was fine, the walk took place early in the afternoon. The King, his head covered (he was the only one to wear a hat) was accompanied by a limited number of courtiers—in fact, his usual escort. Only the holders of the principal offices were entitled to be with him, those who were always in attendance and who were beside him at the *lever* and the *coucher*. However, other noblemen attended at a distance and watched the privileged few from afar.

On foot or in his coach, the King usually drove towards the Grand Canal. As soon as it was finished in 1672, the King devised a means of using it. He had several Venetian gondoliers brought to Versailles. The Marquis de Lengeron, Caffieri and others designed models of ships, the *Grande Galère*, the *Langeronne*, the *Grande Gondole*. Tourville and Duquesne were ordered to supervise the construction of the flotilla. The sailors were housed in Little Venice. Their multi-coloured costume and their language added colour to the majestic but rather static décor.

After 1674 the flotilla took part in every *fête* and was used at other times as well. The ceremony took place with unalterable routine and Dangeau described it often. The King stepped into a gondola with the chosen ladies. The musicians were installed in another; the violins and the hautboys could be heard. The collation was served as the gondolas glided softly over the water. Singers performed too, until they all came back to the landing stage, where the King's coach was waiting. The next day, or some other day, this would all be repeated.

Sometimes the promenade took place at nightfall, replacing the concert or preceding the ball. The King was delighted by the slowly cooling air and the evening ended with a firework display over the water. The Marquise de Sévigné described it several times.

'We left the card tables at six. The King got into his carriage with Mme de Montespan, Monsieur, Mme de Thiange and the Baron d'Heudicourt on a folding seat. The Queen was in another coach with the princesses, followed by everyone else in their own fashion. We passed over the canal in gondolas. There was music and we got back at ten.'

In winter there was another amusement. The canal was frozen. Though not frequent, it is a not exceptional occurrence at Versailles. The flotilla was ice-bound, but one could skate or move around in sledges. The pleasure of doing something unusual made people rather fool-hardy. On December 31, 1684, the ice was too thin and broke. Monsieur le Prince (Condé) was up to his neck in water. The princesses slipped and fell. But the consequences were not serious and at any rate gave the courtiers a subject for gossip.

For this was the chief fault with these daily distractions; everyone was bored, and as it was vital to maintain conversation and never to allow it to languish, people became excited over the most futile subjects. The slightest rumour was exhaustively discussed: Mme de Maintenon's cold or the fact that the King had been bled led to endless commentary.

As relief to the heavy tedium which, from the beginning of the century weighed upon Versailles, receptions, the visits of illustrious persons, kings, princes or receptions for ambassadors, and births or deaths, gave some element of the unexpected to the established routine.

The park and palace of Versailles had been created for splendid occasions. The works had just started when the King made his intentions quite clear. The public knew of it. In June 1663 the gossip-monger Loret wrote these lines:

> *Leurs Majestés vont à Versailles,*
> *Château charmant, tranquil et coi*
> *Où les chasses, les exercises,*
> *Les concerts, les banquets friands,*
> *Les jeux et spectacles riants*
> *Comme passe-temps nécessaires,*
> *Succèdent au soin des affairs.*[1]

Six months later, the *Plaisirs de l'Ile Enchantée,* 'the gallant and magnificent *fêtes* given by the King', carried the glories of Versailles to the four corners of France.

This festival was devised in honour of Mlle de la Vallière, the King's reigning mistress; he loved her passionately. They began on May 5th and lasted for a week. Nothing was ready. Molière had to improvise, but did not mind. The King and his retinue were in fancy dress for the great parade of the first evening: the Prince de Condé was dressed as the Turkish Emperor. The King's suite could be recognized by their colours, flame and silver. Numerous torches lit the park. Open-air entertainments provided Molière with an opportunity to display his ingenuity. The Princess d'Elis was finally freed from the spells of the magician who held her captive. Meanwhile, during the day there was hunting, tilting, and games of skill in the castle moats.

The lucky guests at these spectacles spread everywhere the story of their magnificence. Yet the courtiers were not well lodged. Some of them had to end the night in their coaches, and at Versailles the May nights were far from warm. 'All the courtiers were furious', wrote Mme de Sévigné, 'for the King did not care for them a bit,

---

[1] 'Their Majesties go to Versailles, a delightful, quiet and restful castle, where hunting, riding, concerts, tasty banquets, games and amusing spectacles, all necessary pastimes, relieve the cares of duty.'

and MM de Guise and d'Elbeuf had scarcely a hole to shelter in. Versailles was still only a village, and inns like the *Fleur de Lys* or the *Image St Julien* were not fit to house noblemen. These festivities were repeated in 1665, 1668 and 1674, and they were better organized. That of July 18, 1668, which followed the signature of the Treaty of Aix-le-Chapelle, brought more than 1,500 persons together. The weather was very fine and the park had never displayed so much running water and such an opportunity to produce the shepherds and shepherdesses, and the day ended with a firework display in front of the lighted castle. This time, there was no adverse criticism. The whole of Europe heard of that magnificent spectacle. 'Palaces turned into gardens and gardens into palaces', wrote La Fontaine. But the bill was heavy —more than 100,000 *livres*.

In 1674 the reception given to crown Athénaïs de Rouchechouart-Mortemart, Marquise de Montespan, as the King's official mistress was less expensive. It was then that Racine produced *Iphigénie* and Quinault produced *Alceste*. The Marquise wore a 'dress of gold on gold, embroidered on gold, mingled into a certain kind of gold, forming the most divine material ever devised'. Mme de Sévigné, who described the masterpiece, had a rather fine sense of humour.

The *fêtes* became less frequent when Mme de Maintenon's reign began, and the performance of *Esther*, acted by pupils of Saint Cyr in the King's apartment, had very little in common with what was done when the palace was young.

When ambassadors were received there were solemn ceremonies. Some of them became famous and their memory has been preserved in paintings or engravings. The coming of the Turkish ambassadors became something like a fancy-dress ball. The King did not want to be less gorgeously dressed than the eastern sovereign's envoys, so he was covered with gold and diamonds, feathers and turbans. It is likely that this audience provided inspiration for Molière, who could sometimes be ferociously satirical. The dates, in fact, confirm this hypothesis, since the ballet-comedy *Le Bourgeois Gentilhomme* was created in 1670, and Soliman, the Grand Turk's envoy, was received in 1669. Soliman had not shown the King enough respect and had laughed at Louis XIV's Turkish masquerade.

The ambassadors of the King of Siam showed more respect and

surprise. The King received them in 1686 and great consideration was shown them. They were taken round the orangery. One of them remarked: 'The King's fortune must be very great indeed, for he has erected such a magnificent building to house his orange-trees!' The party ended on the Grand Canal. The Siamese found the slow progress over the calm water much more pleasant than they had experienced on the ocean crossing to Brest.

A visit to Little Venice and a trip on the Grand Canal were now part and parcel of the ritual. When Potemkin, the Czar's envoy, was received by Louix XIV, the eight Venetian gondolas were shown to the ambassador, and huge negroes assisted the guests into the boats.

As usual, there were few courtiers with the King. On some days, on the contrary, there were terrible crowds, as when the Doge of Genoa came to Versailles. It is true that he was eagerly awaited, as his visit had a political purpose in sealing the reconciliation of France with the Republic of Genoa. A huge crowd surged through the palace galleries. 'In spite of all the precautions taken to avoid disorder during his reeption', Sourches wrote, 'the crowd was so frightful that it was impossible to keep a passage free through the Gallery between the Salon de la Guerre and the Salon de la Paix, where the King was waiting. The Doge could scarcely pass through the crowd.'

One of the last ambassadorial receptions took place on February 19, 1715, when the Envoy Extraordinary of the Shah of Persia came to France. As usual, Saint-Simon has left a description of the ceremony which is as picturesque as it is biting:

'This ambassador was very badly dressed, and his presents beneath contempt. The King had put on a black and gold habit, with the finest diamonds of the crown. He sat on the throne with the Princes of the Blood and the bastards standing beside him. The Ambassador came up the Grand Staircase and crossed the Gallery. The splendour of the scene disconcerted him. On leaving the audience he was treated to dinner by the King's officers, as was customary.'

'Pontchartrain had neglected nothing in order to flatter the King, and made him believe that this Embassy had revived the heyday of his glory . . . no one was more easily deceived than this monarch. . . .'

And yet, Saint-Simon had grudgingly to recognize the fact that the courtyard, the roofs and the avenue were swarming with people. Possibly the show was not so very contemptible, after all.

## BIRTHS, DEATHS AND MARRIAGES

On August 6, 1682, the birth of the Duc de Bourgogne, Louis XIV's first grandson, was greeted with tremendous enthusiasm. The Dauphine had given birth to her baby in one of the rooms of the Superintendance of Buildings, where she had her apartments. In fact, the court had just moved into Versailles, and the suite Maria-Christina was to live in was still so full of masons that she had taken refuge in Colbert's apartments, as the banging of hammers ruined her sleep.

To be present at the event, the King had a mattress taken there for his use. When it was known that the baby was a son, 'there was such a tremendous shout of joy in the castle that in a moment the news had reached to the other end of the town . . . one was stifled in the galleries and the apartments, as everyone wanted to be seen there by the King, and the rabble, not wishing to show less pleasure than the people of quality, in a kind of fury broke all the windows of the Superintendance. Some clapped their hands as the King passed by; others lit fires into which they threw all they could lay their hands on. They burnt down the cranes and the scaffolding of the buildings. Some even threw their own clothes into the fire. If they had not been prevented, they would have burnt all the wood stored by the merchants of Versailles. The King was told of this while the *Te Deum* was sung in the chapel. "Let them do as they wish", he answered, "so long as they don't set fire to us!" '

Weddings caused less disturbance, but the crowding was still very bad. In July 1685, when Louis XIV married Mlle de Nantes' legitimized daughter to the Duc de Bourbon, Condé's son, the festival, as described by Sourches, was charming. The sun was shining. 'The whole company embarked upon the Canal and was slowly rowed to the sound of the King's music, he following in his yacht. Supper was served at Trianon. The rooms were magnificently lit with crystal chandeliers.'

Seven years later, Mlle de Blois, another legitimized daughter of Mme de Montespan, was married in her turn to the Duc d'Orléans' son, the Duc de Chartres, the future Regent of France. For once,

Saint-Simon agreed that the bride was very beautiful, but could not refrain from making a remark which he thought was witty. 'Tall and full of majesty, she always behaved as a Daughter of France, even on her *chaise-percée*.' Such pieces of furniture, of course, played a leading role in eighteenth-century conversation.

The most gorgeous wedding, the one which Saint-Simon relates in the greatest detail, was obviously that of the Duc de Bourgogne, the King's grandson, to Marie-Adélaide of Savoy. The Duke was fifteen and his bride barely twelve. Louis XIV was so pleased with that marriage that he had made it known that 'he would be pleased if the court was made to look magnificent'. Everything was done to satisfy him. There was a fantastic display of resplendent costumes. The women vied with one another in luxury and extravagance. And Saint-Simon actually wrote: 'It went so far that the King regretted having made that remark and said that he could not understand how there could be husbands mad enough to allow themselves to be ruined by their wives' clothing' . . . and by their own wives! In fact, Saint-Simon confessed that, between his wife and himself, they spent 20,000 *livres* (40,000 gold francs)!

The Cardinal de Coislin blessed the pair. There was such a crowd that one had to queue up for a quarter of an hour before passing through the doorways. At seven at night everyone met in the King's apartment to play cards. Then they all went to watch the firework display on the *Pièce d'Eau des Suisses*, but wind and rain spoiled the spectacle.

The wedded pair retired to their separate apartments. Four days later the State ball in the Great Gallery was attended by such a crowd that the King himself was overwhelmed. The Duc d'Aumont fainted and Monsieur was jostled and crushed without regard to his rank.

The ceremony of presenting the wedding night-shirts to bride and bridegroom was always a treat, and a great honour when the King condescended to present the bridegroom's. He did so for the Duc de Berry, his grandson, when he married Mademoiselle d'Orléans. Louis actually made a pun: 'You often handed it to me; now it is my turn.'

And yet this wedding was rather quiet. War and defeat had compelled the court to reduce expenses. The King gave the lead and everyone followed his example.

For Versailles it was a period of mourning. Mourning, too,

was regulated and the Grand Master had merely to follow the rules.

No king went through so many family bereavements as Louis XIV. He lost the Queen, his wife, on July 30, 1683. She had given him six children, and five of them died in infancy. The King lost in succession his daughter-in-law, his grand-daughter-in-law, his only surviving son, the Dauphin, two grand-children; also his brother, Monsieur, in 1701, and his great-grand-children. Louis XIV bore these losses with constant stoicism, which was neither indifference nor weariness. He sincerely mourned Maria-Thérèsa of Austria, and his remark when hearing that all was over, has been often quoted: 'I lived with her for twenty-three years and she never gave me any reason to be displeased, nor did she oppose any one of my wishes.' One may guess what was the real meaning of those last words.

Every piece of the King's mourning was strictly regulated as to colour and length. Eventually, he could not stand the sight of them any longer and, when Mme de Maintenon lost her brother in 1703, he forbade her to drape the outside and inside of her coaches in black.

The loss which touched him most was that of his son, the Grand Dauphin, who died at Meudon. When describing the Prince's last moments (April 12, 1711) Saint-Simon allowed himself to relate the grotesque or ridiculous incidents which always happen in such cases, and which never fail to draw a smile, even on faces of the stricken. For instance he recounted the quarrel between the doctors at the bedside of the dying man: 'Boudin suggested to Fagon that they should summon the Paris doctors. Boudin became angry, refused, swore he needed nobody . . .' And an hour later, while the King was supping calmly in the room next to the one in which his son was dying, he suddenly rushed in, shouting, 'Everything is lost!' The King wanted to go to his son, but the Princesse de Conti (the Dauphin's half-sister) barred the entrance: she pushed him back with her hands, saying that he should think of himself only. Mme la Duchesse and Mme la Princesse de Conti were attending both the dying man and the King, while the doctors, in a state of confusion, the terrified servants and a crowd of courtiers were jostling round him.

The King left for Marly, meaning to see the Duchesse de Bourgogne at Versailles on the way. He sent word to her, requesting that she meet him in the avenue between the two stables. As soon as he arrived (about half-past twelve) she stepped to the ground and approached the King's coach. Mme de Maintenon shouted to her: 'What are you doing, Madame? We are all plague-stricken!' For the Dauphin had died of small-pox and infection was dreaded.

Meanwhile, at Versailles everyone was massing in the Queen's former apartments, the ladies having hurried there in *déshabillé*. 'One noticed among the courtiers those who revealed by their look which shop they used to sweep.'

Gradually the situation calmed down. The Duchesse d'Orléans and a few friends withdrew into a salon near the Great Gallery, and happy to be free for a few minutes, started discussing what had happened and what might be the consequences. Nothing in the usual etiquette had changed and the camp-beds of the Swiss Guard had been set up in the usual fashion. The group drew near to one of them. The beds were surrounded by curtains. Suddenly, Mme de Castries, who was leaning against one of them, felt it move and was greatly afraid. A moment later, she saw a large, almost naked arm pushing aside the curtains and a large Swiss soldier, half-asleep and wondering what was happening, appeared, rolling in his bed-sheets. 'Feeling that it was not proper to rise in the presence of so many people, he slipped back into bed and went back to sleep.' This incident made the ladies laugh, but they were rather worried, as they feared he might have overheard their conversation. 'The sleepiness and uncouthness of the man reassured them.' In Versailles, the least word could be repeated, altered and made the object of endless discussion.

Meanwhile Louis XIV had reached Marly. No one was expecting him. The keys of the apartments were not to be found. Only the stumps of candles were available. The castle was ice-cold. Sitting in a corner of Mme de Maintenon's ante-chamber, the King wept bitterly. Finally, keys were produced. The King went to bed. It was almost four in the morning. He was seventy-three years old.

Another loss struck him deeply ten months later: that of his grandson, the Duc de Bourgogne, and of his wife, dying one after the other within a week. They were buried together. 'The King felt the deepest sorrow, and at the Palace there was the dreadful sight of those two bodies, side by side on the same great bed.'

February 11, 1712, the Duchesse de Bourgogne's death. February 18, the Duke's death. March 8, the death of the new Dauphin, their son, the King's great-grandson, aged five. May 3, 1714, the Duc de

68

Berry's death, the last of the King's grandsons. A little later, the little Duc d'Anjou, who was to become Louis XV, was carried to the King. He took this child of four in his arms and, weeping bitterly said: 'Here, then, is all that is left of my family.'

Feasts and mourning, Versailles experienced them throughout the reign. They were the endless punctuation of the daily life of the palace.

# CHAPTER FIVE

# THE DAILY LIFE OF
# A COURTIER

The lives of courtiers were changed profoundly by the creation of Versailles. Until then they were a group of noblemen serving the King and his family. They were the King's friends, held office and were indispensable. They were not numerous. At the beginning of his reign, Louis XIV did not change those habits, and his court resembled that of his ancestors. When he began to stay in his new chateau, he took only a limited number of attendants with him. 'There are hardly any women here, and very few men,' wrote the Duc d'Enghien to the Queen of Poland on June 27, 1667. 'Never has the court been so small and one hardly knows what to do.' We know that at the *Plaisirs de l'Ile Enchantée* there were six hundred guests.

Thirty years elapsed before the town of Versailles was built and the courtiers, moreover, were rather hostile to the thought of settling there. Primo Visconti wrote: 'The air is unwholesome. It is so poisoned by foul water that in August the courtiers all fell sick. Yet, the King is determined to stay there.'

Gradually the charm of the new residence made itself felt. It became evident that nothing could be expected from the King if one did not join the large crowd which settled at Versailles. The court swelled immeasurably. There are no lists and no statistics, but we may safely assume that when it reached its full glory it counted something like ten thousand people.

A small minority were housed by the King. When about a century later a list was made of the dwellings in the castle, there were 226 and twice that number of single rooms. Of course, in order to have the joy and the pride of saying that they lived in the palace, courtiers were ready to accept the darkest garret or the meanest attic. One would have crawled to anyone to be granted a 'rat-hole'.

## COURTIERS AT VERSAILLES

It was in 1671 at Dunkirk, where he was preparing to invade Holland, that Louis XIV signed what can be regarded as the charter of the new city. Until then, as a large borough in the vicinity of Paris, with its old church of St Julien, inns for carters and cattle drovers from Brittany and Normandy, Versailles had altered little. The constructional work done by the King and his father, the organization of the gardens and the basins, had drawn a crowd of workmen there, most of whom were housed in the sordid barracks which sprang up all around. A new city—*Ville Neuve*—a name which survived until the end of the eighteenth century, had been planned to the north of the palace. Plans were made, but the streets and squares were no more than gutters full of mud in winter and of dust in summer. Here and there a few small houses and even fewer larger ones were being built for the noblemen who had sought to follow the King's lead without delay.

The Act of 1671 changed the situation completely. Louis XIV granted not only a tax-free building site to anyone who asked for it; he also granted a tremendous privilege to houses built on such sites—they could not be confiscated by law. All legal experts thought the privilege exorbitant.

In order to understand the full significance of that favour, one of the permanent characteristics of the French nobility—and of the courtiers above all—must be remembered: the lack of money. They lived an expensive life. Courtiers, transplanted far from the source of their income, their lands, had the greatest difficulty in facing up to the innumerable expenses forced upon them by the life at Versailles. They usually counted on inheritances, and borrowed on them long before the testator's death. They reckoned, too, on the wife's '*dot*'. They borrowed without intention of repaying. It was an old tradition never to pay one's debts. Molière invented nothing. This is something not usually appreciated and the habit lasted until the end of the eighteenth century. When going through the archives of families who emigrated at the time of the Revolution one is staggered at the sight of so many unpaid bills.

Throughout Louis XIV's reign, the French nobility was in

continuous debt. It was thought bad form to pay one's bills. One of their creditors puts his point rather coarsely in a satire:

> *Car un lion plutôt me sortirait du cul*
> *Que de leur vaine bourse un misérable écu.*[1]

All creditors were not as patient as Monsieur Dimance in Molière's *Amour Medécin*. Of course, it was flattering to have among one's customers some of the greatest names in France, dukes and marquises who boasted of attending the King's Grand Levee or supper every day, but it was also pleasant to pocket hard cash, and they grew tired of being paid only with fine words and empty promises. Soon they started legal proceedings, and their attorneys would pursue the debtors into their very coaches. If they still did not pay, wages were seized. Numberless big houses in Paris were thus mortgaged or threatened with sale by order of court.

It is therefore easy to see what a windfall the King's offer was for new inhabitants. Their houses could neither be seized nor sold by law. At Versailles everyone flouted his creditors. Noblemen flocked there. The King had found the best way to populate his city and gather there the whole French nobility. That privilege lasted until 1713.

The consequences were soon felt. Numerous courtiers applied for building space, and within a few years some five hundred grants were made. The Noailles, La Feuillade, Condé, Turenne, Gramont, Gesvres, all the greatest in the kingdom soon had their houses at Versailles. Between a courtyard and a garden, the lay-out was quite simple. Let us look at the Duc de Bouillon's mansion in the Rue de la Chausée de Clagny—the present Rue des Réservoirs —though the building itself was pulled down early in the nineteenth century. The ground floor had large windows on either side and a single storey with smaller bays, and was surmounted by an attic emphasizing the slate-covered roof. A large portico, supported by twin columns and crowned by stone vases, opened on a rotunda-like drawing-room. There were six rooms on the ground floor. On the garden front a few steps led down to the flower beds. The house was built by Mansart and completed in ten months.

This was one of the characteristics of the town. Everything was conceived, begun and finished with frantic haste. The King was

---

[1] 'It would be easier for me to produce a loan from my * * * than to extract a paltry coin from their empty purses.'

in a hurry and so were his courtiers. A traveller who had stayed away from Versailles for a while would not recognize the town when he returned. Where there had been empty spaces, puddles or cornfields, there would now be a street lined with fine, gay houses, in the same colours as the castle: red brick, white stone and blue slate. And here would be a square and at its centre a fountain, and around the proud home of the King's mistress an elegant park would be taking shape.

The young, crowded and animated town of Versailles was the very reflection of the King's youth. Courtiers did not mind too much that they had left their castles or their fine Paris mansions. For they were close to the Sun King and they no longer feared their creditors. They had their parts to play in the daily spectacle of the court.

Besides those who lived their daily lives at Versailles, there was the numberless crowd of favour-seekers. These people usually spent only a few days, or at most a few weeks, in town. To secure an office, an employment or a benefit one had to be seen, to dance attendance on the ministers, to haunt the offices. If the stay was short, one made do with a room in one of the town's inns: they were innumerable. If it was longer, one rented a furnished room. The small provincial nobleman, the judge from the third-rate jurisdiction, the mayor of a distant city had the impression of being temporarily part of the closed, envied, magnificent and sordid world of the courtiers.

Who really belonged officially to that social class? First of all, the members of the Royal Family. They surrounded the King but were no better treated than the rest. The Grand Dauphin and his sons, His Majesty's grandsons, used to be present at the *petit couvert*, standing in a respectful attitude. Then came the Princes of the Blood, entitled to an apartment in the palace; members of the house of Bourbon, the Grand Condé, known to Saint-Simon as Monsieur le Prince, and his son; his brother Armand, Prince de Conti, and the latter's two sons. On a level with the Princes of the Blood were the Princes of the Church, cardinals and archbishops. Then came the dukes and peers of the realm. At Louis XIV's accession, they were not very numerous, about twenty including the foreign dukes and those who were not peers, whose titles had been conferred by Parliament. The King was to create more of them and to give what was at first a life title to some of his friends. Below this rigidly fixed hierarchy came the great State dignitaries, Secretaries of State, the Comptroller-General of Finance or of the Army, the Marshals and Admirals of France, holders of high offices (Grand Almoner, Grand Chamberlain, Grand Equerry), who were all entitled to some accommodation in the palace or its annexes. Of these there were about a hundred.

Offices were filled quarterly, consequently there were usually four persons for each of them.

'The offices in the King's household are numerous', wrote Primo Visconti, 'on account of the quarters, which quadruplicate the number of holders, so that there are more than seven thousand of them, without counting the soldiers of the King's Household, four thousand foot soldiers of the French Guards, the Swiss regiment, a company of halberdiers, another of archers, another of guards of the gates, and some three to four thousand cavalry.'

Those different bodies, with a few exceptions, like the guards of the gates or the Swiss, were not housed at Versailles, but in surrounding towns, like St Germain or Rueil, and they came in turn each day to discharge their duty, which brought animation to the town.

Finally, there was a vast anonymous crowd, the various household officers, the King's musicians, and artists working on the castle. But most of the musicians lived in Paris.

It is difficult to determine the exact number of all those who lived in the palace. Under Louis XV, the Chief of Police, Narbonne, put it at four thousand, and he may have over-estimated. Under Louis XIV those who drew salaries were never more than three thousand, but on some special occasions the court probably counted some fifteen thousand people.

One understands why Primo Visconti wrote with harshness and brutality: 'I wish you could see the court. It is a complete muddle of men and women. Well-known people may enter anywhere. As the national temper is somewhat light, it is a mixture of people, a continuous turmoil, so that the Duc de Palestrina said to me: "It's a real b..." '

## DAY BY DAY

The first and imperious duty of a courtier was to be seen or, at least to try to be seen. Consequently, he had always to be in attendance. However late he went to bed, he could not remain in bed in the morning. The lucky ones who attended the *petit lever* were required to be there by seven-thirty in the morning, and as full dress, tidy and be-ribboned, was obligatory, they had to be up very early. Monsieur le Grand, who discharged his duties with the greatest punctuality, attended the grooming of the horses in the stables at five in the morning. It is true that to save time he hardly washed.

The ordinary courtier, who was not obliged to be at the King's side each morning, tried to push his way into the crowd in attendance, and into some important person's favour. 'This winter is spent like the rest,' wrote handsome Bussy Rabutin to his cousin, the Marquise de Sévigné. 'In the morning I attend the King; then to the Cardinal's apartment, but just to have my presence noted, for he is hardly ever seen; then to M. le Tellier, sometimes to Marshal de Turenne. . . .' Four visits in a few hours, merely as a matter of routine. A good courtier was kept very busy.

When Louis XIV went to chapel, it was quite seemly to rush ahead and grab a seat. One sat down and turned towards the King, which shocked La Bruyère very much:

'The nation's great assemble each day at a certain time in a temple they call a church. At the back of this temple is an altar dedicated to their god, where a priest celebrates mysteries termed holy, sacred and awful. They form a wide circle round the altar, standing with their backs towards the priest and his holy mysteries, facing their King, who is seen kneeling on a tribune, and to whom they seem to dedicate their minds and hearts. One can see in such a custom only a form of subordination, for the people seem to adore the prince and the prince to adore God.'

'These people seem to adore the prince:' La Bruyère was right. The nobility was filled with adulation for him.

While the King attended his council, the cabinet doors were closed. In the palace galleries courtiers promenaded, forming groups or passing from one group to another. 'They are chameleons, wind-sniffers and dish-lickers,' said an old actor of the Hôtel de Bourgogne. Courtiers would often lean against a dresser to relieve their fatigue.

Courtiers became bored and occupied themselves by passing on the latest gossip. They were bored, but nothing in the world would induce them to abandon their post. Louvois was indignant. He roundly told a certain captain whose company was in a very poor state: 'You must choose, Monsieur; either to be a courtier or to do your duty as an officer.' The trouble was that officers would rather lose their companies than their places at court.

So the day passed in this fashion: courtiers met the King when he was walking or returning from hunting, or in his apartment. In the evening, still standing, they waited for the time of the *coucher*. One could see the Prince de Condé's son, completely exhausted, dozing on a stool in the corner of a doorway, waiting for the King to come and undress. To enliven their lives, they had nothing better to do than intrigue, gamble, gossip and indulge in witticisms that were passed from one to another.

## NAIVETIES AND REJOINDERS

An unexpected remark by the King often provoked a reverential fear in the man addressed. In spite of his mediocre stature, about five feet four inches, though his wig and high heels added another ten inches to his height, Louis XIV had succeeded in giving himself an aspect so majestic, so solemn, that his presence always seemed formidable. 'One was very small at court, and however proud one might be, one realized the fact. But this afflicted everyone, and even the great felt small.' This completes the remark of Saint-Simon that 'one had to get used to the King's appearance if one did not want to feel awed into silence when talking to him. The respect carried by his presence left one speechless and quite awe-stricken.'

When the tapping of the King's cane announced his approach, when the usher who preceded the procession announced: 'Gentlemen, the King!', absolute silence replaced the uproar of the crowd. Louis would walk in, addressing a remark to one and asking a question of another. It was then important to have words ready that would flatter the master. The cleverest and most intelligent minds often felt lost. It can be easily understood that some responses were no more than silly or naive. Others, on the other hand, did succeed in displaying their cleverness. A great many of such dialogues have been preserved.

For instance, let us quote what Cardinal d'Estrées once said. He was clever and witty and had the honour of supping at the King's table. Louis XIV was growing old and toothless and complained bitterly of his condition. He really suffered from his lack of teeth. His dentist, Fagon, had removed several of them at one sitting, with such brutality that the King's palate had been injured.

'Teeth, Sir?' remarked the Cardinal, displaying a magnificent set of faultless teeth. 'No one has teeth these days.'

The remark was rather like Le Brun's clever compliment in reply to an embarrassing question. As the King's favourite painter, he began a new portrait towards the end of the reign. 'Don't you think I have aged?' the King suddenly asked. Too sincere to lie and too wary to be frank, Le Brun managed to behave as a perfect courtier: 'Sir, I perceive a few more campaigns on Your Majesty's brow.'

At this game the men of letters were as wise as the painters. The King liked Racine and held him in great esteem. He had made him sleep in his room in 1696, when he was suffering from carbuncles, in order to have the pleasure of hearing him read Petrarch's *Lives* 'better than anyone else'. He had made him his historiographer. But the poet kept a certain independence of mind when dealing with his illustrious master. When summoned to take part in the Dutch campaign of 1677, he preferred to stay in Paris. When the King was back, he did not fail to show surprise at the fact that Racine had not turned up.

'How could you not have wanted to see a siege? It was not a long journey.'

'Sir,' answered Racine, 'the fault was my tailor's, who was too slow. I ordered a campaign suit. When he brought it, the cities Your Majesty was besieging had been taken.'

Assuredly Louis XIV was not taken in by such flattery, which was kin to a remark made by the Duc du Maine, one of the King's sons by Mme de Montespan:

'Sir, I shall be an ignoramous all my life! My tutor gives me a holiday every time Your Majesty achieves a victory.'

Besides such witty repartee, there were many silly rejoinders by men who were certainly not stupid, but utterly paralysed by the King's presence. One day, the King asked the Duc d'Uzès, whose wife was pregnant, when the child would be born.

'Sir, the day it pleases Your Majesty . . .'

Some remarks sounded very funny in their desire to please. It is well known that Racine, at the point of death, wanted to give proof of his faithfulness to his Port-Royal friends by asking to be buried among them. This was the height of the Jansenist persecution. The King could not avoid showing displeasure. M. de Custine remarked at once: 'He would certainly not have done it when alive!'

### DEVICES FOR LIVING

An agonizing problem constantly haunted the majority of court gentlemen: how to keep their rank and yet live with adequate magnificence.

Life was terribly expensive in Versailles. To be able to live ostentatiously, huge sums of money were spent daily. One had to have servants, coaches, horses and fashionable clothes, both magnificent and varied. An ill-dressed courtier was lost.

Now, the nobility's fortune was mostly landed. All their incomes came that way. As long as they had lived in their family castles, able to control their estates and see how they were exploited, they had resources enough. But separation had terrible results. Owners had relinquished the supervision of their estates to business men who were not always honest and who were very irregular in paying rents. There was always a storm which had ruined the crops or a flood which had spoiled the vintage. Agents joined with the peasants in robbing an absentee master. Nothing but his active presence on the spot provided sufficient supervision and prevented waste. Mme de Sévigné, though she used often to visit her favourite estate of Les Rochers, would complain: 'Oh, if they would pay me what they owe me in Brittany and Burgundy!' She confessed she could rely on only a quarter of her income.

A courtier who had to rely on only a meagre income, irregularly sent, had to find other means of subsistence. He subsisted on expedients, relying on business which his presence at court gave him some means to discharge. To be admitted to court was an asset he could make use of, a 'capital'—Georges Mongrédien's phrase—which he could bank on. Consequently, courtiers attempted to trade on their influence, and to reap something out of their position near the King and his ministers.

One of the usual things for a Secretary of State for Finances to do, in order to acquire fresh resources, was to ask the King to create new offices, which were sold—as is still the case in France today with notaries, attorneys and auctioneers. Those offices were very expensive and brought in a very small income, but those who

bought them were rewarded by honour, with privileges, consideration, and exemption from common taxes, and they were sometimes
a means of acquiring parliamentary nobility or marrying well.
That is why the King always found noblemen ready to become
either Governor of H.M.'s Carp, or Head of the Queen's Drinking
Cup, or Master of the Revels. 'Each time Your Majesty creates an
office, God creates a fool to buy it,' said Pontchartrain, and it was a
very apt remark.

As soon as a courtier heard of the creation of a new office, he
hurried to tell those whom it might interest. Once the office had
been established, the new officer did not fail, out of gratitude, to
present his advisor with a donation which was really a tip, which
the courtier put into his pocket without embarrassment.

There are dozens of instances, some quoted by Dangeau and
d'Argenson. The Duchesse de Guiches made 75,000 *livres* out of
the creation of an office of tax-collector on the removal of street
garbage in Paris. The Comtesse de Fiesque made 2,000 *écus* out of
the commission of a frigate captain. On the other hand, the Duc
de Saint-Simon admitted he had given 3,500 *livres* to the man who
told him that there was a regiment for sale. In this traffic women
were very eager, and royal mistresses were among the most greedy.
Louise de la Vallière agreed to pass petitions to the King provided
she got a little profit out of each of them.

Money was made out of everything. Titled ladies acted as intermediaries in arranging marriages and took a commission on the
bride's dowry. The Princesse d'Harcourt priced each invitation to
Marly at 6,000 *livres*—nothing less! She was well-known for her
greediness: 'A gambler and even a cheat,' wrote Saint-Simon. 'She
would do business for anything from an *écu* to the largest sums
of money.'

One other way of making money was to tell Secretaries of State
about abuses they could suppress. In exchange for the warning,
the 'giving of advice'—an almost official title—received substantial
reward. It may seem a strange and even unpleasant attitude, but
it was accepted as perfectly natural. It was not within anyone's
reach, and only the highest at court could indulge in it. The Prince
d'Armagnac (Monsieur le Grand, the King's Grand Equerry) got
10,000 *livres* in 1685 for having denounced some misappropria-
tions. Even Monsieur, who was always complaining about his lack
of funds, suggested to his brother that he could make an enquiry

into war profiteering, but he asked for a million *livres* and Louis XIV refused.

The *droit d'avis* (a right to inform) was an exceptional opportunity. Courtiers would bribe office clerks and eagerly waited for irregularities to be reported to them. Valincourt described this rather shabby activity:

> *De là viennent tant de bassesses*
> *De là marquises et comtesses*
> *Genre de courtisans nouveaux,*
> *En foule assiègent la porte.*
> *Attendant que le commis sorte,*
> *Pour demander d'un air soumis:*
> *'Puis-je espérer un droit d'avis?'*[1]

How well one understands why Mme de Motteville wrote: 'The King's houses are a big market-place where one must go to buy things necessary to sustain life and help those to whom we are attached by duty or friendship.'

## GAMBLING

In order to emulate the King the people at court were keen to risk their fortunes at cards. They might win; they might also lose and contract heavy debts which they would have to repay. Then they would not hesitate to turn to the King and present him with a petition. He provided the money, but kept the man who had sought his help in even closer bondage.

Gambling was one of the scourges of Versailles. Courtiers were not satisfied with gambling at the royal tables; they gambled among themselves. François Truffier, Seigneur d'Ogicourt, whom Saint-Simon called Augicourt for short, was one of those hard-up noblemen who stuck to the court and tried to gain at cards what they could not get from the King's pensions. His partners were men of rank: the Marquis de Livry, Monsieur le Grand and even the King's brother. 'They kept open house where one gambled the whole day from the morning onwards, and even all night,' wrote Saint-Simon. 'Augicourt played heavily and cleanly. He could not be reproached with cheating; only with being very bad-tempered

---

[1] 'Hence such baseness and hence the reason why marquises and comtesses and a new sort of courtier, go down to the offices, lay siege to their doors and wait for the clerk to come out, to ask him shyly: "May I hope for a *droit d'avis?*" '

5. Louis XIV and his Heirs, by Le Largillière

BAL A LA FRANCOISE

ALMANACH ROYAL POUR L'ANNEE M DC LXXXII

Rejouissance de Henriux et retour de ... Majesté

Court Ball in 1682

when he lost.' Then he would turn to Louis XIV, 'with whom he used to talk at length as the King went to mass or to see Mme de Maintenon'. This story is very revealing concerning court habits. The King's mistresses were uncommonly eager gamblers. Mme de Montespan, at her Chateau de Clagny, preferred *lansquenet*, to anything else. 'Stakes have gone so high', the Marquis de Feuquières wrote to his father, 'that losses of 100,000 *écus* (600,000 gold francs!) are common. On Christmas day, the Marquise lost 700,000 *écus*. She staked 150,000 *pistoles* on three cards and won. At this sort of game one can win or lose fifty or sixty times one's stake within a quarter of an hour.'

In the eyes of the Marquise, the King's opulent and beloved mistress, losses of some ten millions were negligible. Louis XIV would not have left Athénaïs in any sort of embarrassment, while others could get into dire straits when the cards let them down. Here is Mme de Rupelmonde, a particularly daring adventuress: 'As red as a cow, with plenty of wit but with unparalleled effrontery, she stuck to the court and with the nicknames *La Blonde* and *Vaquà-tout*, she gambled with the highest stakes in the world.'

Her husband was a sad-looking man, resembling an apothecary's servant. He tried to restrain his wife and prevent her from squandering the family money each night. He could do nothing, for Mme de Rupelmonde had a passion for gambling. She often had the Duchesse de Bourgogne as partner. One evening, at Marly, the court was playing *lansquenet* with great zest. Suddenly a Swiss guard entered and shouted: 'Mme de Rupelmonde, go to bed! Your husband is there and is calling for you.' These Swiss soldiers may not have known all the refinements of the French language, or the man may have spoken deliberately in order to humiliate the lady. But everyone burst into laughter. Half-ashamed and half-defiant, Mme de Rupelmonde refused to go, but the Duchesse de Bourgogne forced her to leave. 'The husband was killed shortly afterward', added Saint-Simon negligently, 'and through impudence, insolence, complacency and love of intrigue, the lady finally became lady-in-waiting to the Queen (Marie Leczinska) at her wedding.'

It is characteristic of gambling at cards that there is always the hope of being lucky in the end. It does sometimes happen. Then it is better to be careful, like the Marquis de Dangeau: 'to limit one's fortune and charges' at that point and not at the end of the month, some two or three thousand *livres* on credit. For most courtiers, debits and credits cancelled each out in the end. Funds as a result of gambling were precarious. Only a small number of passionate gamblers were constantly successful at the game. Did they cheat? A few women certainly did not hesitate to do so. Maria-Thérèsa's ladies-in-waiting made use of their artlessness and from cards were able to pay for their dresses. But who knows if the Queen, in her extreme generosity, did not deliberately shut her eyes? At the King's table, or even in his presence, cheating would have been extremely risky, but elsewhere gamblers were less wary, though one had to be very circumspect. The Swiss and the valets constantly watched the games in progress; a bad reputation could ruin a courtier, and cheats were few.

Gambling provided them with excitement—a good way of avoiding boredom for a few hours. For the same reason the King organized lotteries of jewels. The hope of winning a valuable prize occupied their minds, provided them with a subject for conversation and kept them alive until the numbers were drawn.

### LOTTERIES

Lotteries had a long history in France. From the beginning of the seventeenth century Louis XIII had allowed certain establishments to offer them publicly in order to obtain funds for some undertaking rather like we offer a loan. Thus, in 1624, the Oratorian monks of Angers sought to obtain by a lottery the funds they still required to build their college. The King was not so fond of such high-minded plans. For him, the 'bank' was just a game, a means to maintain the courtier's cupidity. Lotteries were numerous and of various kinds.

The most famous lottery was that of February 1681. According to the *Mercure Galant*, the whole of France was deeply involved in it. The chief prize was of 100,000 francs, 'and everyone dreamed of spending that money according to his fancy'. Louis XIV supervised the draw. He sat at the centre of a table covered with a carpet and was assisted by the Marquise de Croissy, Colbert's sister-in-law, and by the Marquis de Dangeau. A valet held the tickets. Courtiers thronged the entrance to the room. Only a few of the most illustrious were allowed in. Bossuet was present, as if to give a sacred character to this game of chance. He agreed to seal the bags.

The great moment arrived and the draw was made. Louis XIV, who as an example had taken a large number of tickets, won the first prize. He immediately put it back to be drawn again, to the benefit of the losers. Among the happy winners the *Mercure* named the Dauphin (10,000 *livres*), Le Nostre's valet (5,000 *livres*), and M Desmarets' servants and his butler (400 gold *louis*). A little Versailles dressmaker, the Queen and Mlle de Fontange each won purses of 100 gold *louis*.

Twenty years later another lottery aroused the enthusiasm of the court: in 1700 the Duchesse de Bourgogne organized one for her charities. The profits were to be distributed among the poor. It was an enormous success. The prizes amounted to 20,000 *pistoles* and had to be raised to 46,000 (that is, to 460,000 *livres*). Tickets had been prepared by the Duchesse herself, with the help of the Dauphin and the Comte de Toulouse, and the picturesque way in which they were sealed greatly amused the King and all those who took part. The greatest precautions were taken to ensure an honest draw. The biggest prize (80,000 *livres*) fell to a King's guard named Damblart, from the de Lorge company. A hatter won the second prize. Out of despair at not having won anything, a rag-man and his wife committed suicide.

'It was a way of attracting public greed,' wrote Saint-Simon. Once more he was not quite fair. The poor received nearly 50,000 *livres*. Other lotteries organized by Louis XIV to amuse court ladies were merely innocent games. Prizes were dress materials, jewels, small pieces of silver-ware. Mme de Maintenon drew the prizes, and everyone won!

## THE END OF THE REIGN

Mme de Maintenon has been accused of making the court dull and ponderous. The former governess of the Marquise de Montespan's children had changed the King's character. She had turned him towards piety, had given him a preference for intimate living instead of grandiosity. But every-day lfe did not change. The former Françoise d'Aubigné was too shrewd to force changes which would have been displeasing, and Saint-Simon, who was not over-indulgent, recognizes that she modestly kept her place, 'and even drew back politely and pleasantly when faced with titled ladies, in the manner of a woman who assumes nothing and reveals nothing, but makes a deep impression'.

It was Louis XIV himself who, with increasing age, abandoned spectacular entertainments. He had become a great bigot. He had long interviews with his confessor. He went more regularly to vespers and the courtiers imitated their master at once.

In this respect Saint-Simon told a story which deeply mortified the ladies of the court. In winter they used to go to chapel with candles, which served less to illuminate their prayer-books than to light their faces and display their pious zeal to the King. He did not always come and, when the officer in charge had told the guards to withdraw, the devout ladies also hurried away, blowing out their candles and leaving their piety behind on their prayer-stools! One day, in order to play a practical joke, a Major of the Guards named Albert de Grillet came to the front of the platform and proclaimed in a loud voice: 'King's Guards, you may withdraw: the King is not coming!' Immediately, all the women present blew out their candles and rushed into the galleries . . . where they met the King, surrounded by his guards. He entered the tribune and saw that the chapel that evening was practically empty. Grillet told him about the trick he had played. Louis was highly delighted, but his victims less so!

Those numerous religious ceremonies often led to conflicts of precedence and other rivalries which were a fine subject for gossip. In 1704, Monsieur le Grand, during the Good Friday celebrations, insisted on taking precedence over the Dukes: was he not Prince of Lorraine and a cousin of the Emperor of Austria? The King settled the matter by deciding that no one was to accompany him to the Adoration of the Cross but the Princes of the blood and the bastards. On her side, Mme de Maintenon had to calm the ladies who wanted to take the collection in church and tell each of them what rank she held.

How easy it is to understand why the King was happy to spend his evenings with her in his apartments, far from the courtiers whose presence only wearied him. The scene had often been depicted: an ageing couple seated side by side, of whom Saint-Simon said:

'They sit in armchairs, a table in front of each, on either side of the fireplace, she on the side of the bed, he against the wall, on which was the door of the ante-chamber, with two stools at the table, one for the minister who was to work for the King, the other for his bag . . . While the King was working, Mme de Maintenon would read or work at her tapestry. She listened to what was passing between the King and the minister, as their voices were loud. She rarely added a word; it was rarer still if that word was of any consequence.'

Those intimate meetings were not very amusing. During those dreary years of mourning and poverty the castle was ice-cold and the Marquise had more colds than ever. Louis XIV alone displayed a magnificent firmness. During the terrible winter of 1709, when all the rivers froze to their mouths, the King tried to help the poor people of Versailles. He taxed all the courtiers and topped the list with a gift of 4,220 *livres*. Barley bread was served at the royal table and bakers were forbidden to sell white bread.

The disgruntled courtiers sought distraction in order to drive away the boredom which weighed upon the palace. The least incident was for them a cause of amusement. When it was said that a company of gypsies had settled at the foot of Montbauron, at the entrance to the town, and were telling fortunes and playing the tambourine, they hurried there to look at them. The governor of Versailles, Blouin, had to intervene and tell the gypsies to clear out.

A few years later, a charlatan offered to tell the King's first doctor the secret of the philosopher's stone. He claimed to be able to transform the basest metal into gold and silver—at a time when the King was obliged to send his plate to be melted down, and Chamillard, the Comptroller-General of Finances, had to devalue the gold *louis* every year! To the King the first doctor spoke about this mysterious person. He was allowed to shelter him in a small house in the village of Montreuil. He was given ovens, crucibles, and every necessity. He was also given two body-guards so that the secret might be better protected, and the whole court crowded to Montreuil to see the alchemist and listen to his discourses. Even Chamillard went there, and vainly waited for a miracle.

It was all in vain. Indeed, two months later the knavery was clear to the naivest of them, but appearances had to be maintained. First, the charlatan was taken to Noisy with the greatest secrecy; finally he was locked up. The first doctor was rather ashamed of having been taken in; but the court forgave him, for they had had a few weeks amusement.

The reign had been much too long. In forty years the actors had all changed and Louis was now surrounded by the children or nephews of his youthful companions. The courtiers were weary of Versailles. The rumour was already abroad that the palace would be abandoned after the King's death. Everyone paid court to the future Regent and impatiently awaited deliverance. Narbonne wrote:

'On those days when the King looked as if he had reached a crisis his rooms were empty of lords and courtiers, who flocked to the Duc d'Orléans. Yet, as soon as it was made known that the King was better, the same crowd left the Duke's apartments at once to flock back to the King's. These scenes recurred more than once, and the Duc d'Orléans was alternately alone or surrounded by all the great people of the state.'

At last Louis died on September 1, 1715, at 8.15 in the morning. On that day the gold *louis* suffered a new devaluation and was worth only fourteen *livres*. It was immediately whispered through the galleries: 'Well, didn't the King want it said that his death was a loss?'

Most of the courtiers, without waiting for the departure of the hearse, arranged to leave Versailles. Nobody was left but those who were tied to the palace by their jobs.

# CHAPTER SIX

# USEFUL PEOPLE

Whether he was a Prince of the Blood or a mere gentleman, a courtier at Versailles took part in the same entertainments and yawned in the same places. But at his side, surrounding him and serving him, were those which could be called the 'utilities'. They did not take the leading roles on this vast stage, but they made the performance work and controlled the shifting of the sets. They were indispensable, and their number was immense. Some lived inside the palace and discharged definite duties; others lived in the town and drew their income from the royal residence.

## THE GUARDS

First of all, there were all those whose job it was to protect the person of the King, to surround him, and to defend him against any possible attack. Life guards, *Gardes-Françaises, Cent-Suisses* or *Gardes de la Manche,* all these royal service regiments were part of the military household. Their senior officers mixed frequently with the courtiers and were admitted into the King's private circle. In spite of their noble origin, the men modestly kept to their places, as motionless as statues and immensely proud of the fact that the King relied on them.

There was nothing new in it. Those various regiments existed before his reign. Louis XIV merely issued regulations to some of them. For instance, he gave his Life Guards first place in the French Gendarmerie by a regulation of 1667.

The Life Guards were chosen by the King himself. They were horsemen, though they often served on foot. Their horses had long been stabled in the Grande Écurie. In the eighteenth century, under Louis XV, they were provided with special stables as well as quarters in Versailles. In the seventeenth century, they usually lived in Paris or in its close environs. Some of them were able to rent a room in town.

They were at the King's disposal all day. But their service was quarterly and they could therefore be relieved. Their regiment was formed of four companies, each of which was shared among six brigades. The first company—the Scottish Company created by Charles VII—had kept that traditional name, but under Louis XIV all its members were French. The uniform was blue with silver braiding and a shoulder belt. The lowest rank was the equivalent of a second lieutenant of the cavalry. They had no lack of money and, when not on duty, they well knew how to enjoy the pleasures of living. They were great gamblers. The girls of Versailles were not shy. They often quarrelled among themselves, but an order from an officer would bring them back promptly to their duties. They were deeply conscious of the honour bestowed on them and most of them meant to be worthy of it.

From the noblemen of the Scottish Company the 'Gardes de la Manche' were chosen. They were twenty-four and had to be constantly at the King's side. Therefore their duty lasted for only one month a year. Also they were on duty only two at a time, except for certain ceremonies at which six of them were required. Their normal uniform was a white, gold-embroidered jerkin and a partisan, held in the right hand, its handle studded with gold nails. Daily—and sometimes twice daily—they escorted the King to the chapel. Then they wore old-fashioned shirts of mail and carried halberts instead of partisans. They stood during mass and bowed only at the Elevation.

A celebrated tapestry, the cartoon of which had been drawn by Le Brun, represents the Renewal of the Alliance between Louis XIV and the representatives of the Swiss Cantons in 1683. The solemn oath, taken on the Bible, was the consecration of a long and constant accord. It was in fact Louis XI who, shortly before his death, had decided to take a hundred Swiss into his military household. Together with the *Gardes-Françaises*, the *Cent-Suisses* were the most highly regarded of the foot-guards. They were divided into six squadrons and commanded by eighteen officers. Their parade uniform retained all the splendid elegance of the Renaissance: a doublet with slashed sleeves, a black velvet hat with a white feather, ample hose and shoes decorated with knots of ribbons. They carried halberds in their hands and partisans on their shoulders. The gorget was of silver.

The *Cent-Suisses* escorted the King everywhere. When Louis left the palace, they marched at the door of his coach, and they walked in front of him during solemn ceremonies and surrounded the throne. Their devotion to the King had no limit. Contrary to the Scottish Company, of whom none were 'of the Hibernian nation', the Swiss were authentic Swiss from the Cantons of Bern or Glarus. Some of them belonged to the Reformed Church. When any of them were converted, members of the Royal Family stood as their sponsors. They enjoyed valuable privileges and had their own court of justice. Some of them founded families in France.

Next to the *Cent-Suisses*, the French Guards in six battalions of thirty-three companies, performed on foot the same role as the mounted Life Guards. Their uniform was blue with red facings and gilded gorgets. They were constantly at the sovereign's disposal, whose safety they guaranteed. Each regiment served for a few days only and then was relieved. When the King went out, they lined up in the front courtyard while the drums rolled. The French Guard then stayed in the open, ready to resume ranks the moment the King returned. No one can be surprised that, after that sort of duty, they would gladly stray into the local inns. There was a constant rivalry between the various corps of the King's household, the members of which often came to blows. The NCO's had to intervene.

The door-guards never left the palace when on duty. They had to watch inside in daytime. They were fifty in number, dressed in the blue jerkin of the Life Guards, but their ornaments and stripes were of a different colour. They wore not only swords, but also rifles on shoulder-belts embroidered with two keys. They were commanded by the gate captain. They went on duty at 6 a.m., relieving the Life Guards who, with the Swiss, assured the safety of the castle by night.

Though they also belonged to the King's military household, the guards of the Provost of the Household were rather a police organization. They served under the Grand Provost of France. They searched for malefactors who might have slipped into the drawing-rooms and made their fists felt during some disturbance. They could easily be recognized by their crimson, blue and white jerkins, and the clubs that were the striking insignia of their office.

For here was the astonishing contradiction to be seen at Versailles. Several hundreds of men-at-arms, belonging to the highest nobility of the land, were constantly on duty throughout the palace, carrying out precise functions. In spite of the discipline—or because of it—everyone was jealous of his mission and strictly refused to go beyond its limits—the palace was in constant disorder, which afforded a fine opportunity for thieves and robbers.

### THE PROVOST OF THE HOUSEHOLD

The Provost-Marshal was the head of the palace police. He judged all the crimes committed within the boundaries of the chateau, either by strangers or anyone belonging to the King's household. The latter could also bring their civil proceedings before the Provost-Marshal and never failed to do so. He was a nobleman and an officer, and was assisted by two lieutenant-generals, magistrates of the long gown and law graduates, which was more useful. In fact, at the court of justice the latter completely superseded the holders of the office. This jurisdiction had to attend the King wherever he went, even to the battle-front. But as from 1682 the Provostship was divided: one sat in Paris and the other in Versailles, and each of the lieutenant-generals sat in each town alternately. At Versailles, the quarters of a Provost-Marshal were in the Rue de la Pompe, beside the Hôtel de Duras (later the Luxembourg Hotel). In 1723 the court was transferred to the Hôtel de Baillage, which had just been built next to the New Market. Audiences were held on Saturdays.

Needless to say, there was no friendship lost between the Provost and the Bailiff. The Royal Bailiff, the competent judge for all civil and criminal law-suits in Versailles, had no liking for this out-of-the-way justice which deprived him of very tangible profits. There were many motives for conflict: when a Life Guard quarrelled with a Versailles inn-keeper, who was the qualified judge, the Bailiff or the Provost? How far did the latter's competence go? It went so far that, in August 1684, the King, having heard of the latest disputes between these magistrates, wanted to avoid more trouble and made a regulation in fourteen articles which was supposed to cover everything. He first made a list of the persons under the Provost's jurisdiction: 'Officers of H.M. and of the Royal Households, domestics and others not domiciled in Versailles.' He settled the exasperating question of law-suits between the court and the people of Versailles. The Provost-Marshal came first: 'Instances in which officers and other court people are principal or secondary parties against an inhabitant also come under the Provost-Marshal.' Also under his jurisdiction were 'vagrants and beggars, wherever they might go, even in the houses of inhabitants where guards might enter to seize them'.

Other articles were devoted to the administrative police. There the Bailiff took precedence over the Provost-Marshal. He had to supervise the lighting of the lanterns, the removal of rubbish, and the inspection of inns and taverns. But if anyone responsible for some disturbance or brawl fell under the Provost's jurisdiction, the Bailiff had to arrest him and hand him over.

The last clause is the most amusing. During Lent a single butcher was entitled to sell meat, at a price fixed by the authorities. Obviously, his designation was not given without a certain amount of largesse. If the King, the Dauphin or the Dauphine were in Versailles during Lent, it was the Provost who appointed the butcher; but if the Royal Family left the town before the end of Lent, the Bailiff retrieved his authority and could appoint another. Solomon could not have been more just! However, conflict continued all through the eighteenth century between the Provost and the Bailiff, in spite of minute regulation, and Parliament had to intervene at last to appease the rivals.

Within the very walls of the palace, thieves, burglars and cutpurses were numerous and unbelievably daring. The ease with which one could enter the palace accounts in part for their immunity. So many valets, guards and pages passed to and fro along the galleries that it was very difficult to identify strangers and prevent their evil attacks. The over-familiarity of the visitors who slipped into the palace has often been commented upon: even more numerous were those who crowded into the gardens. If Louis XIV could say: 'I am the State,' these unpleasant guests could add: 'And the State belongs to us.'

Some thefts created such a scandal that memoir-writers could not refrain from mentioning them. One of the most famous took place on June 25, 1691. It was so astonishing that one might wonder whether it was not a trick in very bad taste, played upon the King's first valet and the King himself.

Early that morning it was discovered that unknown persons had removed the gold fringes from the curtains of the ante-chamber to the State Apartments and even a piece of the embroidery from the King's bed. It was difficult to see how the thieves could use their loot, but the theft was the subject of conversation amongst all the courtiers that day. Bontemps who, together with the *concierge*, was responsible for the royal furniture, was furious and desperate. One wondered how such a crime could have been committed 'in a place so crowded in daytime and so well closed at night, and so well guarded always.'

The next day, Louis XIV was supping ceremonially. Saint-Simon (he was present) records: 'When the sweets were about to be served, I noticed something black and big which fell upon the table in front of the King and Madame. The impact on the table was so violent that all the dishes vibrated, but none was overturned. There was a moment of panic: one might have feared an attempt upon the King's life. The King alone, perfectly admirable in his coolness and serenity, half-turned his head and remarked: "I think these are my fringes".'

What happened was perfectly typical of the lack of order and discipline among the various bodies in charge of palace security. Everyone did exactly what he had to, but declined to take the least initiative. There were about twenty various men on guard at the doors. The King immediately ordered all the doors to be shut. If Saint-Simon is to be believed, the order was carried out by the Duc de Gesvres, captain of the duty guard, after a lapse of three-quarters of an hour. The culprit had had all the time in the world to escape. But it is strange to think how a large parcel could have been thrown from the doorway between the two ante-chambers without one witness having noticed who had done it. This was merely another proof of the extraordinary crowding of those courtiers who watched the King at supper, with eyes for nothing else.

The epilogue threw some light on the mystery. Pinned to the pyramid-shaped parcel, about two feet high, was a note. The Marquis de Livry grabbed it and read the following words aloud: 'Take back your fringes, Bontemps. They are more of a bore than a pleasure. I kiss the King's hand.'

'This is very insolent indeed,' muttered Louis.

The handwriting, disguised, looked like that of a woman. It might have come from a lady to whom some favour had been refused by the first valet. She revenged herself on Bontemps, striking at the same time at the King and the courtiers. On the King's order it was assumed that only a madman could have done it, but the courtiers and Bontemps were deeply ashamed.

Other thefts were quite as bad. On the occasion of a ball at Versailles on December 11, 1697, many foreigners and strangers flocked to the palace. Gatien de Sandras de Courtilz, whose satires about the court are valuable despite their asperity, did not fail to mention that cut-purses would not waste such an opportunity. 'They came all dressed like the rest, so that apart from their faces, which were unknown at court, none would have taken them for other than people of quality.' Marie-Adélaide of Savoy suffered a distressing experience as one clever fellow deftly cut off part of her dress, on which a diamond was used as a clasp. When she became aware of her loss the thief was gone. The Chevalier de Sully was luckier than the Duchesse. He succeeded in seizing a man who was trying to steal one of his jewels, and he was staggered at recognizing the thief as a man of good family. Louis XIV was told, but showed less surprise. He knew that his courtiers stopped at nothing to lay hands on money. Rag-men, second-hand clothes-sellers and similar tradesmen were making fortunes at Versailles, and they asked no explanations concerning the jewels offered them. As regards the man taken red-handed, Sandras de Courtilz went on: 'His Majesty wanted to know who he was. The name was whispered to him. He would not have it spoken otherwise because, for love of the man's parents, he was glad to save this unhappy man's honour.' The Provost was not to intervene, but the whole court eventually knew the man's name and he disappeared.

People of lesser rank who walked about in the gardens merely stole the flowers from the beds or branches from the trees. Thefts were sometimes worse: the lead pipes put in by Francine were stolen. Protective measures had to be taken. The King had some of the thickets and plantations surrounded by padlocked railings. The Provost issued a set of regulations, threatening the most severe penalties to those who were convicted of having committed offences in the park. Arrested by the guards of the Master of the Revels, they were thrust into the Versailles jail, a damp and stinking hole, and sentenced to the humiliation of the pillory. This punishment, however, did not stop the depredators, and the Provost's archives are full of edifying records of the prosecution of malefactors.

Only once did Louis XIV issue orders that such measures were not to be taken. It was during the winter of 1709. The misery was so great and the population so wretched that he let anyone gather wood in the royal forests. With this the poor could fight the cold which lasted for more than three months.

In spite of his impassivity, Louis was lacking neither in generosity nor delicacy. His attitude towards the palace pages provides further examples of a character too often misunderstood.

### THE PAGES

The pages brought their smiles and the gaiety of their youth both to the palace and the town.

Ever since the Middle Ages it had been customary to send boys of noble family to the great lords to be taught how to ride, hawk or hunt. These boys—aged from twelve to eighteen—were also taught the rules of courtesy, and their education went on until they were accomplished. In the seventeenth century, they were sent to the Royal Household only. The deputies of the nobility at the States General held in Blois in 1614 had insisted that the King should retain his pages, and Louis XIII had had a book of rules drawn up about their education. His son left it unchanged except for increasing their number.

There were several groups of pages. The first were attached to the bed-chamber. They were twenty-four, allotted in sixes to the four principal gentlemen of the bed-chamber. There were about sixty attached to the Grande Écurie and a few less to the Petite Écurie. In all, there were about 150 pages in the castle.

To be admitted, one had to produce quarters of nobility dating back to 1550. They were strictly checked and the proofs of nobility minutely controlled. The candidates had to be 'well built, of good morals, 5' 2" tall, good-looking, and aged between fifteen and sixteen'.

Service to the King was quite absorbing. The pages had to be up at 6.30 a.m. and, once they had made their beds—at least once a week, for on the other days the valets made them—they had to go to the First Gentleman of the Bed-chamber to enter the King's room at the hour of the *petit lever*. They silently approached their august master and removed his slippers. Their function ended there. The rest of the morning was devoted to lessons: riding, fencing, even dancing, and in addition some general education, as a perfect gentleman had to have ideas about everything. When the King went out hunting, the pages surrounded his coach in strictly regulated positions. The pages of the Chamber were in front and those of the Écurie at the rear, but the order was reversed when shooting began. The former brought the King his dogs, while the latter handed him his gun. Either was allowed to pick up the game that had been shot.

On returning from the hunt they were with the King when he removed his boots. But even this was not the end. When there was an *appartement,* they stood near the buffets and helped the ladies and gentlemen. They took turns in carrying torches for the King, whom they had to escort everywhere. They had to show discretion and skill. According to custom, they had to hold two lighted torches in the same hand, keeping the other free to brush away importunate people coming too near the King. The Marquis de Monconseil, who was Louis XIV's page towards the end of the reign, told how, one evening, while escorting the King, who was coming from Mme de Maintenon's, he leant too low and set fire to the royal wig! This fire, which almost amounted to high treason, had no consequence whatever, not even for the guilty lad, though he was so terrified that even seventy years later, when telling the story to his daughter, Mme de la Tour du Pin, he still trembled.

There was one last task that the pages had to do: during the *petit coucher* they brought back the King's slippers. After that they were free to repair to the palace garrets allotted to them . . . or to find some more pleasant occupation in the town of Versailles, to shake off the ceremonial atmosphere.

They led as gay a life as they could. Their duties obliged them to accompany the King to church. As has been stated already, towards the end of his reign Louis XIV put on a show of piety. Prayers were long and the pages got bored. So they slyly slipped away through the small staircase and climbed to the chapel roof. What a wonderful viewpoint! From the top of the chapel, the truant pages watched the movements of courtiers in the park, admired the basins and canals, and made fun of the people they saw. They shamelessly carved their names and titles in large and awkward characters, which are still to be seen near the staircase door. When the bell rang for benediction, the pages scampered down and returned to their post behind the King, who pretended to have seen nothing, and may in fact not have done so.

These were innocent amusements, but others were less futile. Inns and taverns offered them dangerous temptations. The bar-maids of Versailles made eyes at them, and there were many quarrels as a result. There were also violent rivalries between the pages of different groups. They fought among themselves and the Provost had to step in. When Monsieur le Grand or Monsieur le Premier got word of what had happened, they stepped in to remove the culprit from the clutches of the royal justice, to shut him up in the prison of the Grande or Petite Ecurie: a small room on the ground floor, with barred windows and thick walls, where the page had plenty of time to meditate on the inconveniences of freedom. But he was soon back among his companions.

There was nothing hard about a page's life. If a fair number of them late in life felt tempted to write their memoirs, that was because they had a nostalgia for the time when they were young, gay, well treated and well fed. One of them wrote to his mother: 'At dinner we have soup, boiled beef, four entrées, two roasts and four sweets.' Definitely, pages ran no risk of starvation in the King's service.

### THE KITCHEN

What piles of food had to be collected each day to feed this huge caravanserai! It is strange that these administrative problems have never so far received adequate attention. And yet, when at the beginning of Louis XV's reign Narbonne listed the various groups living in the palace, he totalled 1,500 people working in the Grand Commun, while there were not more than 1,400 persons all told in the military household. Under Louis XIV, the kitchens required some 2,000 servants.

When the King decided about 1670 to prolong his visits to Versailles, accommodation to house these officers had to be found, for the kitchens of Louis XIII's little castle were much too small. In one of the wings, just built by Le Vau—the South Wing—were housed what the court called 'the King's seven offices': the royal kitchen, cellars, bakery, the drink department, wood store and the out-kitchen, where the meals of persons who were fed at court were cooked. Soon were added the kitchens of the Queen and the Dauphin. But all those offices eventually became an encumbrance. They occupied the whole ground floor and part of the first floor. On entering the palace one was met by an army of valets, kitchen

7. Louis XV, by Nattier

8. Marie Leczinska, by Elle

boys and cooks, all of them noisy and foul-mouthed, who milled around under the King's own windows. Louis XIV then ordered the Grand Commun to be built to house all those various offices. It was built by Mansart between 1682 and 1685 where the village church once stood.

The King's architect knew how to combine majesty and utility. The Grand Commun comprised four buildings surrounding a large square courtyard and each had four doors. Mazeline, Nouvenet, Lecomte and Mazière were commissioned to sculpt the pediments. There was a chapel traditionally under the patronage of St Roch, who protects us against epidemics, and therefore against food-poisoning and spoilt dishes; here cooks could perform their weekly religious duties without abandoning their kitchen ranges. It was served by six chaplains of the King's household, and better attended by courtiers than by kitchen staff. The King and Queen sometimes heard mass there.

The basements were used as store-rooms. Their thick walls were protection against damp. They were surrounded by a passage with many air holes and supported by arcades. In one of the basements were the ovens where the King's bakers baked his bread.

The kitchens occupied the whole ground floor. On the first floor lived people of quality who had been granted a King's office, noblemen on quarterly duty and almoners. Valets, ushers and police officers were on the second floor. The garrets were kept for the kitchen boys and other menials. The King also put there people to whom he had granted lodgings within the palace. Pellisson lived there for several years and died there on February 7, 1693. Louis XIV did not hold against him the fidelity he had shown to Superintendent Fouquet. A century later, Louis XVI housed in the Grand Commun his first doctor, Joseph Lieutand, a book-lover whose library is still famous.

Above all, the Grand Commun was crowded with a whole population of kitchen boys, pastry-cooks and confectioners, who made a great noise, often fighting among themselves and compelling the Provost's guards to step in to maintain the peace.

The butlers on quarterly duty, however, kept their dignity. Theirs was the task of ensuring that everything was ready for dinner for the *grand couvert*, after they had each morning received instructions from the First Gentleman of the Bed-chamber. When the endless series of dishes was ready, they were taken to the palace

97

in a heater, but the journey was made in the open air without protection. The procession came through the main doorway, up a stone staircase which led to a gallery in the south wing, through which they proceeded in ceremony towards the King's chamber or the Queen's ante-chamber. Despite the covers which protected the dishes, and of a heater which did not heat very much, soup at Versailles was scarcely ever hot.

Each of the officers of the Grand Commun had a definite task. One of them, for instance, had to provide the fruit eaten at the King's table, another to provide the vegeables, the *hâteurs* supervised the roasting of joints and their coat-of-arms was the *hâste*, or spit, which speared the meat. Together with the butlers, they had to supervise the whole of the provisioning.

These provisions were bought by tender, prepared by the Versailles Bailiff. Posters were affixed to the gates of Notre-Dame and at the main cross-roads. Always phrased in the same way, they announced that 'contracts would be made to the lowest tender for two or three years, in accordance with his Majesty's convenience, for the following quantities of . . . (meat, fruit, vegetables, firewood, candles, etc.) necessary for the provisioning and use of the Chateau of Versailles, Marly, Trianon and the Ménagerie'. On the day fixed, each candidate made his offer and the most profitable won. Those who were selected could proudly boast of being 'purveyor to the King'.

Despite the Bailiff's efforts to tax food and try to prevent the Versailles tradesmen from exploiting their privileged position, prices were very high. Fearing to run short, the Grand Commun officers stored as much as they could. Waste was very great; neither the food nor drink that was produced at the King's table, or at the collation buffets on Appartement evenings, could be offered twice. A certain amount of it was eaten by the Grand Commun officers; most of it was sold.

The *serdeau* was one of the most unusual offices at court. By origin, the *sert de l'eau* or *sert d'eau* officers served the King's drink. Their office changed with the centuries, and under Louis XIV they merely received from the serving men the dishes taken from the royal tables and carried them to the room where the servants ate. But the *serdeau* officers took the largest part themselves, for they enjoyed a privilege which they exploited savagely. They were authorized to sell surplus food.

On the left of the Place d'Armes, in front of the castle, there was a terrace on top of a wall which ran along beside the Rue de la Chancellerie. Against that wall, on the street side, stood a line of one-floor stalls called the *serdeau*. It was there that the officers offered for sale the scraps from the royal table. As numerous dishes had not been touched, the people of Versailles could buy very cheap food. It was said that some noblemen did not hesitate to send their servants. A chicken bought at the *serdeau* had a royal flavour and was cheaper than at the market.

The *serdeau* officers made large profits out of their business. At carnival time in 1714 the Duc de Berry, the King's grandson (who was to die a few months later of the results of a fall from a horse) gave balls which everyone agreed were magnificent.

'The buffets', Narbonne wrote, 'were covered with all sorts of refreshments and a large number of waiters were carrying them to the spectators and dancers, so that no one had to leave his seat.'

The final note comes from the supervisor: 'It is said that, out of the business they carried out during the balls, the Duke's officers made just about the cost of their office.' So the job of *serdeau* officer was very expensive.

The King was not unaware of the waste. He preferred to ignore it. Sometimes, however, he was very bad-tempered about it, and a poor *serdeau* valet on one occasion had to bear the brunt of it. Though the scene took place at Marly it has to be recorded because it reveals a strange aspect of the King's temper. Saint-Simon describes it with savage pleasure.

The King was leaving his table after supper and the officers of the *serdeau* were beginning to clear the tables when the King noticed a valet who, while removing the fruit, slipped a biscuit into his pocket. Completely beside himself, the King jammed down upon his wig the hat which was handed to him, rushed upon the poor fellow who did not know that his act had been observed and began to beat him over the head and the back so violently that the stick was broken. The King stood nonplussed and the valet rushed away. Still furious, Louis XIV strutted away to Mme de Maintenon's apartment. An hour later the King returned to his courtiers and, addressing Father La Chaise, his confessor, said: 'I gave that blackguard a good beating, but I committed the sin of anger, Father, and I confess it.' Saint-Simon added that the King's cane was a mere reed, which was why it broke so easily. As for the valet,

99

the memoir writer does not say whether he was forgiven or ignominiously dismissed.

## THE TOWN IN THE SERVICE OF THE PALACE

By 1670, before the major alterations which turned Versailles
into a city, it looked like most French villages. One could find the
usual tradesmen there: the baker, two smiths, two carpenters, a
joiner, a mason; also two grocers and a pastry-cook, a less usual
sort of trade, but justified already by the number of courtiers
present.

The first people to move in were workmen. They flocked there
from Limousin or the Marche. It is well-known that from those
barren districts many men went each year to Paris to find work.
For their use, and so that they could gather together in the evening,
barracks were built and given the rather ironical name of 'The
Limoges Hotel'. Contractors to the Ministry of the King's Buildings, who were numerous and busy, hired them.

From the palace to the edge of the town, Versailles was one
immense workshop. Everything had to be created: the water supply
for the park's basins, the paving for the courtyards, the lighting.
There were thousands of workmen, and the number of accidents
increased proportionately. The parish registers bear witness to
this. 'Killed while working on the chateau' was recorded more than
one hundred times a year. The most elementary precautions were
never taken, and though it was a small percentage of the thousands of men employed, the number was still too high.

Louis XIV was not indifferent to the cost and in 1693 he had a
new hospital created, partly for the sick and injured. He awarded a
pension to the widows. As the works became bigger and bigger,
tradesmen flocked to the new city, hoping to make quick fortunes.
First came inn-keepers and hotel-keepers. In a city which suffered
a permanent housing shortage, where a peer of the realm willingly
slept in a garret, inns arose like mushrooms in autumn. At the
end of the century there were almost one hundred and twenty of
them, even in streets where building had scarcely begun. The
proprietors had used the whole catalogue of normal names, including the *Image St Julien*, The *Pied de Biche*, the *Chasse Royale* and
the *Tour d'Argent*. Any name served.

Inn-keepers thought themselves very important. They knew they
were indispensable for, while furnished houses appeared gradually,

the noblemen lodged their servants in the inns. Noblemen who were merely passing through and courtiers who still lived in Paris (or elsewhere) also had to find rooms at the inns. So prices were high, so very high that the Bailiff had to intervene twice, in 1670 and 1672, and fix a maximum, which still left handsome profits to the proprietors: a double room cost forty *sous* a day. To establish some sort of comparison, one might mention that, on the same list of taxed prices, a pound of veal cost five *sous*! There was a whole scale of rooms, from unheated garrets with bare walls, where three or four workmen had to make do with two beds, to a comfortable suite fit for a rich bourgeois or a man of quality.

We are not certain if the inn-keepers abided by the taxes. They completely ignored police regulations. One rule reminded them that they must not serve drinks during High Mass. To the ushers who came to serve him with a warrant because he had not obeyed the order, the landlord of the *Épée Royale* on the Petite Place answered that he did not care two hoots and, if they came again, he would 'put their noses into his pot'. They prudently retired.

In order to feed their customers economically, inn-keepers used to breed their own domestic animals. The town had a surprising appearance, for fields and kitchen gardens adjoined the most magnificent buildings and country lanes turned suddenly into urban arteries. Hens and rabbits were reasonable, but pigs needed more room; nevertheless, they were allowed to roam freely in the streets. One can easily understand the disgust of a magnificently attired nobleman who, on descending from his coach, was met by a pig that grunted and sprawled in the mud and ordure. Once more the Bailiff intervened and, as his orders were not obeyed, he became more stringent. On November 8, 1696, the Royal Attorney's assistant, escorted by his secretary and three ushers, solemnly walked about the city, reporting the presence of 'several pigs in streets and public places'. He made a report and his ushers seized the animals. The inn-keepers looked on with sneers and continued with their pig-keeping.

To workmen far from their families, a few inns were especially welcoming and even some courtiers took advantage of what they had to offer. The maids, by definition, were pretty and easy of access. The Chevalier de Quincy related that at the *Thirteen Cantons*, where he stopped with a friend, two pretty girls called on them and offered to come back to their room after a ball given that night by the Duc de Bourgogne. Which they did with all the simplicity in the world, so that everyone was 'perfectly happy'. This happened in 1707, when Mme de Maintenon was enforcing a period of the dullest possible virtuousness. One has only to glance at the regulations laid down against prostitution to understand the lightness of morals at Versailles.

Other more respectable trades were practised profitably in the royal town. As the palace grew, more shops were opened, not without difficulty, as the most wretched premises cost the earth. Thus, a vinegar seller sold his wares from a pork-butcher's shop, and a baker sold his bread in a carpenter's shop. One could easily get back the cost of the lease by hiring out a furnished room, for a great number of workmen were not yet settled. They had secured the privilege of being recognized as 'merchants attendant upon the court' and only stayed in Versailles when the King was in residence. Only after 1682 were they settled permanently. At that time, in order to secure some control, the Bailiff decided to open a commercial register. All the people practising some art or trade in the town had to be registered. Tradesmen totalling 467 complied with his orders, each of them declaring his name, profession and his native place. Thus, to decorate the drawing-rooms of the gentlemen there was a flower-girl—the King's flower-seller, and to satisfy the gluttony of the ladies a seller of sweets and liqueurs. There were sculptors and gilders and several fiddlers for the pages and the King's guards. Some of those tradesmen were born in Versailles, but most of them came from Paris or the rest of Ile-de-France. Next came Normandy and the Loire districts. There were few Bretons or Burgundians.

A very popular trade was that of public writer. All the masons and building workers wanted to send news home to their families far away. They could neither read nor write. The public writer helped them by composing their letters, and as his handwriting was obviously good, he also taught the children how to read and write. But the lay and religious authorities intervened. Before assuming the title of schoolmaster, one had to have their agreement. Everyone complied with their order. Signs designating a secretary, quill in hand, multiplied throughout the town. Side by side with this extremely elementary schooling a few establishments developed that gave the rudiments of knowledge to the children of officers. As early as 1684, a certain Jean-Marie taught grammar and Latin and took in boarders. Two sisters, Marie Madeleine and Marie-Thérèse Barré, from Tours, kept a girls' school, 'to teach them how to read, and work with a needle at embroidery and tapestry; in a word, all that can give the sex a good education and good behaviour'. Molière's Chrystale would have been delighted by that programme.

Tailors, dressmakers and linen-drapers were almost as numerous as inn-keepers. Of course, few noblemen had their clothes made in Versailles, but they bought their servants' liveries there. Middle-class women, whose husbands had offices at court, and small noble-men employed there, were less particular. In the eighteenth century there were 170 master-drapers and many wholesale dealers who provided the necessary material. They were the first to get together to defend their interests and avoid trouble. In fact, the most frequent bankruptcies were those of tailors, with inn-keepers next.

The inhabitants did not govern themselves. There was no town council. The Bailiff and the Governor (the King's first valet of the bed-chamber) ruled the town. They had just been allowed to elect representatives from each quarter (*quarteniers*) to help the police to maintain order by keeping watch over the safety of the streets. Moreover, the churchwardens of Notre-Dame administered the church's finances and were proud of it.

*Quarteniers* and churchwardens were of modest origin, small tradesmen and artisans chosen for their honesty. Yet they were the inhabitants' delegates. For that reason, they asked Bontemps, their natural guardian, to present them to the King. It was under-stood that the first churchwarden, a grocer named Collette, would make a speech (which he took great care to learn by heart), that the King would thank them in a few words and then the whole group would start singing *Domine salvum fac regem*. The whole thing had been carefully organized.

But one had not taken into account the intense emotion with which these men were overcome. Bontemps took them into the royal chamber, saying: 'Sir, here are the citizens of Versailles whom I will present to Your Majesty.' Completely overcome, poor Collette could not open his mouth. To make things easier for him, his companions started singing at the top of their voices *Domine salvum fac regem*.

The King could not refrain from laughing. All the courtiers

followed suit. Bontemps was furious. He hustled his guests away, saying: 'I had been told you were b . . . . . fools! Go away!'

The poor men retired in confusion. This scene had occurred on the Holy Innocents day, and the occasion did not fail to prompt a popular song, of which the refrain was as follows:

> *Laissez passer ces bêtes*
> *Conduites par des bedeaux.*
> *Voici venir la fête*
> *Qui en fait de nouveaux.*[1]

Narbonne, who told the story, added that the song was heard all over the town, to the great shame of the churchwardens. Narbonne, just like Bontemps, was unjust. The King's first valet was not only lacking in charity; he forgot that some of the greatest noblemen were often tongue-tied in the King's presence.

---

[1] 'Let these beasts pass, led by the beadles. Soon will come the feast when new ones are made.'

# CHAPTER SEVEN

# FASHION AND FOOD

## MALE COSTUME

For a courtier it was quite essential to be in fashion. If he did not want to cut a poor figure, he had to comply with the rules laid down by the master tailors. When Vardes came back to the palace after twenty years of exile, everyone noticed that he was wearing an old jerkin of a style that had not been seen for a long time. A jerkin had to be renewed every other year.

The King set the example. He wore magnificent clothes. So courtiers ruined themselves buying ribbons, jewellery and wigs. At least, they could not be accused of niggardliness. This was another aspect of the King's policy. Crushed by his debts, a courtier had to beg for a pension, an annuity or a gift. He was more than ever chained to the King's chariot.

Fashion was not created at Versailles, but the court consecrated it and all had to follow.

Early in the reign, rhinegrave and doublet were favoured by gentlemen. The rhinegrave had not been imported into France by the brother of the Palatine Princess. This elegant and complicated suit had already been worn, twenty years before the marriage of Philip of Orléans to Charlotte-Elizabeth of Bavaria. The rhinegrave consisted of a little skirt 'in the shape of a stiff hooped garment under which was fixed very full breeches'. Above the belt was a very short doublet, the sleeves of which scarcely came below the elbow and were slit on either side. The rhinegrave thus showed the shirt at the back and at the waist, if it were not covered with multi-coloured ribbons. Such superabundance was the sign of wealth . . . and of bad taste. The *précieuses* would rave with admiration. Molière made fun of the fine marquises who wore, instead of hose, 'hooped breeches as broad as from here to Easter; instead of a doublet, tiny coats which did not reach as far as their breastbone, and yards and yards of ribbons'.

Shoes and wigs completed the outfit. The former disappeared under more yards of ribbon, and compelled their wearers to walk slowly, with legs well apart, so as not to trip. This accounts for the use of walking sticks, brought into fashion by Louis XIV. Wigs were large and heavy. They might weigh as much as two pounds and could cost up to 1,000 *écus* (6,000 gold francs). Ervais and Quentin were the fashionable wig-makers. In order to pull down the 'large tow bonnets' with greater ease, gentlemen had their own hair clipped and shaved; as a man did not wear a wig in bed, one can only imagine the strange impression made upon the partners of fashionable little marquises in bed, with heads as bald as eggs!

Louis XIV wore the rhinegrave: it was a youthful, elegant, rather charming dress. But he began to give it up by 1670. He had put on weight and was not slim enough to wear so many ribbons and fripperies. He also liked to don military dress and reckoned that civilian dress should imitate its comparative simplicity. Finally, the rhinegrave required little material but was very costly. Colbert's political economy was all for using woollen textiles. Thus fashion has often been subjected to considerations quite estranged from its original object.

Then the jerkin came into fashion. It lasted until the end of the reign. It was made of two close-fitting tunics, buttoned all down the front, with pockets low down in front. The first jerkins were made of silk; soon, ratteen, drugget and stamin came into fashion. Lace was no longer used except for the neck-tie, which was very broad and tied with a large, bright-coloured ribbon. M de Miramond, Louis XIV's tie-maker, was very proud to be able to offer him a selection each morning. The King took those which best matched his mood of the day. Ribbons were only worn on the right shoulder. A wide shoulder-belt was worn across the jerkin and the sword was suspended from its lower extremity.

It was, in fact, Louis XIV who set the fashion for the jerkin. The first to be made for him was the work of Baraillon, the court tailor. Noblemen copied the King immediately. When they appeared in the streets of Paris dressed in this fashion, everyone mocked them and the fish-wives of Les Halles made fun of them; they returned to Versailles in fury. Molière has alluded to this unrestrained sarcasm in *Le bourgeois gentilhomme*, when M Jourdain, advised by Dorante, puts on his new suit. His wife and servant make fun of him, Nicole hoots with laughter and Mme Jourdain roundly tells him: 'Do you take people for a pack of fools, having yourself apparelled in such a fashion?' Yet, if the tailor's word is respected, the suit was the court's finest costume, with everything matching perfectly: 'It is a masterpiece', the tailor adds; 'we have created a sober habit which is not black'—for the jerkin was gaily-coloured. According to a contemporary engraving, this is 'a nobleman's winter costume for January 1678: jerkin of Holland, light brown; black beaver hat with a heavy seal-embroidered ribbon; embroidered shoulder-belt of coloured plush; sleeves with double facings; a thick "Prince-coloured" fringe; coloured plush in tufts at the lower part of the shoulder-belt, to hold the sword. Rolled stockings the colour of the coat; a scarf or cravat loosely tied at the neck in Spanish lace or gold and silver net.'

In such trappings courtiers certainly looked their best.

Louis XIV strengthened the fashion by issuing an edict in 1661 that made the wearing of the jerkin into a regulation. To distinguish certain privileged courtiers, the King granted them a warrant, according to which they had the right to wear a jerkin of a certain colour: blue with a red lining, and with gold and silver embroidery. This magnificent costume had to be changed fairly often to look fresh. It cost a fortune. An ordinary jerkin cost up to 800 *livres*; a more ornate one might cost 1000 or 1200. It is true, however, that courtiers usually forgot to pay their tailors.

When the War of the Spanish Succession forced the court, and even the King, to try to economize, court dress became simpler. Mme de Maintenon recommended austerity, and the King obeyed her. Embroideries, lace, ribbons and shoulder-knots gradually disappeared. Dangeau, who so often described the royal dress, noted that Louis XIV took to darker colours, gave up lace except on his tie and cuffs, wore rings no longer and only a few very fine stones on his shoes and garter buckles. Edicts were issued regulating the wearing of gold and silver ornaments. The King wore a hat with a white plume.

From head to foot, the courtier had to follow the new fashion. Smaller hats replaced the large plumed ones; silk stockings were replaced by stockings of cotton, which came from Africa and was woven on hundreds of looms in Paris and Orléans. Shoes were

*à la cavalière* with loops and buckles and with red heels on
ceremonial occasions. Habits were brown or amaranth. The only
new feature was a long, broad ribbon that dangled from the
shirt collar, the *chaconne*: so great was the King's passion for
music that even the names given to costume accessories were
musical.

The appearance of the court remained majestic, but its youthful
brilliance was gone. When the King was in mourning, he wore
hose, doublet and a long cloak of purple cloth; the sleeves were
closed, the collar was decorated with a plain Dutch linen band,
the shoes were of purple cloth with simple steel buckles; a black
hat with a long purple crepe veil at the back; plain purple gloves.
The royal family, the princes of the blood, the high officers of the
Crown put on black costumes, the length of which varied with
the rank of the wearer. The King, who 'hated all that sounded
mournful', shortened the duration of mourning. Otherwise, he
could scarcely have abandoned those funereal garments at all
during the last five years of his reign.

### FEMALE COSTUME

Though it was less fickle than it is today, women's fashion had
changed a lot since the court had settled at Versailles. The royal
mistresses, of course, imposed their will, and all the ladies complied
promptly with the new rules. The main items of everyday dress
were a gown and skirts, with bodices to match. The top skirts
were full, revealing other, narrower, skirts which were worn
beneath. A lady of quality could not do with less than three
skirts: the first, decorated with knots of ribbons, was the *modeste*;
the second, which was likely to be rumpled by too ardent a lover,
was the *friponne* (from *friper*, to rumple); the third was called the
*secret*, because only husbands—or the ladies' intimate friends—
knew its secrets. These three skirts broadened the hips and, inter-
twined with lace and ribbons, their removal was a real test of
patience. A lover's enthusiasm might well be quenched, or contrari-
wise, inflamed.

The turned-back top skirt bore the misnomer *manteau*. It ended
in a train, the length of which was determined by the wearer's
rank: a duchess had to make do with a train of three *ells*, a Princess
of the Blood was allowed five, the King's grand-daughter seven, a

Daughter of France nine, and the Queen had the longest with eleven. Protocol in this respect was rigorous and no lady dared to transgress.

The tapered bodice was very tight at the waist. It was completed with short sleeves. Cut very low, it revealed the tops of the breasts. It was laced up and trimmed with silk ribbons, enamelled buttons, Alençon, Valençiennes or English lace. English lace was black.

The King's passion for the Marquise de Montespan was endless; she reigned over the court for twenty years and established a fashion in dress for pregnant women; she was seven times pregnant between 1669 and 1678. The robe was very long and unbelted, which seemed astonishing; it was known as the *Innocent*—more innocent, no doubt, than the haughty Maintenon herself, who had shady dealings with poisoners.

So much for everyday costume. In the evening, however, for all the receptions or for supper, the women put on full evening dress: a ball dress of brocade, satin or velvet, the sumptuousness of which was proportionate to the wearer's fortune. The bodice was cut very low and was extremely tight, to make the waist look smaller. The trimmings were both numerous and costly. These garments were the ruin of those who wore or paid for them. For a long time, women had been dressed by male tailors. Eventually, female dressmakers got the upper hand, after struggling for twenty-five years for the right to form a guild. The Versailles dressmakers were of no great repute, and court ladies ordered their dresses from Paris, from Mme Charpentier or Mme de Villeneuve. These ladies were no cheaper than their male rivals. Georges Mongrédien noted a few prices: an *ell* of purple velvet on a gold ground cost twenty-four *livres*, so did crimson velvet; Genoa velvet cost twenty. A skirt, with its long train, required a large quantity. In 1679 Mme de Maintenon spent 330 *livres* on a skirt of black and purple satin for her sister-in-law. A flame-coloured bodice cost no more than thirty-eight livres. But Scarron's widow was still only governess to the King's illegitimate children and had to be very careful with her money.

At court, the ladies' main problem was their hair. It is an inexhaustible subject. Fashion had to be followed and it changed according to the whims of Mme Martin, who was hairdresser to all the duchesses and marquises. In 1671 she invented the *hurlupée* or *hurluberlu*. Mme de Sévigné wrote to Mme de Coulanges:

'Picture to yourself a peasant's head-dress, two inches lower than a round bonnet. On either side, the hair is cut to various lengths and made into large careless curls, which don't fall lower than an inch below the ear. The result is something very young and very pretty, like two big bunches of very short hair . . .'

The *hurluberlu* was to last all through the reign, and was even named after Mme de Maintenon, who was no longer either young or pretty, but only the bourgeoises and provincial ladies stuck to it. At Versailles, after 1680, the *fontange* was the rage.

The origin of the *fontange* is well known. It went back to the time when Marie-Angélique de Scoraille de Rousille was triumphant, of whose estate at Fontange Louis XIV made a duchy. While out hunting, an awkward branch had played havoc with the hair of the divinity La Fantaine was to describe as:

> *Pallas y mit son esprit si vanté,*
> *Junon son port et Vénus sa beauté,*
> *Flore son teint et les Grâces leur grâce.*[1]

The girl quickly untied her lace garter and fastened her hair above her head. Louis XIV was delighted with this coiffure and admired his mistress' deftness. He was not long in changing his opinion, for all the ladies at court wanted their hair done *à la Fontange*. The fashionable milliners stepped in and, instead of the charming improvisation, they built a complicated contraption of lace and wire reaching to impossible heights above the head. By that time, the poor girl had been dead a long time, and the head-dress she had improvised was still a success. Finally, the King could stand the fashion no longer. He came to loathe those kiss-curls, and sky-high pyramids of hair. Eventually they became so huge that the expert who came to do the ladies' hair had to take with him a locksmith to fix the iron framework. Louis XIV struggled in vain: fashion was stronger than the most powerful king. It took the mockery of the Duchess of Shrewsbury, the English Ambassador's wife, for the women to give in. The *fontange* had lasted for thirty years.

---

[1] 'Pallas endowed her with her much-praised intellect, Juno with her deportment, Venus with her beauty, Flora with her complexion, and the Graces with their gracefulness.'

## FOOD

The cuisine reflected the situation in fashion; it was heavy and complicated. The King liked dishes that had taken a long time to prepare. His kitchen officers were at work at dawn to get dishes ready in time to be served to His Majesty by one in the afternoon. Each service comprised several dishes, but Louis XIV did not eat them all: he chose those he liked. Soups, with which every meal began, were either thick or thin. The *Potage à la Royale* was made of the white meat of the partridge cooked in an aromatic broth and served on toast in veal gravy; with it would be a soup of lettuce stuffed with eggs, herbs, spices and mushroom juice.

The King sat down before a silver plate that was raised on a silver table-mat; beside it was a silver cruet with spices, pepper and vinegar. He seized his knife and used it with great skill (according to Saint-Simon), eating a chicken fricassée, for instance, without staining anything but his fingers. But after each service he was presented with a moist napkin kept between two silver plates.

To the entrées the King helped himself generously: to the leg of mutton *à la royale*—not roasted but boiled in on an offal broth, the King preferred ham 'stuck with cloves under the crackling, seasoned with cinnamon and sprinkled with sugar'.

Joints came next. They were no longer offered heaped on a single huge dish. Each roast came on a large plate of its own: fillet of venison with truffled partridge, beef flavoured with marjoram and surrounded with pheasant stuffed with cloves and capon stuffed with oysters. The dishes were artistically laid out on dressers and were a delight to the eye before enchanting the palate.

As a new and quickly popular fashion, these roasts were accompanied by endive, beetroot and lettuce, dressed with oil and lemon, which the King preferred to vinegar. One added every possible herb, for far more seasoning was used than today: fennel, tarragon and even violets. The salads came from the King's kitchen-garden, supervised by La Quintinie.

La Quintinie also provided the vegetables, which were the leading items of the last service, the *entremets*. Under that somewhat vague name, the chef included all that was neither entrées nor roasts; even omelettes with a variety of fillings, pies of great variety, and the vegetables in season as well as fruit from the orchard, could be found there.

As regards vegetables, Louis XIV was very exacting. He demanded asparagus in December, melons in June and peas in May. La Quintinie worked for seven years to raise such unseasonable vegetables from the poor soil at his disposal. It is true he had plenty of manure (from nearby stables) and workmen. Thanks to hot-houses, glass frames and his own ingenuity, the master could be offered six different kinds of strawberries, seven kinds of melons, lettuce in March and cucumbers early in April.

Louis XIV was very fond of vegetables. He preferred them to heavy pastry. To please him, La Quintinie grew at Versailles plants which must have greatly surprised the inhabitants of the old village. There were cauliflowers, new to France, the seeds having been imported from Cyprus. Salsify, artichokes and cardoons arrived from Italy. There were cucumbers, much appreciated by the King, spinach, sorrel, aubergines and haricots. Tomatoes were still used only for decoration and potatoes were a botanical curiosity.

Above all else, Louis XIV preferred *petit pois*. A certain Audiger had imported them from Italy about 1660. They became a craze, but it was not within everyone's reach, as one paid up to one hundred *livres* (200 gold francs) for three-quarters of a pound. Their rarity increased their popularity and their price. When they came into season, the King could not resist satisfying his greed; he would gobble a whole dish of them and be sick during the night. Then everything would begin again the next year. The following lines from one of Mme de Sévigné's letters have been often quoted: 'The pea business still goes on. Impatience to eat them, the pleasure of having eaten them and the hope to eat more of them are the three questions constantly discussed by our princes. Several ladies, having supped—and supped very well—went home and found more peas there to eat before going to bed, and ate them at the risk of indigestion. It is a fashion and the rage.'

Hard-boiled eggs were served with the vegetables. According to the Palatine Princess, Louis XIV was almost as fond of them as of peas. 'I saw him devour three or four hard-boiled eggs at the end of his meal,' she wrote. But she may have exaggerated a little.

On the other hand, it is true that the King liked fruit. Most of what was served at his table came from his own orchards. While

out for a walk, he had the gardeners tell him all about trees growing
either in the open or along the walls, where a covering of plaster
and chopped straw kept the heat and hastened the maturation.
Pears were the most successful. La Quintinie listed 300 species,
twenty-five of which were reckoned the most fragrant: *Beurrée,
Louise-Bonne, Cuisse-Madame* or *Gergamotte rayée*. Only seven
varieties of apples were known—(pippins, *Calville* or *Pomme
d'Api*). Plums were not mentioned. Peaches were the royal
gardener's pride. The *Violette Hâtive,* the *Téton de Vénus,* the
*Belle de Vitry* grew along the walls. The King showed them to
visitors, 'telling them that the Greeks and Romans used to call the
peach "the Persian apple" '. Cherries were mostly used in tarts.
The various local cherries, those of Montmorency, or the black
or red-heart varieties, were not very flavourful. Blackberries were
grown with great care. The King used to consume large quantities
of strawberries, but Fagon forbade them in 1709. He had to make
do with figs, which he also liked. Versailles or Argenteuil figs were
delivered daily. As for grapes, they came from Touraine or
Champagne, for the local vines, still quite numerous near Versailles, did not produce fruit worthy of the royal table.

Oranges came from Portugal. Those which decorated the King's
gardens so gaily never ripened, and if he presented them to the
ladies, it was to heighten the colour of their lips. Lemons,
quantities of which were used to season the salads, were imported
from warm countries.

The King had finished eating. Several times he had asked for a
drink; we have already seen how complicated that service was.
The wine that was presented came from Champagne. It was red,
natural and not sparkling. Fagon, who always advocated the
opposite of d'Aquin's prescriptions, induced his royal patient to
drink Burgundy instead, as according to him, Champagne wine
produced acidity in the stomach.

During collations guests drank orangeade, wine, chocolate, tea
and coffee. Tea and coffee were very expensive: a pound of China
tea cost seventy gold francs and Japanese tea was twice as dear.
They were offered on special tables. But as Louis XIV was not
attracted by tea, the courtiers did not take it; they were more
easily tempted by coffee. The King drank it for a few months, then
tired of it.

When the King retired to his apartments, courtiers dined in

their turn. The royal family had already dined, each of them in his own apartment. 'There is nothing more tedious than eating alone, surrounded by twenty lads who watch one chewing and count one's mouthfuls,' grumbled the Palatine Princess. We must assume that their unwelcome presence did not spoil her appetite, for the Princess, though she made fun of the King, ate much and did not bother about her weight. Charlotte-Elizabeth of Bavaria wrote this unflattering portrait of herself: 'My waist is monstrously thick; I am as square as a dice. My skin is red, spotted with yellow; I am beginning to go grey and my hair is all pepper and salt; my forehead and eyes are all wrinkled; my nose is always crooked and, on top of everything, it has been embellished by small-pox, like my flat cheeks. I have a double chin and decayed teeth; my mouth is larger, more wrinkled and slightly spoilt. You can judge my lovely face.'

The King's officials, whose appetites must have been sharpened by all the dishes prepared for their master, usually ate together. Tables and trestles were erected for them in the guard-room. The dishes were brought from the Grand Commun. By the end of the eighteenth century, when economies were again in force, they were sometimes fed by Versailles eating-houses. Here are some of the menus offered to them:

| | |
|---|---|
| Sausage | Broth |
| Fresh eggs | Herrings |
| Large cutlets | Scrambled eggs |
| Chicken | Pig's trotters 'Ste Menehould' |
| Salad | Salad |
| | |
| | Thick soup |
| | Boiled beef |
| | Larded veal |
| | Capon |
| | Pie |
| | Spinach |
| | Dessert |

Plentiful and heavy food. The guards sought quantity rather than quality. Then drank large bumpers of red Orléans wine, and various white wines, sometimes from Mantes, a vintage very much appreciated at Versailles.

High officers, the Grand Equerry, the First Equerry, the Master of the Hounds would drive hurriedly back to their hotels, for it was now about two in the afternoon. They kept open table and their guests awaited them. Having presented Grandet, the mayor of Angers, to the King, who took him into his cabinet, the Prince d'Armagnac took three courtiers home with him to dinner: 'There were very many people there', Grandet wrote, 'for his nobleman kept open table.'

Dinner had to be swallowed within an hour. They had to be back at the palace to go hunting. The Marquise de Sévigné complained of being forced to dine very late, but the supper hour was getting later and later too. Ordinary people would sup at six; at court, on days when there was no reception, it was served at eight. 'When silly people want you to sup at six', wrote the Marquise, 'I laugh at them. I sup at eight. But on what? A quail or a partridge wing.' The King's supper was more substantial.

What about the Versailles bourgeois, the ordinary people who made their living out of the castle? They tried to eat cheaply by going to market at the *serdeau* or at the market in the new city, precariously organized where the Rue du Plessis and Rue de la Paroisse met. Numerous provision merchants made fortunes out of them.

Courtiers had to spend a lot on food, and they ate in haste and badly, so as not to miss their place at the chateau. There was coercion here as in everything else.

# CHAPTER EIGHT

# THE DESERTED PALACE

Louis XIV died on September 1, 1715, early in the morning. In the afternoon, the Duc d'Orléans called on Procureur Général d'Aguesseau in Paris to see what should be done. The next day Parliament met, in the presence of the Princes of the Blood and the peers. The palace was surrounded by the French and the Swiss guards. The Duke made a long speech and ended by claiming the Regency by right of birth. Despite the remonstrations of a few councillors, who asked that the late King's will should be read, the magistrates, 'coaxed into compliance by the Duke's flattering remarks', decided in his favour and declared Orléans Regent of the Realm during Louis XV's minority.

The Council instituted by Louis XIV did not meet, the Duc du Maine was deprived of the command of the troops of the Royal Household and of the supervision of the future sovereign's education.

The people of Versailles, who had gathered each day in front of the palace during the King's illness, had gone home. The Parliament and councillors were very soon to regret their decision. The Regent did not wait long before humiliating them. In Versailles these words were sung everywhere:

> Le parlement fait pénitence
> Je pense
> De quelque gros péché.
> C'est, dit-on, pour avoir cassé
> Le testament du roi de France
> Je pense
> De quelque gros péché.[1]

The people sang, but not for long.

---

[1] 'Parliament does penance, I think, for some great sin. It is said it is because they have annulled the King of France's will. . . .'

### THE KING'S DEPARTURE

As the representative of a nobility kept in bondage for half a century, the Duc d'Orléans did not like Versailles, where he had been mortified so often. On the pretext that Louis XV had a cold and that the air of Versailles did not agree with him, he decided to take him to Vincennes. Louis XIV's body had not yet been removed from the palace when, on September 9th, early in the afternoon, the royal coach started for Paris. The news was already abroad, and many of the inhabitants had gathered at the bottom of the Place d'Armes. Louis XV had some money thrown out to them as he passed.

The King had gone. The whole court followed in haste. It was a general stampede. Within a few weeks the town was deserted. The officers of the King's Household, the office holders, courtiers who had merely come to breathe the air of Versailles, and even tradesmen, disappeared and the proprietors of furnished or unfurnished houses were reduced to a most difficult situation. Until that day there had been competition for the meanest garret at any cost, and the inn-keepers were making fortunes; then suddenly there was a crisis of a quite different kind. Tenants demanded the cancellation of their leases, and this was the cause of numberless law-suits.

The Regent settled the matter: 'After we had left the town of Versailles and ceased to regard it as our usual residence, the majority of the merchants, artisans, workmen and others, who were dependent upon our court and our councils, having left, the city was deserted overnight.' Consequently, to give some help to 'those who have to stay there because of long residence or large expenditure on the construction of their houses', he decided that the land tax would be definitely suppressed.

This resulted in an abrupt collapse of rents and in the selling price of houses, so that numerous proprietors preferred to keep their properties rather than to sell them at a loss. Clever speculators profited from the situation. An attorney-general of the *Cour des Aides*, Bosc, bought for 100,000 *livres*, payable in notes of Law's banks (already depreciating) the splendid Conti mansion, now the Versailles town hall. He even succeeded in getting back most of that price by selling the outer building and the rich interior decoration.

Lodgings were obtainable at ridiculously low rents: the valet Lebel rented a fine large mansion on the Petite Place for 250 *livres* a year. It would have been five times that price two years earlier.

Versailles was like an emaciated body in clothes too big for it. The priests who were attached to the Royal parish had nothing to do and were too many for a population that had been reduced by half. Was it to find something to do that they decided in 1718 to shave off the tiny goatees they wore on their chins, which had got them the nick-name of *barbichet*, coined by Saint-Simon? This change greatly shocked the police commissioner Narbonne!

What was to become of the palace? One can realize the hatred inspired among the nobility by a proposal made by the Duc de Noailles, to whom the Regent was thinking of confiding the Ministry of Finance: declaiming in front of Saint-Simon against the huge organization Louis XIV had contrived in Versailles, Noailles coolly suggested destroying the chateau and carrying its treasures off to St Germain-en-Laye! Saint-Simon was appalled by the idea and words failed him for a while. Then he recovered. 'Sir,' he said at last, 'if you could get the fairies to help you with their magic wands, then I would agree with you.' Noailles did not insist.

The palace had not been entirely deserted. A few offices stayed on. The building department, which looked after the chateau, remained at Versailles. Blouin, who was simultaneously the King's valet and governor of Versailles, did not leave his lodgings: the young King did not need him. The stables and the school for pages also continued.

After so many years of strenuous activity, the palace looked empty. Windows were opened and cleaned. Gusts of fresh air, to quote the words of a contemporary, came to blow away the miasmas which were slowly poisoning the inmates of the palace. It had become one of those impressive historical buildings in which one conjured up the memory of a prince and his reign, and in which royal guests were put up for a while.

This happened in 1717, when the Czar Peter I spent some time in France. He wanted to see Louis XIV's palace: his wish was immediately complied with. He arrived at Versailles on May 2nd, where he was met by the Duc d'Antin, Superintendent of the Buildings. The Queen's apartments had been hurriedly arranged for him. He slept in one of the little rooms. The next day he made the classic trip by gondola along the Grand Canal. He was shown the Ménagerie and Trianon, where he spent a second night. He spent a week in Versailles in all. As a sovereign who wanted to have a good time in France—an old tradition—the Czar had brought along with him a number of ladies of little virtue. They were housed near him, in Mme de Maintenon's former apartments. Blouin, who had been the King's faithful servant, was deeply shocked.

For seven years the chateau was poorly maintained. The Regent had made heavy cuts in the subsidies paid for its upkeep. Repairs were carried out as best they could. The future was uncertain.

Cardinal Dubois' policy saved the Sun King's achievement. As time passed the Regent's influence upon Louis XV was increasing and becoming dangerous. Law's failure had created a violent crisis in public opinion. To protect himself from an aristocracy whose ambitions he had set free, Philip of Orléans thought of relying on the people of Paris. The lesser branch of the Royal Family always verged on demagogy. Dubois, who thought only of keeping peace within the kingdom as well as abroad, thought that bringing the court back to Versailles would help. He claimed that the young King was keen to go back to the palace he had known in his childhood. It is more probable that he was never consulted.

### LOUIS XV'S RETURN

In April 1722 the inhabitants of Versailles heard that the King and court were likely to return. It was a happy rumour. Proprietors and inn-keepers got busy. In the palace, the Superintendent's office was working to death. Everything had to be got into fit condition. In two months the most urgent work was completed.

At last the great day dawned. On June 15, 1722, according to Narbonne, the King returned to Versailles as his permanent residence. In his coach were the Regent—whose rule was soon to end, since the King would be of age the following August—his son, the Duc de Chartres, the King's tutor, the Duc de Bourbon, together with Marshal de Villeroi, his guardian, and the Bishop of Fréjus, his teacher.

A large crowd was waiting along the Avenue de Paris and on the square, shouting with delight, and the King responded gaily. He looked delighted. Saint-Simon related how, as soon as he arrived, he drew all his attendants into a mad race across the park. This boy of twelve had kept a vivid remembrance of those wonderful gardens, of the running water, and of the fountains round which he had played when a child. He wanted to see everything and recapture all the past. After a two-hour walk he was so tired that he lay down on the floor in the Galerie des Glaces, as if to take physical possession of it. What he really wanted to do was to look comfortably at Le Brun's ceiling. He then agreed to withdraw into his apartments.

When alighting from his coach, he had gone first to the chapel to say a prayer, for Louis XIV's great-grandson was very devout at that time. When evening had come, the people of Versailles, to show their satisfaction, asked permission for a firework display. Narbonne was their ambassador to the Duc d'Orléans. The latter thought it not seemly, and the firework display did not take place.

For seven years, there had been no court in France. The nobility had dispersed and little groups had been created. Noblemen and office holders were quickly brought together again. The castle and its neighbourhood quickly recovered all their animation, but the tone was different.

Louis was a shy boy, more studious than is ordinarily thought. He had been brought up by the Marquise de Ventadour and by Marshal de Villeroi. The former had once been very gay, but in old age had become very devout; she had neither intelligence nor authority. Villeroi was an old man, 'frivolous and conceited'. He had tried to give his ward court manners and language and a complete contempt for the courtiers. 'One must hold ministers' chamber pots while they are in office and empty them over their heads when they are out,' was one of his theories. Louis XV never forgot this advice and was soon to use it in respect of Villeroi himself.

The court had hardly been at Versailles for a month when a scandal broke out. In the park a group of young men from the King's own entourage was discovered indulging in pleasures frowned upon by the more conventional. Most of them were married men. To console themselves, their wives had taken lovers, with whom they were living publicly. Among these young men, most of them scarcely twenty years old, were the Duc de Boufflers, the Comte de Ligny, the Marquis de Rambure and Villeroi's own grandson, the Marquis d'Alincourt. The most guilty were sent to the Bastille and the others exiled in distant chateaux, together with their wives—a bitter punishment!

The King was surprised by their disappearance. He could not be told the real story—only that they had torn up some railings in the park. The culprits got the nick-name of 'fence-breakers'. Marshal de Villeroi was the subsequent victim of his grandson's unpleasant exploits. On August 15th, coming from an interview with the Regent, he was forced into a sedan-chair, taken to the Orangerie, where a coach was waiting for him, and exiled to Neuville, in the neighbourhood of Lyons.

The King did not regret the removal of his former tutor. Two months later (on October 25, 1772) he was crowned at Rheims. His reign was now beginning.

# CHAPTER NINE

# THE COURT OF LOUIS XV

Superficially etiquette and ceremonial remained unchanged, but the spirit was wholly different. The King himself had taken responsibility for these changes, which made the old courtiers shake their heads regretfully.

## THE KING'S CHARACTER

Louis XV has been severely dealt with by nineteenth-century historians. More recent studies enable us to see him in a better light. Yet one must agree that his character is often difficult to grasp.

He was intelligent and knew the court well. What he had been taught by Marshal de Villeroi had not been wasted: he had little confidence in those who served him. He soon showed himself sceptical about their devotion. He was never to be as hard-working as his great-grandfather. He was lacking in will. When the War of the Austrian Succession broke out, he remarked: 'As for us, we merely withdraw on Mont Pagnotte.' This was a hillock near Chantilly from which one could follow the hunt without actually participating. He meant that the present business did not concern France, and it was a wise reflection. Louis XIV would have stuck to his decision; Louis XV, who was more easily influenced, was drawn into it by his councillors.

He was not really lazy. He held a council every day and often received ministers and ambassadors. In the evening, after supper, he liked to discuss the affairs of the kingdom with his own friends. He had his private informers and his own politics, that celebrated 'King's Secret'. Never had the secret censorship of letters been more active. Every Sunday the King received the Postmaster-General, who gave him an account of what his men had discovered in his courtiers' correspondence. The King was as interested in gossip as he was in politics. This was in order to shake off his boredom, as he never made the least allusion to the stories he had thus discovered. But his scepticism increased.

Boredom was Louis' main trouble. It was to escape it that he acquired his first mistresses and tirelessly pursued fresh distractions.

This boredom was so great that it was accompanied by the most mournful thoughts. His morbid turn of mind may have been inborn, for within a few days, when he was two, he had lost both his father and his mother. When he heard of anyone being at the point of death, he relished every detail. He used to ask the courtiers whether they had chosen where they wanted to be buried.

'Where are you going to be buried?' he once asked the Marquis de Souvré.

'At your feet, Sir,' the old man pointedly answered, and the King was taken aback. Such a reply would have been unthinkable under Louis XIV.

Macabre fancies often haunted him. If on a journey he passed a country churchyard he stopped and sent one of his men to see whether there were any newly dug graves. When the man came back, saying that there were, 'it really makes one's mouth water', the Maréchale de Mirepoix scoffed; she was in the Royal coach with the Marquise de Pompadour. The King looked at her reproachfully and said nothing.

To shake off his melancholy and escape such thoughts, the King travelled a great deal. It would be going too far to say that during his reign the court returned to its itinerant traditions. Louis XIV also went to Marly and St Germain, but he spent the greater part of the year in Versailles. His great-grandson escaped from it as often as possible.

Narbonne has made a list of the King's journeys between 1722 and 1742. Here, for instance, are his notes for 1725, a particularly memorable year, as it was the one in whch the King married Marie Leczinska.

'The King left Versailles for Marly on January 17th and came back on February 1st. On February 3rd he went back to Marly until April 7th. On June 8th he left for Fontainebleau. During his stay there he married Marie Leczinska, the King of Poland's daughter. There were magnificent feasts and, despite public distress, the King made a great show. Most noblemen wore stockings of pure thread of gold, costing three hundred francs . . . On December 1st, the King came back to Versailles with the Queen.

So in 1725 Louis XV spent only 131 days in Versailles. In 1733 he stayed there for only 125 days; in 1737, 272 days; in 1740 for 257 and in 1742 for 226. Marly, Choisy, Rambouillet, Fontainebleau were his favourite residences. It is true that he grew more sedentary after Mme de Pompadour's death.

Finally, one last aspect of his character must be emphasized: the King was shy. Constantly on show, he took little notice of the unknown people who slipped in between his courtiers. On the other hand, as he had a remarkable memory, he identified all the gentlemen of the court. He did not like to meet newcomers. Was it on account of his education or was it a trait of the period? He found happiness with a small group of people. As he was the King, he had to comply with all the official ceremonies, but was only happy and restful in an intimate circle. That is why he was so happy with Mme de Pompadour in the Little Apartments she had organized for him. Those rooms, with their refined taste, were a relief after the huge State Rooms downstairs.

## TWO ASPECTS OF THE COURT

The King divided his life into two: one part was devoted to the public, and the other was private.

Of course, Louis XIV had also set apart a good many hours during which he disappeared from sight and went to see his mistresses. Memoir writers have been singularly discreet on that subject. One of them wrote that the King received Mme de Montespan in the evening, but even she could not change the ceremonial.

Louis XV, on the other hand, went to see his mistresses as soon as he was free. It was in Mme de Pompadour's rooms, and in her presence, that he discussed the affairs of state with his ministers. Never would such a break with etiquette have been committed in the time of the fair Athénaïs.

His first change was to his bed-chamber. The young King, as a matter of course, first settled in his great-grandfather's room, and the first years of his reign were spent there, and those of his connubial faithfulness. After a while, he came to dislike it and probably abandoned it for intimate reasons. About 1735 he decided to alter all the rooms on the right wing of the Courtyard, where Louis XIV's collections had been displayed. To Gabriel's drawings, Verbeckt and Rousseau built the most elegant ensemble ever seen in France up to that time. The first room, the nearest to the Council Room, became the King's bed-chamber. Louis XV moved there in 1738. He did not regret his great-grandfather's room, so large and so badly heated that he caught colds. The new room was furnished with a bed *à la Duchesse,* two narrow armchairs and a chest of drawers. In the alcove were also a *chaise percée* which at last provided the King with some privacy. This 'English chair', provided with taps and plugs, was decorated with J. P. Boulle's marquetry. Medieval privies were coming back into fashion in the eighteenth century. There were *chaise* cabinets throughout the palace, not only in the King's apartments.

Another change: while Louis XIV was awakened at the same time each morning, Louis XV told his valet the previous evening when he wanted to be called. If he had gone late to bed, he wanted to be allowed to sleep the next morning.

There was now a first private *lever* and then a public one. Having awakened, the King would rise, put on his dressing-gown, pass through the Council Room and go to the official bed-chamber where he was supposed to have spent the night. He would even lie down for a few minutes in Louis XIV's bed. Then the various entries would take place: no part of the ceremony had changed. The King's toilet lasted longer. He was shaved every day and he washed more: the barber would wipe his face with a soft sponge dipped in water and alcohol, and then with pure water.

Louis XV was no longer satisfied with his great-grandfather's cup of broth or herb tea. When his toilet was finished, he was served with more substantial food, with a cup of black coffee and fruit.

The rest of the morning unfolded in accordance with the usual rules; after saying a prayer, the King would go into the Council Room, attend the meeting, receive ministers and ambassadors. The latter often complained of difficulties in securing an interview. The solemn meetings and the big public audiences took place in Louis XIV's former room. The King stood alone behind the balustrade and no one was allowed to cross it without the King's permission. For having committed that offence in April

1746, the Cardinal de Tencin was asked to leave. Etiquette was still very strict and Louis XV enforced it on his courtiers.

Mass was always said at the end of the morning, and then the King had dinner. He still ate alone surrounded by his officers watching over the proceedings. On the other hand, there were considerable changes concerning supper arrangements. When he returned from hunting or from a walk, the King would withdraw into a private room which he had turned into a dining-room, near the Clock Room, which was reached through the Dog's Room. It was a small room, to which only the ruling mistress had access and a few friends. It was in 1735 that a special room was set aside for meals. This arrangement became the fashion at once and in all big houses built thereafter, this new room was provided for.

For some time Louis had two dining-rooms, one for winter use on the second floor, another for summer, under the roof. He then had the original idea of taking a walk on the roofs after supper, together with a few ladies and friends. This did not last long: Louis XV never did anything for long. The courtiers envied the privileged few who took part in those small supper parties, but they did not take place every evening. As a duty, the King supped also in Grand Couvert with the Queen and the whole Royal Family, where everyone could approach him. This made him all the happier to return to his small rooms and private suppers. As he had a robust appetite, he sometimes supped again with his mistress.

The evening was prolonged. The *Bien-Aimé* did not follow the strict time-table of his predecessor. He would play cards, chat, brew his own coffee. He consequently went to bed at irregular times which somehow played havoc with etiquette. Bored with waiting for him to perform his evening prayers, his almoners would sit on the stools in the King's room, and some valets had the audacity to sit on Louis XIV's bed, taking care to draw the curtains.

At last the King would come. The morning comedy was repeated. The King slipped for a while into the former King's bed, and as soon as the last courtier had disappeared he got up, put on his dressing-gown and returned to his rooms. By a small inner stair-case he could either leave the palace or climb to the second floor, where Mme de Pompadour was waiting for him. A time came when the King merely pretended to undress, but kept his clothes on in order to escape more easily.

Early in the reign, he would discreetly send word to the Queen telling her not to worry. With a friend, the Duc d'Ayen or Luynes, he would go incognito to the Opera Ball, or to dance *chez* Mme du Chalaise. He later visited some girls of small virtue, and came back very late—or very early. In March 1737, after a carnival night, it was six in the morning when he got back to his apartments. The doors were closed. The guard was half asleep. Someone scratched on the door: 'Open, sentinel, it is the King.' The man was both surprised and sceptical. 'The King is in bed, I won't open and you shan't pass, whoever you are, except with light.' A candle had to be fetched. The guard opened, recognized the King, saying: 'Sir, I beg Your Majesty's pardon, but my orders were to let nobody in. So do, please, excuse me from my orders.' The King congratulated him and went to bed at last.

Thus the King led a double life, the one he had inherited from his great-grandfather and which he maintained, since Versailles was inconceivable without ceremonial and etiquette; the other of a man who, though King, sought to enjoy life to the full.

## THE KING AND THE QUEEN

His engagement to the Infanta Marie-Anne-Victoire having been broken, the King married the King of Poland's daughter, Marie Leczinska, on September 5, 1725. The Queen was twenty-two, Louis barely fifteen. He was a handsome, strong lad with a fine face; 'He had the finest head you ever could see,' wrote a contemporary. Another thought he looked like Cupid.

The Queen was no beauty: she had a fresh complexion, expressive eyes and a slightly upturned nose. She was pleasant to look at. The King, who was not very sentimental but very pious (so was she: she always attended a private mass before going to the King's), immediately fell in love with the girl Heaven and Cardinal Fleury had selected as his wife. If we are to believe the Duc de Bourbon, who may exaggerate, during their wedding night, the King 'proved his love for her seven times'. We may wonder how the Duke knew! It is unlikely that the King had confided in him, and even less so the Queen.

It is true, however, that the Queen was soon with child. In the room where Maria-Thérèsa of Austria and the Dauphine had lived and died, she brought into the world ten children in twelve years: twins, Madame Première and Madame Seconde (Marie-Louise-Elizabeth and Anne-Henrietta on August 14, 1727, at 10 a.m.); Mme Troisième (Louise-Marie) was born on July 28, 1728. The surgeons had proudly stated that it would be a boy and a firework display had already been prepared at Versailles. It was called off and there was only a modest *Te Deum* the next day in the chapel and in Notre-Dame.

At last, on Sunday September 4, 1729, at 3.40 a.m., Marie was delivered of 'Monseigneur le Dauphin, in the presence of the King, the Duc d'Orléans, the Duc du Maine, the Comte de Toulouse, the Chancellor, the Ministers and a great number of lords and ladies'. This time, joy was unchecked. In Versailles every house and hotel was lit up. Shops remained closed for forty-eight hours and the firework show took place as planned. There were seventy rockets, fired all at once on the Place d'Armes at 10.30. They lasted for seven minutes.

But that was not all. One after the other, Marie produced six other children, the Duc d'Anjou (who died at the age of three), Marie-Adélaïde, Victoire, Sophie, Félicité and Louise. The Queen is reported to have said, with a sigh of weariness: 'Well!—always to bed, always with child, always being confined . . .'

The words may be apocryphal; yet they render fairly well the feelings of a woman who had aged before her time and liked to live with her own circle of friends in her rooms.

Here too, much had been done to alter the setting Maria-Thérèsa had known. On Gabriel's plans, Verbeckt had sculpted gilded wainscotting and François Boucher had painted a camayeu ceiling. At the same time, the inner rooms behind the State Apartments where the Queen gave audiences and supped in Grand Couvert, were also given a new look, in accordance with the Queen's excellent taste. She even had a workroom built, where she would indulge her favourite pastimes of tapestry and painting under Oudry's direction.

The Queen's day was fairly busy. For a long time she shared the life of her husband and master. Then, little by little she organized her days to her own liking. She visited the King each morning in full court dress, then went to mass. She saw the King again in the evening when the family supped in public, once or twice a week. During the rest of the time she enjoyed a freedom

9. Madame de Pompadour, by Boucher

10. The Jeu du Roi in the Galerie des Glaces, to celebrate the Dauphin's marriage in 1745

'unknown to Queens of France until then'. Her dress was simple. She dressed in white brocade with the fleur-de-lys-studded cloak only for official ceremonies. On other days, she had dresses like those of her ladies-in-waiting. On her head she wore a mantilla or a lace kerchief. She had renounced all coquetry.

After audiences she devoted some moments to her children, then retired to her workroom with her tutor who used to guide her brush and himself paint the most tricky parts.

She dined alone, according to custom. Her appetite matched the King's. She was very greedy, and as Louis XV was drawing away from her, she lapsed into piety and became fonder and fonder of food. The courtiers gaped at her as she silently gobbled up the dishes put before her. She sometimes felt a little ashamed of displaying her immoderate taste for good food in public. She would then address one of the noblemen around her and tell him how good was the dish she was eating. He would solemnly agree.

Feeling a little heavy, the Queen returned to her rooms after the meal. She liked music and played, without any real talent, the guitar, the hurdy-gurdy and the harpsichord. Her daughter Louise was more gifted. She also liked to colour pious pictures and on her little private press print drawings she would present to her attendants.

Towards the end of the afternoon the Queen drove out in her coach. Generous and charitable, she visited convents she had taken under her protection. In 1767, she brought to Versailles the August-ine nuns of Compiègne, whose house was falling into decay. For those nuns, Mique, the King's architect, planned a large house in which to educate young girls and house elderly ladies. The Queen went over the plans and signed each page.

Sometimes the Queen preferred to meditate. Did Louis XV's taste for macabre things contaminate his wife? She created the fashion of *belles mignonnes*: skulls that one looked at for a long time to convince oneself of the vanity of worldly things. The Queen's *belle mignonne* was ornamented with tresses of hair and lit with candles. It was supposed to be Ninon de Lenclos' skull. At any rate the Queen believed that it was.

At six o'clock, on returning from her drive, she would hold her circle, always with more or less the same people: Président Hénault, a ceremonious man of law; Maurepas, who had a pleasant way of relating all the gossip of the chateau; Moncrif, the Queen's reader, who loved cats and wrote about them; and Cardinal de Luynes and a few others.

The Queen would play *cavagnole,* a game played with dice for rather low stakes. The Queen was not very quick and seldom won. As she was very generous and spent all she had on charity, she was sometimes at her wits' end to pay. Once, she lost some 1,000 *livres,* which she borrowed from Luynes and Noailles. They were too gallant to make allusion to the debt and Marie did not dare to ask the King for such a sum. However strange it might seem, it was Mme de Pompadour who got the Queen out of trouble.

When there was no Grand Couvert, supper took place in the Queen's private apartment or in those of the Duc and Duchesse de Luynes, 'my honest people', as the Queen called them. There were few people around the table and Marie again ate a large meal. Then everyone returned to the drawing-room. One would discuss the events of the day. The Queen was not a prude and memoir writers have told many stories which make it clear that she was no hypocrite. *Cavagnole* was resumed. The Queen and her friends would work at some needlework for the poor. Little by little the voices would die down and some would doze off. One evening, Cardinal de Luynes woke up suddenly, shouting: 'Summon the chapter!' He thought he was in his abbey. The court laughed about it for a whole month.

Meanwhile, the King was with his mistress, or had gone incognito to a show. It should not be imagined that Marie, in the early years, did not resent her husband's infidelity bitterly. Of course, after 1738, she made him aware that for her health it was better that he should abstain from his conjugal duties. The King complied without remorse. But the insolence of his first mistresses, the Duchess of Chateauroux above all, was very painful to her. Even after the Duchesse had died, the Queen dreamed of her.

'I had an awful nightmare,' she once said to a friend. 'I thought I saw her ghost.'

'What could Mme de Chateauroux be looking for in the Queen's rooms?' the courtiers mockingly wondered.

Marie Leczinska suffered by her desertion, she was happy when Louis paid her some attention. In 1745 all her rooms were re-decorated on his orders, while the court was in Fontainebleau. The bed was recovered with a new spread decorated with religious motifs. Marie almost wept with joy. She suffered, too, at being separated from her children.

## NO CHILDREN AT VERSAILLES

It is one of the strangest aspects of that huge building that shel-tered the court, that no children were seen there, and above all no babies. Whether they were born of the highest or the lowest officers of the court, from their birth onwards they were put out to a nurse. An agency from the town was to found for this sort of thing. The new-born babies were sent to surrounding villages, Villepreux, Noisy or even further afield. Many died. Parish regis-ters are edifying from this point of view. They were buried at once and their parents did not attend the funeral.

Royal children were an exception. They were brought up inside the palace but, taken away by those who were responsible for their education, they were hardly ever seen. A part of the park was reserved for their games. Their parents could see them for only a few moments each day. Marie Leczinska loved her daughters dearly. She received them in her private apartments. Louis XV, though busily occupied by his functions, entertainments and mistresses, liked the company of the young. When he happened to meet in one of the galleries a page playing truant from his duties, he would playfully pull his ear. That was how he playfully punished the young Bontemps in 1747, when the lad had hidden himself behind a curtain, whip in hand, to play a nasty joke on his companion Villepail. Louis XV received the stroke. It was no use for Bontemps to shout: 'Forgive me, Your Majesty! Villepail had beaten me and I thought it was him!' The King roughly pulled his ears and laughed heartily; Bontemps less so.

Those were unusual scenes. There was no room for children in the palace. That is why Louis XV, accepting Cardinal Fleury's advice, decided to send five of his daughters away. Barbier claimed that the decision was for reasons of economy. With Thérèse, Vic-toire, Sophie, Louise and Adélaïde gone, a good many jobs could be suppressed. It is not certain that this was the only reason for the King's decision, for he loved his children dearly. He may have wished to remove them from the restless atmosphere of the palace. He decided to send them to the Abbey of Fontevrault, one of the most highly reputed in the kingdom. The Abbess was Mme de

Mortemart, Mme de Montespan's own niece. To house the Daughters of France, a lovely little house, the Little Bourbons, was built and surrounded with gardens.

And yet the King hesitated long before depriving himself of his daughters. Little Adélaïde, who was only seven, implored her father to keep her and sobbed her heart out. Louis was deeply moved and granted her wish. The other four left with a large retinue and their journey—about sixty leagues—was very expensive. Thérèse died at the Abbey; Victoire came back in 1748, Sophie and Louise only in October 1750. The Marquise de Pompadour described their home-coming: 'Mesdames Sophie and Louise arrived yesterday. The King went out to meet them with the Dauphin and Mme Victoire. I had the honour of following them. Indeed, nothing was more touching than their meeting. The King's tenderness for his children is unbelievable and they responded with all their hearts.'

The poor Marquise also loved children and had only one daughter, Alexandrine. She would have liked so much to give proof of her love to the *Bien Aimé*! She miscarried several times. A luckier mistress, Mme de Vintimille, had had a son by the King, whom courtiers nick-named the 'Demi-Louis'. Mme de Pompadour's dream was to marry the 'Demi-Louis' to little Alexandrine. The King pretended not to understand his mistress' allusions, and the project came to nothing. Alexandrine died of appendicitis when nine years of age.

CHAPTER TEN

# PLEASANT AND UNPLEASANT ASPECTS

When reckoning the number of inhabitants at Versailles, shortly after the King's return, Narbonne wrote: 'Within the castle boundaries, princes, lords, officers and servants: 4,000 people.' But not included in the figure were the members of the military household or those persons who were housed in the outer buildings, like the Grand Commun, the Stables or the Kennels. But the figure is difficult to accept; however huge, it would seem impossible to cram so many people into the chateau. Narbonne had accepted a rather rough calculation.

Lodgings were always scarce in Versailles. Proprietors, having had one bad experience, were now intent on getting the most out of the houses and flats they had to let. Tenants tried to recoup themselves by sub-letting rooms at high rents, and everyone complained.

A nobleman felt he had to have a mansion in town. Buildings around the castle were modernized or transformed. The new district of St Louis grew increasingly in population. Court officials, musicians and workmen found shelter there.

It was still a favour to obtain a flat in the palace, and Louis XV could not satisfy all those who begged one from him. He was enslaved and persecuted by his court. When the King uttered this final verdict: 'This man shall never have a dwelling in Versailles as long as I live,' the wretched creature could only vanish.

Rivalries and jealousies were innumerable. In December 1743, Louis granted Maupeou, First President of the Parliament, a lodging in the castle: 'he was the first to be so honoured', wrote Barbier, who added: 'He is treated like a minister. He owes his position to the Comte de Maurepas.' For no decision was taken in Versailles without people trying to discover what really had happened, who helped and what was its hidden meaning.

A few years later, Mme de Pompadour, who had originally been lodged on the second floor, in the Little Apartments she had so delightfully decorated, intrigued to be transferred to the ground floor. In spite of her flying chair, a real hand-operated lift was installed for when she was tired of walking up and down stairs. To please her, the King granted her a suite near the chapel which until then had been occupied by the Comtesse de Toulouse and the Duc de Penthièvre, her son. The suite was divided into three parts: The Duke and Duchess kept the first, the Countess having nothing but two little rooms. Mme de Pompadour was given the rest. 'Everything has been divided and parcelled out, and compromises have been made,' wrote Luynes, 'and everyone is displeased.' The Comtesse de Toulouse refused to sleep in her two rooms and came there only to welcome the King (her grandnephew).

Most of the lords housed in the palace saw nothing in it but a privilege and the glorious evidence of Royal friendship. They had a room but did not always live there. These rooms were used to receive friends or to change their clothes or to take a few moments' rest. In the evening, they preferred to return to their own houses, either in Versailles or in Paris. Louis XV set the example by running away from Versailles whenever he wanted to have fun.

### A NEW STYLE

While the nobility's fixed idea under Louis XIV was never to leave court, but to cling always to the King's person, courtiers now came to Versailles out of duty only. From the high officers of the Crown, dukes and peers of the realm who had to attend certain ceremonies, down to the lowest valets, chair porters or fire-makers, everyone played a part in the palace. The useless unattached nobleman had completely disappeared. And, as soon as his duty was finished, every one of them hurried home.

To be admitted permanently into the King's retinue one had to be presented. The ceremony was always carried out according to the same rule. The applicant, whether male or female, had to be provided with a 'godfather' or 'godmother', that is to say, a sponsor. At a fixed time the candidate, if a lady, escorted by her sponsor and ladies-in-waiting, was taken into the King's study. Louis waited, standing beside the fireplace; she would curtsey, the King would bow and utter a few words; the new lady would answer, blushing deeply. Only trivialities were spoken. Then she would curtsey again and the little group would walk out. The same ceremony was repeated in the Queen's apartments. They were received in the Queen's bed-chamber. There was further curtseying and a brief dialogue. Marie Leczinska, who did not lack shrewdness, sometimes tried to put the new lady out of countenance. Instead of the insignificant, expected remark, she asked some unexpected question. When Jeanne-Antoinette Poisson, as the brand-new Marquise de Pompadour, was presented on September 14, 1745, the Queen amused herself by countering all the hopes of the courtiers. They were expecting a vague compliment about the favourite's dress. Instead, she asked:

'Give me news of Mme de Saissac,' (she was one of the Marquise's friends). 'I was very pleased to have seen her sometimes in Paris.'

Mme de Pompadour replied in a few words. She was upset and troubled. It must be admitted that the situation was as difficult for the Queen as for the mistress. She ended with this declaration of faith: 'Madam, I earnestly desire to please you.'

She curtsied very low in order to kiss the hem of the royal dress —after having pulled off her glove so fiercely that she broke her bracelet, Luynes noticed. It fell to the carpet. Courtiers went all over the palace, relating that story.

These presentations were no mere formalities required by an old-fashioned etiquette of which everyone complained, so that Dufort de Cheverny, an usher for ambassadors, who had to be most careful of these rites, denounced them in his memoirs. When they had been presented, the lady or the courtier had a right to enjoy 'the honours of the court'.

It was not a new institution, but after 1732, on the King's order, it had taken a more regular and official aspect. Whoever was admitted to the honours of the court, after having been regularly presented, enjoyed several privileges. He was invited to the palace banquets, balls and receptions, and became a member of the 'circles'. He could be asked to the King's 'little suppers'. That happened very seldom; the King selected only a small number of friends, and the Prince de Croÿ was once all in a tremor, hoping that the King, on emerging from his cabinet, might look favourably upon him. Croÿ had nothing to complain of: he was often asked to the 'little suppers', though the courtiers who never had such luck were many.

It was also a privilege to be admitted to the King's coaches. When no longer they lived in Versailles, courtiers had to make their way to and fro between Paris and the royal city. There was a constant traffic of carriages of all sorts on the road. How proud were those who had the right to ride in one of the coaches that bore the King's coat-of-arms! How delighted to squeeze oneself—together with eighteen or twenty other persons—into one of the gondolas (with seats for twelve) which followed the King's hunt, but not without an element of danger.

One was not admitted to the honours of the court without references. One had to prove the right degree of blue blood. To be put on the official lists of nobility, one had to give proofs of nobility as far back as 1400. The genealogists, Clairembault and Chérin, were very strict and turned down doubtful applications without mercy. It is true that the King could always grant special dispensations, as he did for Jeanne-Antoinette d'Étioles (born Poisson) who would have been totally unable to prove four centuries of nobility, as hers was barely four years old. The fact that the King ignored the rules was as fantastic as it was understandable. Other families were also elected by royal favour, since it was the King's intention to reward those who were devoted to his service.

Yet, the rules regarding accession to honours limited the number of courtiers.

### 'IN THIS COUNTRY'

Nevertheless the palace was still terribly crowded. Each nobleman had a retinue of valets and chair-carriers. Galleries were crowded with valets who rushed to open the doors when an important person was announced. Rules of precedence, to which old courtiers clung tightly, made traffic even worse. Should a Princess of the Blood, on her way to the Queen's suite, alight from her chair on entering the guards' room, or could she be carried as far as the ante-chamber, a privilege technically reserved for the Daughters and Grand-Daughters of France? Luynes discussed the problem seriously. The princess might be sent back, but beggars would invade the Dauphine's ante-chamber, as the police were no better than in the earlier reign. 'Merchants, following the court', still occupied the ground-floor galleries. Booths and shops still displayed their frail and graceless architecture in the forecourt and along the castle façades. Some of them, leaning against a wall, would block the windows of the latrines and thereby make the stench and filth of the place even worse.

Scriveners had their booths inside the palace. Some of them were doubtful people and the Grand Provost, Louis de Bouchet, Marquis de Sourches, had to take steps to control them. It had been discovered that they used equivocal words in what they wrote and copied libellous texts, handed to them by dangerous people. They were forbidden to transcribe prohibited texts on pain of corporal punishment.

The consequence of this new style of life at Versailles was an increase of coteries and groups, which were fiercely jealous of one another and exchanged the most perfidious accusations. Louis XV was warned of the trouble caused by such rivalries, but preferred to ignore them, showing a weary indifference.

The awe inspired by the royal person had lessened. Courtiers no longer took off their hats when passing Louis XIV's bed. They sometimes quarrelled in the King's presence and he had to intervene to calm them. When the King was playing whist or backgammon, the Duc de Couillon maintained that he, and he alone, was entitled to hand cards to the King. The Duc d'Aumont took for granted that it was he who had that privilege, and the two dukes argued so bitterly that Louis XV had to silence them. Ladies of quality also forgot their etiquette in the presence of the Queen, and Marie Leczinska, in spite of her meekness, had to call them to order. A Duchess had dared to drop her white satin pelisse on one of the stools in front of the royal bed. According to rule, a valet took the pelisse and put it on a bench in the ante-chamber. The Queen's cat found the cloth to its taste and did what was to be expected. On leaving, the Duchess discovered what had happened. She was furious and re-entered the Queen's room, brandishing her pelisse and complaining of the impertinence of careless valets. Marie replied: 'Remember, Madam, that you have servants and I have none. I have officers of my chamber who have paid dearly for the honour to serve me. They are cultured, well-bred men. If you had observed the forms suited to your rank, you would not have run the risk of having your cloak thrown into the ante-chamber.' (Quoted by Kunstler.)

It is doubtful if the snub served any purpose. On Maundy Thursday, 1731, at the ceremony of the washing of the feet of the children of the poor, Mme de Gontaut-Biron quarrelled with Mme de

Rupelmonde, both being in the Queen's service. The former, as a Duchess, demanded precedence. The latter, not being patient, grabbed her arm to hold her back. The two ladies grew shrill, called each other whores and ended by telling each other to be off in the coarsest possible way. Those words did not disturb Marie and she managed to quieten the ladies in spite of their fish-wife manners. The next day, with great dignity, Cardinal Fleury decided in favour of the Duchess. Mme de Rupelmonde swallowed her displeasure.

Among people of quality it was good form to use the coarsest language, rejecting with contempt the bourgeois style. 'This country' had its own vocabulary, and one had to use it unless one wanted to look ridiculous. One did not speak of a play seen at the 'Français', but at the 'Comédie Française'. The word cadeau was forbidden; one had to speak of a présent. One never drank champagne but vin du Champagne. And one did not slip a louis d'or into a collection plate but a louis en or. Pronunciations too were different. One did not carry a sac, but a sa, and one offered a pinch of taba. Other pronunciations retained the regional accent of the reign of Louis XIV, who would say: 'The State is moué (moi), for I am the roué (roi).' Similarly, a courtier who had spent some weeks on his lands would say that he had been 'chess (chez) lui'!

Those archaic turns of phrase and special words distinguished the people of 'this country' from the rest. Those who did not know them were mercilessly laughed at. Mme de Pompadour had this unpleasant experience. Being a bourgeoise she used words which were not accepted there. As the King was passionately in love, he just smiled at the colloquial language used by his mistress. Courtiers discussed it endlessly and made fun of her vocabulary. 'Lacking a perfect fluency in the language used among people with whom she was not accustomed to living,' wrote Luynes cruelly, 'she used words and phrases which sounded extraordinary in this region. It is likely that the King is often embarrassed by her speech.'

It was a mere guess. Louis XV was not embarrassed. He knew that the Marquise, who was refined and clever, would soon drop those bourgeois habits. The writers she liked were quite used to the Versailles customs and trained her. Voltaire's anecdote is well-known. At a supper where both were present, quails were served and Mme de Pompadour thought they were grassouillettes (plump).

138

'*Grassouillettes entre nous, me semble un peu caillette. Je vous le dis tout bas, belle Pompadourette,*' said Voltaire in a whisper.[1] She did not forget the remark.

Under the Marquise and her friends the court language developed gradually. The bitterest courtiers turned their rage into songs:

> *Sans esprit, sans caractère,*
> *L'âme vile et mercenaire,*
> *Le propos d'une commère*
> *Tout est bas chez la Poisson.*[2]

Such were the things one could hear in the palace galleries in 1745, the year when the King triumphed at Fontenoy and the Marquise triumphed in Louis's heart.

### SONGS, NICK-NAMES AND LIBELS

The song ended thus:

> *Mais pour si sotte créature*
> *Et pour si plate figure*
> *Exciter tant de murmures,*
> *Chacun juge le roi fou, fou, fou.*[3]

So, Louis XV was openly regarded as mad! This tells us much about the loss of respect for the King. Could one conceive of such insolence at Versailles in the days of Louis XIV?

Despite all the regulations put forward by the Grand Provost, pamphlets and libels were passed around from hand to hand. Some persons were daring enough to stick some of them to the very doors of the King's private apartments.

Courtiers delighted in creating nick-names. Which inns would be appropriate for the important people at court?

For the King: The Crowned Beauty, near the Innocents.
For Cardinal de Fleury: The Diamond Head in the Rue Mauvais-Conseil.

[1] A pun that cannot properly be translated. *Cailette* means a young woman of easy virtue, or vulgarly, a 'bird'.
[2] 'Without wit or character, with a low, mercenary soul and the style of a fish-wife, everything about the Poisson is low.'
[3] 'But to cause such grumbling for such a foolish creature, with such a dull face, everyone reckons the King is mad!'

For the Chancellor: The Turncoat in Judas Street.
For Cardinal de Rohan: The Good Valet in Peacock Street.
For the people: The Beggar's Bag, facing the hospital.

The last pun underlines the ange rsecretly rising against the court. When playing the animal game, nick-names were less perfidious.

The King: a horse.
M. d'Argenson: a sucking calf.
M. de St-Florentin: a sucking pig.
M. de Maurepas: a cat that spins.

Louis XV's immoderate tendency to move from one palace to another was sharply criticized:

> Tu vas à Choisy, tu vas à Crécy,
> Que ne vas-tu à St Denis?[1]

Songs were equally venomous. They spared no one, neither the Prime Minister nor Parliament. Here are a few verses which are a fairly good example of the taste of the time.

> Après la mort du grand Louis
> Nous étions tous ébaubis
> Mais le Régent nous rassurit,
> Sur le ritata, tantaleri.

> Pour ministre, le roi fit choix
> De ce grand cardinal Dubois,
> C'était un bigre bien bâti
> Sur le ritata, tantaleri.

> Après dans le gouvernement
> On a fait un grand changement,
> Il est devenu tout Fleury,
> Sur le ritata, tantaleri.

> Ceux-là qui sont du Parlement
> En ont jasé bien autrement,
> Disant que le roi est trahi
> Sur le ritata, tantaleri.

[1] 'You go to Choisy, you go to Crécy. Why don't you go to St Denis?'

*Des conseillers et présidents*
*En ont été bannis aux champs,*
*Et la Grand Chambre en est aussi,*
*Sur le ritata, tantaleri.*[1]

The rather flat inspiration drags on for about twenty verses. And yet, this song is not one of the worst. Other writers displayed their talent with a cruelty verging on ignominy. The Marquise de Pompadour was pelted with *poissonades*, which resembled the *mazarinades* of the Fronde. A few little poems ascribed to Maurepas are so vulgar that they cannot be reproduced here. Some are slightly more witty:

*Autrefoise de Versailles*
*Nous venait le bon goût;*
*Aujourd'hui la canaille*
*Règne et tient le haut bout.*

*Si la cour se ravale*
*De quoi s'étonne-t-on?*
*N'est-ce pas de la Halle*
*Que nous vient le poisson?*[2]

There were also cartoons. After the Treaty of Aix-la-Chapelle, against which public opinion was violent, one engraving had a great success at Versailles. It represented the Marquise dragging the King by the nose from one end of the Great Gallery to the other. But royal mistresses were not interested in politics in 1748. She was entirely devoted to her love affair.

What with pamphlets, songs and cartoons, the French court felt as if the wind of revolution was blowing over it.

---

[1] 'When Great Louis died, we were all very much upset. But the Regent gave us back our confidence . . . As his minister, the King selected that big Cardinal Dubois; he was a well-built lad . . . Then, big changes were made in the government, which became full of flowers' (a pun on Fleury's name) . . . 'Those in Parliament chattered their heads off, swearing that the King had been betrayed . . . Councillors and presidents have been rusticated and so is the Grand Chamber . . .'

[2] 'In former times good taste began at Versailles; today, rascals reign supreme. If the court demeans itself, we cannot be surprised; does not fish (*poisson*: the family name of Pompadour) come from the market-place?'

## INTRIGUES AND QUARRELS

Coteries there had always been and they multiplied. There was the Maurepas party, the Richelieu party, the Marquise's friends. Later, there was Choiseul's party. Louis XV rarely intervened. When he felt that the air of Versailles was unbearable, he left for Marly or Choisy with a few close friends.

After the publication of the lines against the Marquise, which were as widely known as if they had been published in newspapers, the limit had been reached. Richelieu, who hated Maurepas, took the favourite's side and, in front of the King, pretended to be indignant. Courtiers counted the score. Courageously, Mme de Pompadour went to see Maurepas, who, among other things, supervised the police.

'When are you going to discover the authors of those poems?' she asked.

'When I know them, I will inform the King.'

'You have no respect for the King's mistresses.'

'On the contrary, Madam, I have always respected them, whatever their origins.'

The reply was given before about thirty people, and Maurepas was congratulated on his daring. Hearing of his minister's outburst, the King said nothing. The next day, at the levee, he laughed heartily at his witticisms, but the same evening he signed the *lettre de cachet* whch informed the minister of his fall and exiled him to forty leagues from court. The letter was delivered during the night. Maurepas disappeared from the stage and Richelieu, who had known of it before anyone else, was beside himself with joy. His radiant manner was obvious. He hated the Marquise as much as ever, but he preferred for the time being to flatter her.

Any opportunity was good enough to start an intrigue. From one reign to the next, quarrels over precedence had lost nothing of their violence. Everyone demanded his or her 'rights', or tried to grab some advantage. Entreaties would be made of the officer who allotted rooms when the court moved to Choisy or Fontainebleau. This man wrote the names of the guests on their doors; some had the formula: 'Pour M le Duc de . . .', others, 'M le Duc' and nothing more. No flattery was too great to obtain the celebrated word *pour*.

Other rivalries were kindled when the blue ribbon of the Order of the Holy Ghost was distributed. The Blue Ribbon was regarded as the highest honour the King could give. As the time of promotion drew near, candidates gave themselves over to every imaginable trick. The unsuccessful courtiers revenged themselves by mocking the newly decorated. In February 1739, young noblemen who 'on account of their birth and merit, expected to be granted that distinction,' relieved their anger by writing these verses:

> *Célébrons tout pompeusement*
> *Le très inepte entendement*
> *D'un cardinal que la mort oublia.*
> *Alleluia.*

> *Il fait dire à Sa Majesté:*
> *'L'esprit Saint s'est manifesté*
> *A neuf apôtres qu'il dicta.'*
> *Alleluia.*

> *Dans le nombre cinq a choisis*
> *D'âge à peu prés égal à lui*
> *Que bientôt on enterrera*
> *Alleluia.*

> *Ensuite trois ambassadeurs,*
> *Assez minces négociateurs,*
> *Puis un neuvième appareille,*
> *Alleluia.*[1]

And so on, with harmless irony, the candidates who were overlooked mocked the ones who were promoted. For an ambassador, the Blue Ribbon was most important. As the representative of His Most Christian Majesty in Rome, the Comte de Stainville (who was to become the Duc de Choiseul), a friend of Mme de Pompadour, did not conceal his ambition when writing to the Marquise. She exerted herself diligently, but was not sure of succeeding at once: 'I do not know if you will receive the Blue Ribbon at Whitsun, but what I am sure of is that I will do all I can to prevent any promotion until you are among the chosen.'

[1] 'Let us celebrate with all pomp the stupidity of a cardinal whom death has forgotten, Hallelujah!' (This cardinal was Fleury, aged about 80). 'According to him the King said: The Holy Ghost has revealed itself to nine apostles, whose names he gave, Hallelujah! Among these he selected five, scarcely younger than himself, who were soon buried, Hallelujah! Then three ambassadors, pretty poor diplomats, then a ninth of his own, Hallelujah!'

There was no promotion at Whitsun. That year, the Holy Ghost did not descend on the court! Choiseul grew restless. 'Be assured that, without exception, no one desires more keenly than I do that little *ell* of blue ribbon,' Mme de Pompadour wrote him.

A few months later, she let him know: 'Except for unpredictable things, I hope to send you a little *blue* note on New Year's Day!' Choiseul was decorated on January 1, 1756. The Marquise's intervention had not been in vain. She had defeated her adversaries' intrigues. It was one more subject for gossip for a few days. What was there to do at Versailles, if there were not all these intrigues?

### FEASTS AND BALLS

Yet, the prestige of the court was not impaired. When an event touching the Royal Family—a marriage or a birth—was celebrated by the usual balls and night feasts, with the unavoidable firework display, guests filled the palace to overflowing. The firework displays were immensely popular. They were the only free shows for which no invitation was required.

When the Dauphin was born in September 1729, the first gentleman of the bed-chamber, M de Mortemart, arranged a firework display in the forecourt of the chateau. The Cardinal grumbled a little, since a firework display cost a lot and Fleury was 'very sparing of the State's money'. No one worried and there was a great crowd to watch, and all were agreed that they had never seen such a magnificent display: 'The road from Versailles to Paris on the way back was but one long line of carriages.'

When Louis XV's eldest daughter married the Infanta of Spain in August 1739 there were more fireworks and Barbier was there. They were fired from the *Tapis Vert,* opposite the Great Gallery. The public was allowed into an enclosure with numbered seats. Barbier had to wait for five hours in the sun, until darkness. It is true that to ease the boredom, they could watch the princes and other lords playing cards in the Gallery. Sometimes, those privileged beings came to the windows. 'Finally, the King, the Queen and Madame came to the central window, standing on a carpet. The King gave the signal by firing a rocket which he held in his hand. The firework display lasted a long time and there were some very fine pieces.'

One firework display nearly ended in tragedy. On September

11. Ball in the Covered Riding School, 1745

2. Versailles, the Terrace

13, 1751, when the Duc de Bourgogne (Louis XV's grandson, who was to die when nine and a half) was born, they were fired at 8.30 in the evening at the end of the Avenue de Paris, between the two Écuries. The site was badly chosen. A rocket fell on the roof of one of the wings of the Grande Écurie, behind the semi-circle, on the Avenue de St Cloud side. It started a fire in the hay lofts: soon, all the roofs were blazing. All the pumps in the castle were set working and the household troops were summoned. The fire was extinguished after three hours; several French or Swiss guards had been injured. Had help not come at once, the whole of the Grande Écurie would have been destroyed. The bill was heavy: repairs cost 157,000 *livres* and fifteen *sols*. On the other hand, the firework display itself cost 664,000 *livres*!

Fireworks were a popular distraction, which the people of Versailles or the capital enjoyed as much as the courtiers. On the other hand, one had to produce the proper credentials to be invited to the King's balls, and produce an invitation signed by M. de Bonneval, the Master of Ceremonies, like those he sent out for the Dauphin's wedding. In the centre of a card elegantly decorated with garlands and cupids, were the words:

*BAL PARÉ*
*À VERSAILLES*
*POUR LE MARIAGE DE MGR LE DAUPHIN*
*LE MERCREDI, 24 FÉVRIER,*
1745.

The ball took place in the riding school of the Grande Écurie. The next day there was a masked ball, this time in the palace. For this no invitations were required. One had simply to come to the entrance masked and to give one's name to one of the Gentlemen of the bed-chamber. But the crowd soon became so great and one had to wait so long at the entrance to the Salons d'Hercule and de l'Oeil de Bœuf (to reach the Great Gallery) that any kind of control was abandoned.

By midnight the scene from the Marble Courtyard was beautiful beyond comparison. The Avenue de Paris was turned into a river of light by the uninterrupted double line of carriages, all lit with torches and cressets. As for the palace, it blazed in the distance like a great and joyful fire.

The Gallery was so crowded that it was impossible to move backwards or forwards; it was difficult to know where to put one's feet. People crowded around four huge tables that had been laid out for a buffet, and the food served was 'lean', for it was already Friday morning. Not only was every kind of wine to hand but fresh salmon, trout pâtés, boiled fish, sole fillets and mountains of fruit. There were such quantities of food that—so it was said—some maskers filled their pockets and resold their loot the next day in the market of Versailles!

Shortly after midnight the Queen entered, unmasked. Her dress was studded with pearls and she wore on her head the two most beautiful crown diamonds, the Sancy and the Regent, blazing in all their glory. She was accompanied by the young couple, the Dauphin dressed as a gardener and the Dauphine as a flower-girl.

The latter, used to the strict etiquette of the Spanish court, was surprised by the liberty and easy-going manners of Versailles. She did not want to look too haughty and agreed to dance with a handsome masked man. He said that he was Spanish, and he had such dignity that it was obvious that he must be a grandee. He was extraordinarily well-informed about the rumours that were circulating concerning the marriage and seemed to know every-one. Maria-Thérèsa was rather intrigued and would have liked to know who he was. But he never allowed her to guess and left before the end of the ball. The next day it was revealed that he was the Marquis de Tessé's Spanish cook. The whole court roared with laughter, and the poor Dauphine, who had not been clever enough to keep silent, was much upset.

Another incident occurred while supper was being served. A masked lady entered one of the drawing-rooms and discovered with much annoyance that all the seats were already occupied. She discreetly removed her mask: she was the Princesse de Conti, the Duc du Maine's mother-in-law. She was quite sure that by making herself known she would be given a seat at once. But the men pretended not to know her and she left in a great fury, declaring that in all her life—an already long one—'she had never seen such unmannerly people. The company here must be very low indeed!'

For the princess, who had known Louis XIV's court, the change in behaviour, the contempt for older people and the indifference for precedence seemed unbearable. There were crowds at the Sun King's balls as well, but the crowds behaved with respect for etiquette.

The night moved on. The King had not yet made an appearance. Finally the door from the Salon de l'Oeil-de-Bœuf opened and a very strange procession stepped in: seven yew trees, exactly like those in the park, entered one behind the other: they were Louis XV and six of his friends!

The idea had been his. The costume had been devised so that the lower part looked like the pot the tree was in, and the upper like the stem out of which branches sprouted: 'Like this,' Louis said, 'because the seven of us will all be alike. No one will recognize me.' The trick succeeded. One young woman, thinking the King had noticed her and hoping to please him, made no difficulty about flirting with one of the yews in a secluded corner, but she had climbed the wrong tree. Louis XV, who was getting very hot in his disguise, had withdrawn with a lovely Diana. The *Bien-Aimé* had recognized Mme le Normant d'Étioles, née Poisson.

C. N. Cochin has left us some engravings of this extraordinary night. As for Voltaire, a friend of Jeanne-Antoinette, he concocted some verses in which he made a discreet allusion to the King's new love, comparing him with Caesar:

> *Ce héros des amants ainsi que des guerriers,*
> *Unissait le myrte aux lauriers,*
> *Mais l'if est aujourd'hui l'arbe je révère. . . .*[1]

\*　　\*　　\*

The Dauphine died in childbed on July 22, 1746, but the future of the dynasty had to be assured. On January 23, 1747, court mourning ended, and little more than a month later, on March 9th, the Dauphin's second wedding—to Maria-Josepha of Saxony—was solemnized. Again, there was a ball in the State Apartments, but times had changed. The war of the Spanish Succession was dragging on and austerity was the fashion. This was noticeable in the buffets. 'All the apartments were beautifully lit,' wrote Barbier, 'but the buffets were not pleasing. There were no trout pâtés as for the other wedding.' He added that the greediness of the guests,

---

[1] 'The hero of lovers and warriors used to twine together the myrtle and the laurel, but the yew today is the tree I revere . . .'

during the night of the yew-trees, had revolted the members of the court. 'It was quite right to suppress such expenditure.'

> *Le peuple, animal ignorant,*
> *N'aperçoit ici que clinquant.*[1]

Apart from the balls, plays and concerts, there were few entertainments at Versailles. One understands why Barbier was so excited about the appearance of a rhinoceros at Versailles in March 1749. It was an astute Dutch sea captain who brought it from India. It was exhibited at Versailles in a cage on four wheels, drawn by eight horses. The King, the Queen and Mme de Pompadour went to see it, praised its interesting face and threw it orange skins, which it swallowed, opening its huge throat. Louis XV thought of buying the strange beast for his menagerie, but the proprietor asked for 100,000 *écus* and the King drew back, horrified.

### LOCAL CUSTOMS

For a week the one topic at the palace was the rhinoceros and its habits. The town's people also admired the phenomenon, paying an entrance fee of three *livres*. The people of Versailles still participated in court entertainments; they collected the gossip and sometimes the surplus food.

Carnival was the occasion for numerous balls and masquerades which went on for several days. People danced all over the town, and some austere magistrates were not the least keen on that sort of entertainment. Some of them got rather rowdy. Protected by their masks, doubtful people sometimes gate-crashed into the best gatherings. One night, the son of an attorney of the baillage of Versailles had a rather unpleasant experience.

He had invited some of his friends to a small party and they were dancing to the tune of a hurdy-gurdy when three masked people came in. Several ladies were shocked and the young man's mother firmly stated that it was disgraceful, not to be able to have a party at home without strangers breaking in to see what was going on. Jean-Baptiste Le Coq, the attorney's son, added that it was a private reception, to which one could not come if not invited, and above all without having given one's name. The three unknown men did not insist. They left, grumbling that such a gather-

[1] 'The people, like silly animals, are only brought here by the false glitter.'

ing was not worth their unmasking, and while going down the stairs they added that they would cudgel the man who had driven them out.

They were sons of a draper. A few days later, they met Jean-Baptiste Le Coq in the street and took him to task. He denied having insulted them. 'You had better know,' they replied, 'that a merchant is as good as a magistrate.' A fight broke out and Le Coq took refuge in a grocer's shop in the Rue du Plessis. Finally they calmed down. Le Coq lodged a complaint, but the matter dropped, and this trivial incident is proof that such quarrels and abuse over-flowed from the palace into the town.

Consequently, the police became stricter. The Governor and the Bailiff issued more and more regulations, for beggars and doubtful people were coming in increasing numbers to a town where the citizens were so rich and generous. It was difficult to get the regulations put into effect, and police officers were very likely to get beaten. In March 1727, two constables and a sergeant of police arrested a suspicious-looking man begging near the Grande Écurie. They dragged him off to the local jail. The man resisted. As usual, passers-by took the part of the prisoner. Even one of the King's musicians was seen to abuse the sergeant. 'You dirty beggar! Set this fellow free! Otherwise I'll slit your dirty face!'

The sergeant solemnly answered: 'Away with you, Sir. I am carrying out the King's regulations; don't oppose them.' There-upon the musician, who very likely had had a little too much wine, hurled himself upon the policeman and beat him about the head and arms. Blue chaise-carriers (public sedan chair porters) who were waiting for clients, some valets and some unknown people struck the constables and forced them to let the beggar go and take refuge in the church of Notre-Dame. Narbonne, who reported the story, complained of not having enough men. The police did not always have the last word at Versailles.

Though the police might be beaten, the people did not love the royal person less, and the hard times they were passing through did not affect that love. When Louis was on the point of death at Metz in August, 1744, public prayers were said in all the churches of the realm. The population queued up in Notre-Dame and the chapel of Saint Louis. Louis XV recovered and there was great rejoicing. His return was a moving occasion. It was not necessary to excite the people's enthusiasm. A huge crowd massed along the Avenue de Paris, and its impatience was great. The King, the Queen, the whole Royal Family had left Paris on the evening of November 18th, having spent five days there. Night had fallen when the procession reached Versailles. Cressets had been lit along the Avenue and in the palace square. A company of townspeople in uniform and on horseback rode towards the King. There were no speeches. Though Paris people had for five days participated in the festivities which marked the happy occasion, they again rushed to Versailles in the evening. The whole court was back. The apartments were crowded with people, watching the King at supper. There were more than two hundred public carriages from Paris drawn up on the Place d'Armes!

The faithfulness of the people of Paris and the enthusiasm of those of Versailles had their reward. At nine that evening a firework display was lit in the Avenue, opposite the King's room.

That night the taverns and inns were full. Who knows whether the joy of the Versailles crowd did not touch the King's heart? He was still a sensitive man. A few months later, his emotions were captured by the woman who gave herself to him without reserve. Mme de Pompadour entered upon the scene. Her influence upon the life of the court was profound.

# CHAPTER ELEVEN

# THE REIGN OF THE MARQUISE

### THE KING'S EARLY MISTRESSES

Louis XV was faithful to the Queen for eight years, but Marie Leczinska's lassitude and the pious penances she compelled the King to suffer eventually turned him from his marital duties. He was a prey to the uninhibited sensuousness of the Bourbons, and he did not hesitate long before taking a mistress: so many young and pretty women offered themselves.

The King was very good-looking, with an attractive face and charming manners. His charm increased with the years. Portraits by Nattier and Van Loo underline the fire in the depths of his soft eyes, his noble nose and warm lips. Was there a woman at court who was not in love with the *Bien-Aimé*?

His first acknowledged mistress was Louise-Julie de Mailly, the Marquis de Nesles' eldest daughter. She was twenty-four. Her affair with the King remained a secret for three years and was only made public in 1737: 'People have said for a long time that this Comtesse de Mailly is the King's mistress. Now it seems quite certain,' wrote Barbier in November.

As lady-in-waiting to the Queen, Mme de Mailly had her own apartment in the palace. She was not really pretty, but well made, amusing, full of wit and fairly disinterested. Louis XV loved her for her frankness and the charm of her conversation. With her he discovered what later he came to like so much in Mme de Pompadour's Little Apartment: intimacy.

In 1739, the Comtesse de Mailly brought her sister Pauline-Félicité along, who was soon to share the King's affections. This new favourite had less wit but she was ambitious. On September 28, 1739, she was married to the Marquis de Vintimille du Luc. She calculated on triumphing over her sister and reigning alone over Versailles, but her plans came to nothing. She died on September 10, 1741, nine days after the painful birth of a son who was to be nick-named the '*Demi-Louis*', as he looked so much like the King.

Always taking great care to amuse the King, Mme de Mailly thought of her fifth sister, Marie-Anne, who was twenty-four and the widow of the Marquis de la Tournelle. Marie-Anne was pretty, passionate and unlikely to agree to sharing a lover. She soon compelled the King to part with his first mistress. On November 3, 1742, Louise-Julie had to move out and leave the palace. In her triumph, Marie-Anne was granted what none of her sisters had got, a title, that of Duchesse de Chateauroux. It made Marie Leczinska desperate.

Courtiers laughed at the faithfulness the King displayed in taking all his mistresses from the same family of five daughters. Little verses were repeated all over the palace:

> L'une est presqu'en oubli, l'autre presqu'en poussière.
> La troisième est en pied, la quatrième attend,
> Pour faire place a la dernière.
> Choisir une famille entière,
> Est-ce être infidèle ou constant?[1]

Others had nick-named poor Mme de Mailly 'the widow'; and the court kept humming:

> Madame Allain est toute en pleurs,
> Voilà ce que c'est d'avoir des soeurs.
> L'une jadis lui fit grand'peur!
> Mais, chose nouvelle,
> L'on prend la plus belle.
> Ma foi! c'est jouer de malheur!
> Voilà ce que c'est d'avoir des soeurs!'[2]

The affair of Louis XV and Mme de Chateauroux ended tragically. The King had joined the army in Metz in 1744, during the war of the Austrian Succession. He was stupid enough to take his mistress with him, possibly to show her the amenities of a military campaign. He fell very ill in Metz and it was rumoured that the Marquise was perhaps responsible for his illness. He was in a high

[1] 'The first is almost forgotten, the second crumbling into dust, the third is in charge, the fourth waiting to make room for the last. By choosing a whole family, are you faithful or faithless?'
[2] 'Mme Allain is in tears. What a plague sisters are! Some time ago, one already gave her a great fright, but something new has happened and the most beautiful has been chosen. What bad luck! What a plague sisters are!'

fever and was thought to be at the point of death. The Queen and the Royal Family were summoned in haste, while Mme de Chateauroux, packed into a coach, was driven away with lowered blinds. It has even been said that as her coach passed the populace shouted abuse and pelted it with rotten fruit.

Before receiving Extreme Unction, the King had signed a declaration in which he apologized and asked God and his people's forgiveness for the scandal he had caused. This declaration was printed and distributed all over France. Louis XV was deeply humiliated. With his usual common sense, Barbier frankly wrote: 'One should respect a King's reputation and allow him to die, not only with religion, but also with dignity and majesty.'

Louis XV recovered. The rapture with which his recovery was greeted has already been mentioned. Back in Versailles, he asked Mme de Chateauroux to return. In her turn, she took sick. To go to her lover, she got out of bed too soon, contracted pneumonia and died a few days later on December 8, 1744. She was twenty-seven.

Her last comfort was to have regained the King's love. The following lines were written about her:

> *Louis revoit le jour pour me rendre mon rang,*
> *Et je meurs sans regret pour lui rendre so gloire.*[1]

## A BOURGEOISE IN VERSAILLES

Most courtiers were sure that Mme de Chateauroux would soon be replaced. Louis XV wept long in La Muette, where he had retired. He felt rather responsible for his mistress' death. Did he really regret her? It may be doubted. She was an imperious character; she was an intriguer, and she was surrounded by a côterie whom she wanted to force upon the court. The *Bien-Aimé* was tired of the Nesles tribe.

But he was quite unable to live in chastity. It was under such circumstances that Jeanne-Antoinette La Normant d'Étioles, *née* Poisson, appeared on the scene.

Louis XV knew her already. Mme Le Normant d'Étioles owned a castle on the outskirts of the Forest of Sénart. In a blue velvet

---

[1] 'Louis returns to life to give me back my rank, and I die without regret to give him back his glory.'

dress, driving her rose-coloured phaeton, she had often followed the royal hunt. Her name had been mentioned to him. It was even said that he had been impressed by her beautiful complexion, the refinement of her features, the charm of her whole person, and that Mme de Chateauroux had taken umbrage.

Jeanne-Antoinette was invited to the palace for the celebrations that marked the marriage of the Dauphin to the Infanta. On the night of the Yew-trees Ball, the King never left her side. A few days later, she became his mistress. 'The kerchief has been thrown,' the old courtiers were saying, 'but it is only a short-lived affair. The King will never bring a *bourgeoise* to Versailles.'

'All those masked balls have provided opportunities to talk about the King's new affair with the young and pretty Mme d'Étioles. Her mother's name is Poisson. It is said that for some time now she has been constantly here, and that she is the King's choice. If this is true, she must be only a passing fancy and not a permanent mistress.'

The court could not imagine that Louis XV would bring to Versailles a woman born outside the aristocracy. It had never happened hitherto. Was it possible that little Mme d'Étioles, the daughter of the profiteers' agent, would rule over the palace? Luynes was correctly describing feeling everywhere when doubting such a fantastic prospect.

Luynes was wrong and so were the courtiers. In July 1745, two months after the victory of Fontenoy, Mme d'Étioles became the Marquise de Pompadour. On September 10th she moved into her apartment on the second floor of the chateau. On the 14th she was officially presented at court.

Her apartment was situated above the Grands Apartments. It was a very simple suite, quite near the King's private rooms. There were three rooms: a drawing-room with carved wainscotting by Verbeckt, a bedroom with an alcove, and a study. From the balconies, at the height of the statues which decorate the northern attics, there was a beautiful view over the northern flower-beds.

The King had easy access to her apartments by a private staircase. 'What I like most is your little staircase,' he used to say delightedly. Sometimes, his ministers would pursue the King to his mistress' apartment, to show him some letter or report. Louis would sigh, listen to some rather pointed remarks, as the realm was in difficulties, and Mme de Pompadour would intervene.

'Come, M de Maurepas, that's enough. You see, you are making the King look quite yellow. So good-bye, M de Maurepas!'

The minister would not insist and withdrew reluctantly. Such was the Marquise's influence. She was all-powerful over the King's heart and mind. High officials who displeased her were dismissed, and the courtiers became angry. This woman, without birth or rank, taking precedence over princesses and duchesses! While the aristocracy was half-ruined, and had so many reasons to hate the rich and proud *bourgeoisie,* the King was providing them with a new reason to be jealous: a woman born a Poisson was all-powerful at court!

In spite of doggerels, libels and plots, her reign lasted for twenty years.

### A SOVEREIGN GRACE

The Marquise's supreme talent was in providing the King with all sorts of entertainments without making him leave the castle to which he was tied by his greatness.

She sang and danced beautifully. Louis XV was fond of plays. If he was not as fond of music as his great-grandfather, he at any rate applauded Rameau's operas and ballets. But how tedious it was to have to sit through the performance in full ceremony, surrounded by court ladies with hooped skirts of such width that one had to leave an empty seat between each of them, so that they would not be too incommoded!

For the King Mme de Pompadour created the Petits Cabinets theatre. It was first situated in the gallery next to Louis XIV's former Medal Room, and then it was transferred to the Ambassadors' Staircase. It was put up or taken down in a few hours. The stage was broad and the auditorium tiny, at most holding twenty people. The one topic discussed at court was the coming first night. Numerous noblemen were refused admittance, among them the Comte de Noailles, Governor of Versailles. He was so furious that he left Versailles the same day 'A good idea,' said the King to the Dauphin. 'The Comte de Noailles will go to Paris to console himself in his wife's arms for a snub he has received at court!'

The actors belonged to the greatest families of the realm. The stage manager was the Duc de la Vallière, who recited the prologue written by Moncrif:

> Le désir de briller n'a rien qui nous inspire;
> Ici, nous pouvons tous le dire,
> Le zéle et le talent sont l'ouvrage du coeur.[1]

The first presentation, Molière's *Tartuffe*, took place on January 17, 1747. Then came *Le préjugé à la mode* by La Chausée, and *Les trois cousines* by Dancourt, to which piece came the Dauphin and the Dauphine. God only knew how much the Dauphin, who loved his mother dearly, loathed Mme de Pompadour! He could scarcely bear to say a few words to her about her dress that evening; and scarcely had she turned her back than he put out his tongue at her! Two years later, under the influence of his second wife, Maria-Josepha of Saxony, who was very generous, he became a little more polite. This change impressed the courtiers. He attended the Petits Cabinets theatre and agreed that the Marquise was delightful in the part of Colette. 'You are the most charming woman in the world,' Louis XV said to her when the show was over, and she was delighted.

Yet she had to fight against endless plots. The Marshal de Richelieu, First Gentleman of the Bed-chamber, was furious. Amongst his duties, he had to supervise the *hôtel des menus plaisirs*, where were stored the sets and stage properties for the various plays. Sets had been borrowed without his permission. He was enraged and decided that nothing whatever could be removed without a note signed by himself. He went even further and forbade the King's musicians to cooperate in the plays without his permission.

The Duc de la Vallière went to see the terrible Marshal and matters between them became very shrill: 'You are an ass,' Richelieu told the Duke.

Mme de Pompadour implored the King to intervene. His prestige was at stake. Louis XV did not want to lose an old companion whose service—and sallies—he appreciated. He knew how

---

[1] 'The desire to shine has no place in our inspiration; here, we may tell you, zeal and talent rise from the heart.'

to bring the affair to an end. On returning from a hunt, while the First Gentleman was pulling off his boots, he casually asked the Marshal:

'By the way, how many times have you been in the Bastille?'

'Thrice, Your Majesty,' Richelieu answered.

He understood completely. The sets were lent and the musicians played. The Marshal and the Marquise made up their quarrel.

However, the Petits Cabinets theatre was soon to disappear. There was a rumour at court that it was terribly expensive, which made Mme de Pompadour indignant. She justified herself one day, in the midst of a group of courtiers who, she well knew, would hasten to repeat her words everywhere. 'Do you know what they say?' she asked. 'That the new theatre has cost two million *livres*! Actually, I can tell you that it has cost merely 20,000 *écus* at most, and I wonder who can dare to object if the King spends that amount on his entertainment!'

She was right. The actual theatre had cost 75,000 *livres*. But she failed to add that the expenses were enormous. New sets had to be painted, new costumes made, and they were always sumptuous. About 300,000 *livres* were spent in this way each season.

In the end, Louis XV was horrified by the cost and he was tired of all the intrigues that went on around him to take a part in the performances as a member of the chorus or merely to sit on the edge of a folding seat. The last curtain came down on February 28, 1750, after a performance of *Le méchant* by Gresset.

Mme de Pompadour was to act for the King again, but it was at Bellevue in her own chateau. There would be no more comedies or ballets at Versailles.

### THE MARQUISE'S SUPPERS

After theatrical performances, it was by organizing intimate receptions that the Marquise succeeded most in pleasing and amusing her royal lover. She had furnished her apartments with the most refined taste: furniture, paintings, trinkets, rare or exotic works of art were selected and laid out with discreet elegance. In her company the King came to love a graceful setting.

At the end of the day, the King would ascend the little staircase to his mistress, abandoning etiquette and ceremonial. He talked freely. The Marquise responded. She had a talent for witty repartee.

She knew all the gossip and all the rumours at Versailles. Sometimes the conversation took a serious turn. Mme de Pompadour, who was fascinated by politics, cleverly gave her own opinion. One evening the King was in a great state of excitement when he came to his mistress' room.

'What is the matter?' she asked him.

'Those long gowns (Parliament Councillors) and the clergy are at daggers drawn. I find their quarrels very distressing. But I detest the long gowns most. On the whole, my clergy is very devoted to me. The others would like to enslave me.'

'Firmness is the only way to break them,' said Mme de Pompadour.

'You don't know what they do and think. They are a Republican assembly. Well, that's enough! Things as they are will last as long as I will!'

The Marquise hurriedly changed the subject.

Usually, their conversation was less austere. Gradually the guests arrived. They had given their names to an usher who, standing at the door of the little staircase, verified that they were on the list. The Duc de Croÿ, who went to one of these parties, has left a detailed account of it.

'We waited for supper in the little salon. The King only came in time to sit at table with the ladies. The dining-room was lovely and the supper pleasant and very free. We were served by two or three valets only, who went out after having put in front of us all we might need.

'The King was gay and relaxed, but with a greatness he never allowed us to forget. He no longer looked shy in the least, but spoke easily and volubly, as a man who knew how to amuse himself. He seemed very much in love with Mme de Pompadour, not restraining himself in this respect, indifferent to criticism.

'He spoke very freely to her, as to a beloved mistress with whom he wished to amuse himself . . . and she behaved very well and had much influence, but the King wanted to be the absolute master and was very firm about it.'

Croÿ went on to describe the supper: 'We were eighteen, sitting very closely together at table.' (One can easily understand him: the dining-room was not very big). The Marshal de Saxe was among the guests, but he did not sit down, as he had just had dinner.

'He merely picked a few morsels in passing, being extremely greedy. We were two hours at table, with great freedom but without excess. Then the King moved into the little salon, brewed and poured out his own coffee, as there were no servants and we helped ourselves. He played cards with Mme de Pompadour, Coigny, Mme de Brancas and the Comte de Noailles, for low stakes. He liked cards very much but Mme de Pompadour hated them and tried to draw him away. The rest of the party formed into two groups, also for low stakes. The King made everyone sit down, even those who did not play . . . Mme de Pompadour, pressing him to retire and dozing off, the King rose at one o'clock and said to himself, gaily and in a fairly loud voice, "Well, let us go to bed." The ladies curtsied and left, the King bowed too and went to his Little Apartments. We all descended by Mme de Pompadour's little staircase to the State Apartments for the usual *coucher*, which took place as usual and at once.'

This was a typical evening at Versailles, one of the many while the Marquise held sway.

On another occasion, Croÿ recorded the subjects of conversation. The Petits Cabinets comedies were under discussion first, then the King's own authority over his ministers.

'Because he loved Mme de Pompadour very much, she had a great influence over him. She was party to almost every grace he granted. But it was not known whether the King told her all about things that mattered, and I am inclined to think that he loved her more as a lover than as a friend.'

Croÿ was right. At that stage of her relations with Louis XV Mme de Pompadour was above all the minister of all the graces. There would come a day when love gave place to friendship, a deep and tender friendship, and Mme de Pompadour then interested herself in the affairs of state.

But here is a last scene, described by the Duc de Croÿ, charmingly simple and free. It took place in December 1748. On that evening the hunt had ended near the little chateau of La Celle at St Cloud, one of the Marquise's favourite residences. She was staying there with a few friends. The King had taken great care not to let her know that he would call. She was taken by surprise and Louis XV was in high spirits. After a moment the Marquise excused herself: she had promised to attend that evening the first performance of her friend Crébillon's tragedy *Catilina,* and the Marquise made a cult of fidelity. Louis XV did not look annoyed and gallantly helped her into her coach. Then everyone returned to Versailles.

In spite of Mme de Pompadour's absence, the King supped in the Little Apartments. He had only six guests.

'The King was charming in that little circle, very easy to talk to and infinitely courteous. Afterwards, in the Cabinet du Tour, he had a fire lit and made us sit round it, like himself, without the least distinction, and we chatted with the greatest familiarity, except that we could not forget that we were with our master. At ten o'clock we saw the Marquise's carriage arrive. He went out to her and we left, very pleased with the special favour we had been granted.'

In this vivid picture the last touch is the most characteristic: 'He went out to her and we left.' After the *coucher* ceremony, for six or seven years of mutual love, Louis XV repaired each evening to his mistress' room.

Everyone at court knew it. And yet, out of discretion and respect for royal dignity, Louis XV did all he could to preserve appearances. Yet on one occasion everything came very near to disaster. Mme de Hausset, the Marquise's Lady of the Bed-chamber and attendant, has told the story.

'Once, at dead of night, Mme de Pompadour came into my room in her night-gown: "Come at once," she said, "the King is dying!" Scarcely taking time to slip on a petticoat, I found the King gasping for breath in Mme de Pompadour's bed. I threw water over him and made him swallow Hoffman's drops. He came round and said to me: "Don't make a sound. Just go to Quesnay [the Marquise's doctor] and tell him your mistress is not well, and tell the servants not to babble".'

Mme de Hausset did as she was told. Quesnay arrived at once, felt the King's pulse and said that the crisis was over. He returned to fetch a drug and poured it over the King, who recovered shortly afterwards. Then the King went back to his own room, leaning on the doctor's arm, without arousing the servants. 'My dear friend must have been very afraid,' wrote the King the next day, in a little note for Jeanne-Antoinette, 'but she can be reassured. I am all right, as the doctor will assure you.' In fact, Louis had merely suffered a violent attack of indigestion, which had provoked a fainting fit. The Marquise had been terrified at the thought that something might happen to the King in her apartment.

Besides the possible scandal, she had been terrified by the sight of the King in that state. Mme de Pompadour was quite sincere.

'His constant companion, involved in all his habits, loving him truly for his own sake, she had become necessary to him, not only because she had the secret of amusing him and relieving his boredom, but also because he could talk to her about his smallest troubles, because she knew everyone around him and knew all about them, and always displayed a judicious mind and gave sound advice. The King could no longer do without her . . . she sacrificed her comfort and rest to the feelings and pleasures of the master.' (Pierre de Nolhac).

### AN EXHAUSTING LIFE

The Marquise wore herself out in making Louis XV happy. She took little care of her health. She would rise at eight and receive her friends and her informers while her maids completed her toilette. She would have discussions with some of them and dictate a few letters. She would then give audiences to those who had sought the honour of being received. Many just came to beg for something. She always listened with great patience, scolding the tiresome and the boring ones. A councillor of Parliament, M de Meinières, was once roundly told what she thought of him. She forcefully denounced the attitude taken by that 'august court' at the crucial point of the quarrel between the Parliament and the clergy, after Damien's attempted assassination of the King. 'Does this so-called wise court always try to put the Government right and then within a few minutes come to such an extreme pass!—they only obey their passions, jealousies, anger and blindness . . .'

Standing against the fireplace, trembling, she was looking at Meinières with a scorn he never forgot.

Other interviews were less stormy. She accepted petitions, gave promises to intervene, tried to oblige her friends. Then came time for mass and she would attend, sitting not far from the King. The King sometimes met his mistress before dinner. When she was one of the Queen's ladies-in-waiting, she had to do her duty at the Queen's side.

In the afternoon she often accompanied the King when hunting. She had no special liking for the King's favourite pastime. Yet it gave her an opportunity to enjoy—provided the weather was fine —the open country air so necessary to her health. And Quesnay had advised her to take exercise.

If she did not follow her lover, she retired into her hermitage at Versailles. It was a small house of one floor and five rooms (three facing the courtyard and two the garden) built on a piece of land ceded to the architect Gabriel, near the Dragon gate. 'I spend half my life in my hermitage,' she wrote to her friend Mme de Lützelbourg. There she would see her servants or her agent Colin who brought her his accounts. The King would join her there when the hunt was over. Sometimes, she would drive to one of the neighbouring chateaux, La Celle-Saint-Cloud, Bellevue or Brimborion— which she had nick-named Babiole—a mere pavilion at the bottom of the park at Bellevue, with a delightful view over the valley of the Seine.

But soon she had to return to Versailles, to a court which spied on her and often hated her. She would change, ask for her writing desk and scribble a few notes. 'I must stop,' she once wrote to her father. 'I have still some sixty letters to write tonight.' Let us hope that this tireless letter-writer had exaggerated.

She would have to begin again the next day, and get ready to take part in all the activities: for the King could not stay anywhere for long. It is easy to understand why she confessed once to her friend, Mme de Lützelbourg: 'Don't be angry with me. Do you think I have a minute to myself? You are mistaken . . . rehearsals, performances, important and indispensable duties, the Queen, the Dauphin, the Dauphine, three daughters, two baby princesses: have I even time to breathe! Pity me and don't be angry with me!'

Her health deteriorated continually. She had always suffered from sore throat and bronchitis. She coughed up blood. Her doctor prescribed a strict diet: rest and ass's milk (which was supposed to be a tonic). How could she follow it at court, with this exhausting rhythm? 'I have had a rather bad cold, which gave me a fever for twenty-four hours,' she wrote to her friend on May 29, 1751.

'It is slightly better. I am going to the drawing-room tonight which, by the way, is diabolical for colds. It is frightfully hot inside, and cold when coming out, so that people cough more now than at Christmas.'

What did it matter, so long as the King was happy? 'I adore him; I only want to please him. I would give my life to please him.' And in order to please him she tried to be on good terms with the Queen.

### THE MISTRESS AND THE LEGITIMATE WIFE

Marie Leczinska had never forgotten the insults which the Duchesse de Chateauroux had heaped upon her. She tolerated more easily Mme de Pompadour's presence: 'As there must be people like this,' she had said, 'rather this one than another.' The Marquise, who suffered as a result of her false position at court, tried hard to please the Queen, but courtiers did all they could to make things even more difficult. An anonymous letter circulated, accusing Jeanne-Antoinette of trying to grab all the offices and to push her favourites into the King's intimate circle, so that she could spy on the princes more easily. She cleared herself of 'these horrors'.

When she found some means of increasing her respectability, she grabbed at it. Twice a week she paid court to the Queen, who received her coolly. The Marquise wanted to take part in the Easter ceremonies. The Queen had to appoint fifteen ladies to wash the feet of pauper girls, and Jeanne-Antoinette hoped to be one of them. 'She's not lacking in impudence,' the Queen grumbled, and made it known that the ladies had already been appointed and there was no vacancy.

'It does not matter,' the Marquise remarked suavely to the Duchesse de Luynes, who brought her this answer; 'everyone knows that I shall take the collection in the chapel on Easter Sunday.'

The Queen answered that there were scandals which should not be displayed in public and made haste to select another lady to perform that task.

Though pious, Marie Leczinska sometimes felt the pangs of bitterness and jealousy. She was often very wounded. She grasped at any circumstance which would allow her to humiliate her rival. Here is one of those little scenes which were so frequent at the palace.

One day the Marquise entered the Queen's room, carrying a large basket of flowers in her beautiful arms, gloveless in accordance with etiquette. Marie could not refrain from admiring Jeanne-Antoinette's elegance and charm. In a loud voice she praised every part of the Marquise's person, as if she had been a statue and not a living woman. Patiently, and still grasping the enormous basket in her arms, Mme de Pompadour waited for someone to take it from her. But the Queen suddenly said: 'Well, Madam, just as you are now, give us the privilege of hearing that magnificent voice which charms us in the Little Apartment plays.'

Mme de Pompadour sought to excuse herself, saying that she was in no state for singing, but the Queen insisted and the favourite could not refuse. Then she sang with full voice the great aria from Glück's *Armide,* 'At last he is in my power . . !' The court ladies who watched the scene could not refrain from smiling and the Queen winced. Mme de Pompadour, triumphant, had had the last word.

The year 1752 marked a turning-point in the relations between Mme de Pompadour and Louis XV. Friendship took the place of love. Those two beings, made for one another, continued to meet daily, for they could not abandon their mutual attachment, but no guilty feature remained in their relationship.

'Our dear friend', wrote the Abbé de Bernis to the Comte de Stainville in 1757, 'can no longer shock any but fools and knaves. It is publicly known that for the past five years friendship has taken the place of gallantry. It would be pure sanctimoniousness to go back into the past in order to blacken the innocence of the present relationship. It is based on his need to unburden his heart to a sure and trusted friend.'

Consequently, Mme de Pompadour wished that her situation at court should be less precarious. She had been given flattering titles. What did they mean if not accompanied by an important office which would justify, in a clear and final fashion, her presence in the palace? Soon after her arrival, she had asked the King that she be made a lady-in-waiting. Marie Leczinska had rebelled and the King did not press the matter. But in 1756 things had changed. The Queen well knew the exact nature of the relationship of her husband and the Marquise, and she had no pretext for refusing the King's request. On February 7th the commission was signed. The Queen was told of it by a note from the King, to which she replied: 'Sir, I have a King in Heaven who gave me the strength

to endure evil, and a King on earth whom I shall always obey.'
Which meant: may the King of Heaven give me strength to endure
what the King on earth compels me to suffer!

The next day, the Marquise was present at the Grand Couvert
in a magnificent dress, and she took her service at the Queen's
side.

'This unexpected event burst out of the blue to everyone's
amazement,' wrote the Duc de Croÿ. 'But that was not all. Mme
de Pompadour declared that she had returned to religious practice! There had been a lean supper in her apartments. She put
an end to her public dressing, and received the ambassadors while
seated at her tapestry frame. Thus she passed from her dressing
table to her embroidery table!'

Jeanne-Antoinette was now trying to follow in the footsteps of
Mme de Maintenon. And Croÿ added: 'Under such circumstances,
the Queen distinguishes herself, as usual, by her sweetness and
moderation.'

It was lucky that Mme de Pompadour's bad health prevented
her from discharging her duties assiduously. Marie Leczinska was
glad of it. The two women tolerated each other.

### AN ATTEMPTED MURDER IN VERSAILLES

The reversal of alliances, increasing taxes, the lasting fight
between the King and his Parliaments had created a very heavy
atmosphere. Early in 1757 the court was in a bad mood. The winter
was severe; courtiers were looking glum, which scarcely pleased
the King. They were cold; draughts blew in every direction through
those galleries. In a way, at Versailles they were supreme.

Louis XV decided to leave the palace for a while and go to
Trianon for Epiphany. There, at least, drawing-rooms were smaller,
the chimneys did not smoke and etiquette was relaxed. On January
5th the Queen and her daughters took the coach to the little
chateau. Mme de Pompadour remained at the palace. She was
suffering from a severe cold, but her condition was not serious.
Louis XV, who loved his daughters deeply, decided to pay her a
visit during the afternoon. He took this opportunity to spend some
time with Mme de Pompadour and to sign a few letters in his
corner study. He had ordered the coaches for 5.30. His own was

to draw up near the door of the new guards' room, at the north-east corner of the Marble Courtyard.

At six o'clock the King came down the staircase with M. de Montmirail, M. de Brionne and M. de Duras. M. de Baudreville, the equerry in charge, walked in front, the Dauphin beside him and the Duc d'Ayen, captain of the guards, behind them all. The night was already very dark. Several guards, carrying torches, lined the staircase and made a lane through the guards' room to the door.

Just as the King was descending the last step and entering the room a man rushed out of the shadow, pushed the soldiers aside and struck the King a violent blow in the side.

'Duc d'Ayen,' cried Louis XV, 'someone has struck me hard with his elbow.' The Dauphin and one of the guards seized the man, who had not even tried to escape. The Dauphin thought he was just some beggar who had managed to slip in and asked him: 'Can't you see that's the King?'

Louis put his hand to his side, withdrew it covered with blood and exclaimed, 'I am wounded!'

Leaning on the arm of the Duc d'Ayen and the Dauphin, he managed to climb back up the staircase. Upstairs there was pande-monium. The news of the attempted assassination had already spread. As the King was supposed to sleep at Trianon, his bed was not made; there was neither linen nor sheets, and no valet could be found. The King felt weak and was made to lie down on a mattress.

His coat was removed. Blood gushed out of his wound and spread over the floor. 'I am going to die,' he muttered. 'Quick, get a chaplain and the Queen.' Then he fainted.

The Dauphine's surgeon arrived in haste. He bled the wounded man, who came round. Then the first surgeon arrived. He probed the wound and found it long but not deep. No vital organ had been touched. But the King was very weak and still sure that he was going to die.

'Madam,' he said to the Queen, 'I have been murdered!'

He again asked for a priest and for Extreme Unction. The Abbé Soldini was there and shut himself up with the King.

A little later, Louis XV had the Queen and his daughters ad-mitted. He asked the former's forgiveness for the insults he had inflicted on her, and told his daughters that he regretted with all his heart the scandals of which they had been witness. He told the courtiers: 'Gentlemen, I am glad to think that the State will henceforth have a good master.'

Everyone was in tears and thought that the King was really going to die. Hope returned in the morning.

Meanwhile, Machault, the Keeper of the Seals, had rushed to the palace and the inquiry had begun. It was discovered that the culprit, a certain Robert-François Damiens, a former servant, had been able to walk all day in the park and through the galleries without anyone observing him. It was also discovered that the King had been threatened several times during the preceding weeks. Insulting pamphlets had been peddled and displayed within the chateau. Louis was no longer the Well-Beloved. He was openly insulted:

> Lâche dissipateur des biens de tes sujets,
> Toi qui comptes les jours par les maux que tu fais,
> Esclave d'un ministre et d'une femme avare,
> Louis, apprends le sort que le Ciel te prépare!
> Si tu fus quelque temps l'objet de votre amour,
> Tes vices n'étaient pas encore dans tout leur jour.[1]

This could be read practically everywhere. Argenson's police constables grew weary of tearing off and destroying the posters which were replaced daily. The postmaster of Versailles revealed that he had found in a letter box a sheet of paper with the following words: 'Warning to the State. One of the conspirators warns the King that he had better be on his guard, and also the Dauphin, when going out. Otherwise they are lost.'

Yet it does not seem that a real plot had been organized, with Damiens as the instigator. He had acted alone, doubtless crazed by all the accusations against Louis XV which he had heard all around him. He wanted to teach the King a lesson. Yet, he was to die an atrocious death, having been found guilty of high treason.

---

[1] 'Vile squanderer of your subject's wealth, you who count your days by the evils you do, slave of a minister and of a grasping woman, Louis, learn the fate that is in store for you. If for some time you were the object of our love, it was because your vices had not yet reached their full magnitude.'

## THE CONSEQUENCES OF THE TRAGEDY

Mme de Pompadour was one of the first to be told of the attempt. She wept. She could not even go to the King's bedside and she expected to be sent away. Towards midnight Quesnay, her devoted friend, came to reassure her. Yet she remained anxious. Would not her tireless enemies take this opportunity to have her banished from the palace and from power? 'You can imagine my situation,' she wrote to Choiseul the next day, 'for you know my attachment to the King . . .'

She decided to remain hidden in her apartments. On hearing of the attempted murder, the people of Versailles had rushed towards the palace shouting, 'Long Live the King!' They also shouted, 'Death to Pompadour!' Jeanne-Antoinette heard those shouts of hatred and revenge.

Louis XV's condition improved. His wound healed very quickly. As early as January 11th he could get up, but he was gloomier and more melancholy than ever. He allowed the Dauphin to preside at the councils and only received a few intimate friends and his chaplain. To those who congratulated him on the lightness of the wound, he answered: 'It is deeper than you think; it has reached to the heart.'

Was Mme de Pompadour going to be Damien's chief victim? Her closest friends suggested that she should leave without waiting for the King's order. Bernis was against this. 'Don't give way to cowardly thoughts. You are the King's mistress no longer, but he loves you all the same. You must wait for his orders before leaving the court.'

It seemed that Louis XV wanted to be rid of the very memory of his former friend. He once asked M de Clermont whence he had come, and he answered: 'I have called on Mme de Pompadour.' The King pretended not to hear.

The Marquise did not even dare to go to the Queen's apartments. The situation became unbearable. Everyone at the palace was weighing the advantages or difficulties that would result from her departure. Those who owed her everything openly abandoned her.

The end came on January 17th: it was another of those unexpected changes, quite frequent in the history of the palace. Louis XV had summoned the Keeper of the Seals, and Machault told him of the coming trial; he also told him about the state of public opinion and of the Marquise's position.

Jeanne-Antoinette was feverishly waiting, the Minister was announced and he came in, cold and severe. Everyone hurried away, leaving the two together. Half an hour later, Bernis dared to come back. The Marquise was alone, seated in an armchair, the tears streaming from her eyes.

'Ah, my poor Abbé!' she cried. 'I must go!'

Machault had told her that, in the interests of the King and the State, she must leave Versailles at once. She rang immediately for her servants, gave orders to have her Paris house (the Elysée) prepared for her and asked that her coachmen should be at hand. She was making ready to go and her apartment was forbidden to all but her intimate friends. At that moment one of them, the Madame de Mirepoix, came in.

'What is the meaning of all these trunks? Your servants say you are leaving.'

'Alas, my dear friend, I must! It is the master's order, according to M de Machault.'

'What does he think personally?'

'That I must leave at once.'

'He wants to be master. He is betraying you. Who leaves the field is lost . . .'

Soubise and Bernis shared her view. After a long talk the Marquise decided to postpone her departure. But so as not to irritate her enemies, it would be said that she was going.

The storm blew over. A few days later, Louis XV suddenly decided to return to Mme de Pompadour. She had no difficulty in convincing him that Damiens was a lunatic, that there had never been a plot and that it was absurd to think that all France hated the King. Louis XV was not convinced, but she brought him peace of mind.

In the palace the courtiers who had expected she would be dismissed were full of consternation. Would she take revenge? All she asked was that Machault and d'Argenson should be sent away. As for the others, she preferred to ignore them. She wrote to Choiseul: 'All those people owe their existence to me. The first grace I asked the King was not to punish them. I do not want to have such contemptible people pitied.'

The Duc de Luynes, with his usual philosophy, wrote in his diary on January 20th: 'The King has gone back to his usual way of living. The whole court and all the ministers were in her apartment yesterday.' A few days later, he added with some humour: 'The King seems to pray very devoutly, and Mme de Pompadour still hears mass every day.'

Versailles had been through another 'Day of Dupes'.

## THE END OF A REIGN

After Damien's attempt at murder, Mme de Pompadour's power was no longer contested. She put her favourites into the ministry, had her say in the choice of military leaders and dabbled in high European politics, for which she had evolved a design. Her plans were ruined by the defeat at Rossbach and the mediocrity of the French generals when faced with Frederick II's skill. She had her friend Bernis replaced by Choiseul, but the Seven Years War ended in defeat and she was in despair. She was utterly worn out: for twenty years she had struggled to keep the King's heart.

She was not yet forty-one, and thanks to creams and cosmetics, she could still show a radiant complexion. She was in the last stages of tuberculosis and was at the mercy of bronchitis. She hardly slept at all, her digestion was bad, she became breathless each time she ascended a staircase, and yet she kept her charming smile and continued to entertain and advise the King.

In February 1764 she fell ill at Choisy: it was a congestion of the lungs and hope was abandoned. Courtiers were already talking openly of her death. Almost every day, the King drove from Versailles to spend a few moments near his friend. He had dearly loved the Marquise and still felt a deep affection for her.

Suddenly the fever abated and the illness receded. She was able to return to her apartment in the palace. But after a few warm days winter returned with renewed vigour, and March was marked by storms. She could not get warm and broncho-pneumonia supervened, aggravated by the condition of her heart.

This time, Jeanne-Antoinette realized that it was the end. On principle, no one, apart from the royal family, was allowed to die in the castle. But the least movement made her breathless, and the King himself insisted that she should stay. For the Marquise etiquette was defeated in a way that would never happen again.

The vicar of the Madeleine, her Paris parish, gave her the Last

Sacrament on Palm Sunday, April 15th. The King was busy all day with religious ceremonies. News was brought to him by Champlost, her valet. Early in the afternoon she received a few friends, Choiseul, Soubise, Gontaut. She became more and more oppressed. She was perfectly conscious and to the end she kept her lovely smile and her wit.

'Now, my friends,' she told them, 'leave me to my soul, my confessor and my women.' And as the vicar was preparing to leave she said: 'One minute more, Monsieur le curé, and we will leave together.'

She died before the end of the day.

Shortly afterwards a small procession passed through the chilly galleries of the castle in the silence of the night. The Duchesse de Praslin, who witnessed the scene, saw, on a simple stretcher, the body of a woman, covered by a single sheet that scarcely disguised the head, breast, hips and legs. The Marquise de Pompadour was leaving the palace she had entered twenty years earlier, in the radiant beauty of her youth.

Two days later, from his balcony above the Marble Courtyard, Louis XV gazed at the procession that bore his friend to her grave. In spite of the storm that raged over Versailles, he stood there for a long time, facing the Avenue de Paris, and the heavy tears ran down his cheeks.

# CHAPTER TWELVE

# THE KING IS BORED

Age had not sobered the King. When he ceased to be the Marquise's lover, he found compensations elsewhere. To maintain a sense of dignity and propriety in the chateau, he hid his affaires in his house in the Parc-aux-Cerfs. Any number of stories have been invented, told and embellished about this famous park. Libellous pamphlets at the end of Louis XVI's reign and during the Revolution have spread the worst possible accusations among the people. The truth is sordid enough, but it is not necessary to make it even more degrading.

The name itself gave material to the demented imaginations of libel-writers. They described a park in which innocent victims were ensnared, vainly imploring Heaven to rescue them. Louis XIII's former game reserve had become a quiet district of Versailles, gradually built over early in the century, but did not deserve such notoriety or indignity.

In 1755 Louis XV bought from Jean-Michel-Denis Cremer, at the corner of the rues St Médéric and des Tournelles, a modest house which he had been renting for several years. There were four rooms on the ground floor and as many on the first, and quite a large garden in the angle made by the two streets. The situation suited the King perfectly. It was at the back of the hostel for the King's Guard, with which it communicated through a small door, so that the King could pretend he was going to see his guards and reach his clandestine house incognito. He usually went there at night, and rarely revealed his identity to the girls of low condition and little virtue whom he had housed in this little villa.

Courtiers did not know the names of the inmates of the Parc-aux-Cerfs and history has no reason to be more inquisitive. Yet, one name has been remembered, that of Morphise. The court gave this name to a certain Miss O'Murphy, of Irish origin, who had sat for the painter Boucher who, according to Croÿ, had brought her to the King after having put her in a religious painting for the Queen!

Little O'Murphy was gay, rippling with laughter, plump and dimpled. Louis XV lodged her in the Parc-aux-Cerfs and seemed to be so much in love that this new passion found an echo in ambassadors' letters. The Papal Nuncio, Monsignor Nerini, who specialized in court gossip, predicted Mme de Pompadour's dismissal:

'By all appearances, the Pompadour's reign is drawing to its end . . . the new Irish star has received diamonds and magnificent dresses. She was expected to make a public appearance, but did not turn up because she shows signs of being pregnant. Arrangements have been made to furnish her apartment with carpets to avoid all danger of a fall.'

Such was the gossip that courtiers murmured to one another and the Nuncio carefully collected. Yet this time his perspicacity was faulty. The dancer's star shone but for a short time. Pregnant or not, she disappeared as quickly as she had come. Other young women took her place.

The house was run by the wife of a clerk of the War Ministry. At court she was nicknamed the Abbess. Mme Bertrand was as discreet as she was careful. She had but few servants, two house maids, a cook, a coachman and a valet.

Neither Marie Leczinska nor Mme de Pompadour were ignorant of the existence and purpose of the Parc-aux-Cerfs. They just shut their eyes to it, but it is not true to write, as the Goncourt brothers did, that the Marquise had aided the King in his weaknesses. She merely tolerated them. The suggestion that she was no more than an entrepreneur is without foundation. She never had anything to do with these paltry intrigues. After her death the King still visited the Parc-aux-Cerfs. He kept it for six more years and only parted with it in 1771, at Mme du Barry's request.

### A GLOOMY KING AND A BORED COURT

Did distractions, which have to be mentioned as they are part of the dreary daily life of the eighteenth century, succeed in entertaining the King? It may be doubted. Louis XV was gloomier than ever. He was bored and could hide it no longer. He was aware of his own low tastes, and of his own weakness. His brain was still clear and this made him even more bitter.

With changeless regularity, days and weeks followed their course at the palace. Nothing was unforeseen. The King attended his council, received ambassadors, was presented with newcomers, and these filled his mornings. In the afternoons he hunted, visited the hot-houses at Trianon, came back to his apartments and read the information his own agents had sent from abroad. 'In spite of everything, he is now too lazy to be really interested in affairs, and too *blasé* to be thrilled by pleasure'; he carried his morose turn of mind with him everywhere. When he left Versailles he could only change the scene and he found everywhere the same crushing tedium.

He was not an egoist. He had wept at the deaths of his eldest daughters. Like his great-grandfather, he had lost most of those he loved: the Dauphin, an honest, upright, rather ponderous man, quite different from his father; the Dauphin's second wife, Maria-Josepha of Saxony, one of the least known figures in history, who had lost her eldest son, the Duc de Bourgogne, though she had five more children, three of whom eventually ascended the French throne. Louis XV still had four daughters, Adélaïde, Louise, Victoire and Sophie. 'Mesdames Tantes' lived on the ground floor of the palace and Louis visited them every day. The portraits painted by Nattier while they were school-girls at Fontevrault bear no resemblance whatever to the heavy and aged faces of these elderly whining spinsters who were only interested in gossip about etiquette and precedence. They took no part at court and their influence was negligible. Out of habit, the King spent some time with them each day. He took more pleasure in his grand-children, and above all in his youngest grand-daughter, Elisabeth, who was gay and vivacious.

The King should have dropped the burden of etiquette, which made life hard for all the people at court. During a century ideas had changed. Public opinion was conscious of its strength, and it no longer took shape in the palace, but in Paris, in the salons and clubs. Since 1768, the most important ministries had been transferred to Versailles, which spared the ministers the trouble of driving each day from Paris to Versailles and back. One of the results was that the number of clerks and agents who crowded the offices and the galleries was increased further.

After Damien's murder attempt, the palace police had been reinforced. The Provost's supervision did not prevent incidents. In

January 1762, a Life Guard was found wounded on the floor of a very badly lit passage. He said that he had been attacked by two men, a priest and a man in a green suit, who tried to slip by into the Queen's apartments. The court was greatly excited. The Comte de Saint-Florentin, Minister of the King's Household, and the Grand Provost started an inquiry at once at the King's request. It transpired that the guard had wounded himself to attract attention, to display his zeal and receive a pension. He succeeded beyond his hope. But the Judiciary did not like such jokes. The guardsman was accused of high treason, and condemned to death and hanged in the Place de Grève. He was one of Mme Adélaïde's *protégés*, but she could do nothing to help him.

This episode was the main topic of conversation for several days. All the inns and furnished houses in Versailles had been searched. The police arrested a few beggars and drove some shady characters away. After that, tedium descended once again upon the courtiers.

And yet, for noblemen who had to leave the court because they were short of money, the palace still kept its old glamour. Provincial noblemen tried hard to put aside a few hundred *écus* each year so as to be able to spend two or three weeks in the shadow of the King and his attendants. How proud they were if granted the honours of the court! What stories they could tell back home! Imperturbable, Chérin had their proofs of nobility checked. The official genealogist, as *blasé* as the King himself about the pleasures of Versailles, wisely wrote: 'A mania for leaving the provinces and deserting the country, which becomes a desert, the desire to enjoy some temporary entertainment at court, an immoderate taste for pleasure . . . these are the evils which are destroying the aristocracy.'

These were the weary reflections of a thoughtful man who had no illusions about the vanity of life at Versailles.

### THE QUEEN'S DEATH

In her own apartments, Marie Leczinska was still leading the life she had made for herself. She had not wept for Mme de Pompadour's death: 'No one mentions her now. It is as if she had never been. Such is the way of the world. It is no use worrying about it.' Her funeral oration was brief.

The Dauphin's death touched her more deeply. She felt a deep affection for her son, though she had few opportunities to display it. She retired even more into the circle of her intimate friends and devoted herself to works of charity.

She suffered another bereavement in February 1766: her father, King Stanislas, who had always adored her, died in his turn. He had been her support, and his letters gave Marie the comfort and tenderness she lacked in her own family. 'You are my other self', he wrote shortly before his death, 'and my thoughts as well as my heart are mingled with yours, as I live only for you.'

Stanislas knew all about the slights his daughter had to put up with: 'I kiss your tears, and those little pearls are of a great price to me.'

Her father's death plunged the Queen in the deepest sorrow, and she spent many hours in her oratory. 'As for me', she wrote, 'I am sad and shall be so all my life. My only comfort is to think that those I weep over would certainly not wish to come back to this vale of tears.'

She had lost her taste for life. She was not old: she was only sixty-three, but her health had deteriorated, and her first doctor, Lassone, treated her in vain. She faded gradually during several months. Louis XV felt a certain regret; he had no official mistress and contented himself with the inmates of the Parc-aux-Cerfs. He had always been full of respect for his wife, but to this he now added an affection that was vaguely tinged with remorse. He formed again the habit of seeing her every day, and gave her back the honours of public life, of which she had been deprived for twenty years. The return of the King softened Marie's last days and she died as discreetly as she had lived on June 24, 1768. Those who had known her wept. The public was indifferent.

'This respectable princess, who had done nothing but good,' wrote the Duc de Croÿ, 'deserved to be mourned by the nation. The goodness of her nature could be seen in her face, which was full of grace.'

When Lassone came to tell the King that all was over, Louis went to the room where she had died, and in the presence of a few witnesses bent over the bed where the lonely woman lay and placed a kiss on her forehead.

The court went into mourning for six months and Louis withdrew to Compiègne. This put the court into a flutter. The King's appetite was well-known and his age—fifty-eight—was far from placing him out of temptation's way. He could easily be dragged into some degrading liaison. 'Mesdames Tantes' were most excited. Choiseul thought of nothing but planning a profitable marriage for the Dauphin, but first of all, one had to find a second wife for the King. Mesdames reviewed the list of possible candidates. Louis XV shrugged: had any King of France married again when nearly sixty? Playing on his recent bereavement, he resisted every attempt.

He was even less inclined to marry again because, thanks to his valet Lebel, who was his usual intermediary, he had discovered a delightful young woman who did not seem very hard to win.

He put her into a small house at Compiègne. She remained hidden all day and only came out at midnight to go to the castle. She left the King's apartment only at daybreak and two liveried servants escorted her sedan-chair.

## JEANNE DU BARRY

She had been born in Vaucouleurs on August 17, 1743, and she was just twenty-five. Her mother's name was Anne Bécu and her father's identity is uncertain. Jeanne had been very well brought up in Paris in the convent of the *Adoratrices du Sacré-Cœur*; then at fifteen she became the companion of a *fermier général's* widow and later still was employed as a shop-girl by a milliner. Her beauty attracted customers and lovers. She had a great many lovers whom she selected from among the men of quality. The Duc de Noailles, who was very frank, even with the King, made a rather cutting remark about her. As Louis XV, rather worried by his favourite's past, remarked one day: 'It looks as if I'm Sainte-Foix's successor.' 'Yes, sir,' the Duke replied; 'just as Your Majesty succeeds to Pharamond.'

Pharamond—who never existed—was the legendary first King of France.

In 1763, Jeanne was the mistress of Jean du Barry, an evil type who had been nicknamed The Rake. Being completely devoid of scruples or dignity, he was well aware that she was fit for a King, and he found a way of offering her to the sovereign.

Louis XV was dazzled by her charm and freshness. Choiseul had been warned by the police about the King's new passion but he shrugged his shoulders: 'We did not think that such a low intrigue could be more than a passing fancy; we wished the King good luck, and it would be his last display of bad taste and bad company that we would witness.'

Jean du Barry was clever enough to marry Jeanne to his brother, a heavy country squire named Guillaume who, in return for substantial benefits, agreed to give her his name and title. He was a Comte. The marriage took place on September 1, 1768. Three months later, Mme du Barry was installed in Versailles. First of all she took the flat left empty by Lebel's death; later, a little apartment was contrived for her in a part of the King's rooms on the second floor; drawing-rooms, a library, a bedroom, all of them newly decorated.

At first, it seemed to be just a mere amusement, the whim of a few nights. Then suddenly this nonentity of a girl took up her place as official mistress! The court banded together against her and the song-mongers worked overtime:

> *Il vous souvient encore de cette Tour de Nesles,*
> *Tivinmille, Limal, Rouxchâteau, Pompadour,*
> *Mais dans la foule enfin de peut-être cent belles*
> *Qu'il honora de son amour,*
> *Vous distinguez, je coirs, celle qu'à notre cour*
> *On soutenait n'avoir jamais été cruelle . . .*
> *Du laquais au marquis, chacun se souvient d'elle!*[1]

Her official presentation did not make them relent. The King pretended not to hear his daughters' remarks, nor Choiseul's discreet warnings. In his mistress' fresh and gentle arms, on her soft breast, he forgot for a while his cares and his business. With supreme tact, Mme du Barry, contrary to the Marquise, was careful never to talk about politics. This shop-girl had mastered the court style perfectly. She was even more at ease than Mme de Pompadour. 'Though she (the Marquise) had been brought up and had lived among the financiers of Paris, who were then extremely refined,' wrote Talleyrand, 'she still had a vulgar way of speaking and the

---

[1] 'No doubt you remember the tower of Nesles, Tivinmille, Limal, Rouxchateau, Pompadour, but in this crowd of some hundred fair ones on whom he bestowed his love, you may distinguish the one who has never been cruel to anyone at court. From the valet to the Marquis, everyone remembers her.' (The 'Tower of Nesles' is a complicated pun on the actual tower of that name, which had had a very bad reputation in the Middle Ages on account of Queen Marguerite de Bourgogne's too lively parties, and the Nesles family.)

greatest difficulties in correcting herself. She was utterly different from Mme du Barry, who, though less well brought up, had succeeded in acquiring a more refined way of speaking. She even knew how to tell stories in a lively way.'

Talleyrand apparently forgot that Jeanne Bécu, before coming to Versailles, had met nothing but great aristocrats for five years. Her lovers taught her the language and habits of courtiers.

Choiseul, who was then all-powerful, dreaded the influence the Comtesse could gain over Louis XV. Was she not likely to gather around her all his political adversaries? The King did all he could to reassure Choiseul:

'I speak to you with confidence and friendliness. It is possible that the public is against you. That is a minister's fate, especially when it is believed he is on bad terms with the master's friends. But, apart from that, the master is still pleased with you.'

'Apart from that . . .' The struggle between Choiseul and his enemies became more acute every day. Mme du Barry, who merely wanted to live in peace with everyone, was the pawn deftly pushed forward. Eventually, Choiseul's attitude irritated her. Their quarrels multiplied, to the great amusement of the court. She would forget to invite him to her suppers. When he was her partner at whist, she would shrug her shoulders, make pert remarks and all sorts of 'school-girl taunts', wrote Mme du Deffant to Horace Walpole.

The fools thought it so very funny. They reckoned on the fall of Choiseul and had already put these lines into the mouth of the minister:

> *Vive le roi! Foin de l'Amour,*
> *Le drôle m'a joué un tour*
> *Qui peut confondre mon audace,*
> *La du Barry, pour moi de glace*
> *Va, dit-on, changer mes destins;*
> *Jadis je dus ma fortune aux catins,*
> *Je leur devrai donc ma disgrâce.*[1]

In fact, Choiseul did not really dread that destiny. He held in

[1] 'Long live the King! Down with love The knave has played a dirty trick on me which could confound my audacity. Du Barry, always cold to me, is about to change my fate, they say. I owe my success to ladies of ill-repute, and I shall owe my disgrace to them too.'

his hand all the threads of a political intrigue. He was negotiating the Dauphin's marriage to an Austrian Archduchess, and the King would never dare at such a crucial moment to part with him. He counter-attacked and distributed a cartoon showing a certain Comtesse du Tonneau[1] riding a cask in full court dress.

## THE DAUPHIN'S WEDDING

After three years, negotiations succeeded at last. It was decided that Louis-Auguste should marry Marie-Antoinette-Josèphe-Jeanne at Versailles on May 16, 1770. The bride was fifteen and the bridegroom, the future King of France, just sixteen. Louis XV meant to have as grand a ceremony as possible, though times were hard, the people who worked in the palace were paid very irregularly and the Treasury was almost empty. But the court's prestige was at stake. The new Dauphine must be magnificently received and at the chateau there was great commotion. The Dauphin was the only one who showed no zest. This immature youth felt that all these ceremonies, in which he was to take the leading part, would simply stop his hunting, his only pastime, and thus made him cross.

The wedding day was blessed with beautiful weather. Never had Versailles known such splendour or such animation. It was a revival of Louis XIV's most glorious days. The ceremony had been organized by the Duc d'Aumont. The Dauphine dressed in her apartment on the ground floor. She wore a white brocade dress with large hoops and needed no make-up to look rosy and fair in all her youthful beauty. The Dauphin had dressed in the uniform of the Order of the Holy Ghost; he looked gloomy and hardly ever smiled.

Several thousands of privileged guests, with invitation cards provided by the Master of Ceremonies, had lined up in the Great Gallery, through which the wedding procession was to pass. At one o'clock they left the King's cabinet. The bride and bridegroom headed the procession, then, in accordance with precedence, the Princes of the Blood, the Dauphin's brothers, his aunts, and lastly the King himself, escorted by seventy court ladies, among whom one of the most noticeable was Mme du Barry. She was ablaze with gems.

The procession entered the chapel. All the guests, who were already seated, rose. The Dauphin and Dauphine's armchairs were

[1] A bad pun on du Barry = *du Baril* (a cask).

at the foot of the altar, exactly on the spot marked by Louis XIV; customs never changed at Versailles. The Cardinal de la Roche-Aymon, the King's Grand Almoner, blessed the couple and ascended the altar steps. The King and the Princes and Princesses of the Blood who had remained standing during the blessing, returned to their seats and the royal choristers sang mass. At the end, the vicar of Notre-Dame produced the parish registers, which were signed by:

Louis (the King)
Louis-Auguste (the future Louis XVI)
Marie-Antoinette-Josèphe-Jeanne (who was so moved that she made a blot on one of the registers)
Louis Stanislas-Xavier (the future Louis XVIII)
Charles-Philippe (the future Charles X)
Marie-Adélaïde-Clotilde (the Dauphin's sister and future Duchesse de Savoie)
Marie-Adélaïde ⎫
Victoire-Louise ⎬ (Mesdames Tantes)
Sophie-Elisabeth ⎭
Louis-Philippe d'Orléans
Louis-Philippe-Joseph d'Orléans (the future Philippe Egalité who, twenty-three years later, was to send his cousin to the scaffold.)

An extraordinary galaxy of signatures, including four Kings of France and the father of the fifth and last.

The Great Apartments had been cleared during mass. While tables were brought into the gallery for the King's game of cards, Marie-Antoinette received the oaths of the officers of her household, who were named to her by M. de Saint-Florentin, and then the ambassadors' compliments, presented to her by the Comtesse de Noailles.

The King began to play cards at six. Balustrades had been erected to control the movements of the guests as they filed past the table where the King was playing *lansquenet* with the Dauphine, as if they were on show. Great patience was required to stay there as an object of such scrutiny. A thousand invitations had been sent out but anyone properly dressed could pass the Swiss guards. The crowd entered the Salon de la Guerre, walked along the Gallery on the window side and went out by the Salon de la Paix.

Fireworks had been prepared for the end of the evening, but a violent storm compelled the huge crowd in the park to seek shelter. The rockets were soaked, the display was called off and people went away disappointed.

Supper took place in the new opera house that Gabriel had just completed, and was inaugurated that very night. The blue, gold and red tones shone softly. The stage was so deep that the balconies had been reproduced on a set at the back of it to suggest a perfect oval. A floor had been erected over the stalls at a level with the stage, where twenty-four musicians, conducted by Rebel, played throughout the supper. The royal table was in the middle. It was twenty-six feet long and thirteen broad. Louis XV sat alone at the top. At his side, in accordance with rank, sat the Dauphin and Dauphine, the Comte de Provence and the Comte d'Artois, Mme Clotilde and Mme Adélaïde, Mme Victoire opposite Mme Sophie, the Duc d'Orléans and the Duc de Chartres, the Duchesse de Chartres and the Prince de Condé, the Duc and the Duchesse de Bourbon, the Comte de Clermont and the Princesse de Conti, the Comte and Comtesse de la Marche, the Princesse de Lamballe and the Duc de Penthièvre (her father-in-law): eleven persons on one side, ten on the other; twenty-two in all, counting the King.

The court was present in the boxes. The first gentleman on duty, to the roll of drums and with his silver gilt wand in his hand, announced: 'The King's meat!'

Supper began. Mme Victoire was gloomy and unmoving. She had been terrified by the storm. The Dauphine, feeling shy and tired, hardly touched the food. On the other hand, her young husband relaxed and for the first time in the day looked pleased. He gobbled the food that was put before him, so that Louis XV leant towards him and muttered: 'Don't have too over-loaded a stomach for tonight!'

Louis-Auguste looked at his grandfather with surprise: 'Why not? I always sleep better when I have eaten well.'

The King shrugged and looked at Marie-Antoinette with compassion; she pretended she had not heard.

The last act of the ceremony was the *coucher*. The court hastened back to the ground floor apartments where the young people were to live. They crossed the galleries once more, all ablaze with light. The bands of the French and Swiss guards had massed in the drawing rooms. They were in 'Turkish' costumes and played very loudly what was assumed to be oriental music. As no one was listening, their cacophony was of no importance. The great moment had come. The Cardinal de la Roche-Aymon blessed the bed, the King handed the Dauphin, who again looked bored and sleepy, his shirt. The Duchesse de Chartres performed the same service for Marie-Antoinette. The curtains were lowered, the wedded pair climbed into bed, the curtains were opened once more, according to etiquette, and the court withdrew.

The Dauphin was already asleep. In his private diary, Louis wrote the next day: 'Nothing', which merely meant that he had not hunted.

The festivities continued. *Persée* was performed at the Opéra, an old piece by Lully and Quinault, slightly adapted to fashion. Sophie Arnould was a delightful Andromeda. Guimard and Vestris were much applauded in the ballet, but the whole work was too *démodée* and it was a flop. There was a great ball the next day, at which the Dauphine appeared. Violent quarrels about precedence had caused the withdrawal of part of the nobility, who were annoyed because the representatives of the House of Lorraine had been granted special privileges in the order of dances: they were to dance before the Duchesses. So, after long discussions, they decided to stand aside, or to participate only by royal command. Some of them took refuge in the railed boxes, to display their displeasure.

There was a public festival in the park. Orchestras were playing in the groves. According to contemporary reckonings, more than 200,000 persons had come from Paris, Versailles and other neighbouring towns. To enliven the atmosphere, the Petite Venise sailors walked about, blowing into their instruments. During the whole evening, people danced and ate at the buffets. As night fell, the King left the State Ball, which was dragging on, and walked towards the Great Gallery. From the central window, leaning on M. de la Ferté's arm, with the Dauphin and Dauphine at his side (the Dauphin was yawning his head off, as he had hunted in the morning), Louis watched the finest firework display ever produced at Versailles.

The organizers had surpassed themselves. They had found new figures: beside revolving suns with the French coat-of-arms, there were 'astronomical wheels' within which were the young couple's coat-of-arms, also waterfalls, suns and pyramids of fire. Despite the smoke which hid it slightly, the finishing piece produced thunderous applause; there were 20,000 'gold and diamond' rockets.

Scarcely had darkness returned to the park than at the end of the Grand Canal appeared a structure all lit up; the Temple of the Sun. The banks lit up little by little and then the Green Carpet and the whole park were but a huge stream of light. So was the palace, drawn in lines of fire. On the canal, the gondolas, ablaze with lanterns, were slowly moving to the sound of the band of the French guards who were aboard. It was a fairy-like display.

The whole court came down and mixed with the people in the park. M. de Choiseul gave his arm to the Duchesse de Gramont (his sister). The Duc d'Aiguillon escorted Mme du Barry. Etiquette had not allowed the King to join them. He was rather tired and was frightened of catching a cold. The Dauphine, who was only fifteen, wanted to go closer to the illuminations but again etiquette forbade it. The Dauphin had already gone to bed.

The marriage festivities came to an end. They had cost nine million *livres*.

The expenses were never fully paid. Twenty years later, when the Revolution broke out, some of the tradesmen were still sending in applications and requests for at least a part of the money owing. At Versailles—and this was a habit of long standing—bills were only paid when it was impossible to do otherwise.

### THE COMTESSE AND THE DAUPHINE

It is said that, at the supper the King gave the day before the wedding, Marie-Antoinette, not well aware of the court secrets, leant towards the Comtesse de Noailles and asked her who was the fair lady with dark eyes and a radiant complexion, seated at the end of the table.

'That is Mme du Barry,' answered the lady-in-waiting, scornfully.

'What is her office at court?'

'To amuse the King.'

'If that is so,' answered the Dauphine, 'I shall be her rival.'

Without realizing it, she had made a remark which was to come true. She soon understood Mme du Barry's true part and conceived for the favourite a violent hatred.

The rival groups had reached a truce for the wedding, but their hostility was afterwards greater than ever. The Duc d'Auguillon led the fight. First of all, Louis XV reassured his ministers:

'You conduct my affairs well,' he wrote to Choiseul. 'I am pleased with you. But beware of people round you and of those who give advice. I always hated them and I detest them now more than ever. You know Mme du Barry. I like her, and I warn her every day also to beware of people round her and of those who advise her, and you may be sure she obeys me. The fury against her has been horrible, and what was said was badly exaggerated. People would be at her feet if . . . such is the way of the world.'

This letter did not reassure the head of the Government, and a blunder hastened his fall. His crass carelessness in a conflict between England and Spain nearly drew France into war. The King was warned by a Foreign Office agent. Pale with anger, he abruptly intervened and settled the matter, but did not forgive Choiseul for his too independent policy. On December 24, 1770, he sent him in disgrace to Chanteloup, his chateau in Touraine.

Mme du Barry did not enjoy his absence for long. A new coterie formed against her, and at its centre was the Dauphine. Marie-Antoinette was still very young. She regretted the dismissal of Choiseul, who had arranged her marriage. She was under the influence of Mesdames, who continued to show the most violent animosity towards their father's mistress. They had tolerated the Marquise de Pompadour while their mother was alive. Now, embittered by their aimless life, they never failed to sneer at the favourite nor to condemn her. Marie-Antoinette took their part with surprising enthusiasm. She should have shown as much reserve as the Dauphin. Possibly she was jealous. As the future Queen of France, she was already the first lady at court, thanks to her youth and gracefulness. 'The Barry', as she contemptuously called her, being thirty, seemed elderly to a girl of sixteen. But jealousy may have had probably deeper roots. The Dauphine was suffering from her husband's inadequacies. She felt rather bitter when she looked at that woman, obviously created for love, who had never tried to hide her bliss. Out of spite, she never missed an opportunity to humiliate her when she could. Mme du Barry was indifferent to her petty insults. Louis XV, when he heard of them, was displeased and sullen. Courtiers revelled in such discords.

From Vienna, the Empress Maria-Thérèsa forced a solution on her daughter.

'You must know and see the du Barry only as a lady admitted at court and into the King's intimate circle. You are his first subject: you owe him obedience and submission. You must be an example to the courtiers, and the court . . . if you let yourself go, I see nothing in the future but great trouble, sorrows and small intrigues which will make your life very unpleasant.'

That wise advice came from a mother who knew all the snares of the court of Versailles, and dreaded that her daughter's icy attitude, by exasperating the King, would endanger her policy of alliance with France.

Marie-Antoinette agreed to be more pleasant with the lady of Louveciennes. Usually, when she met Mme du Barry, she managed never to speak to her. On January 1, 1772, the Dauphine was giving her New Year audiences in Marie Leczinska's bedroom, into which she had moved when the Comte de Provence had married. Accompanied by the Maréchalade de Mirepoix and the Duchesse d'Aiguillon, Mme du Barry came forward and, with regal elegance, made the customary curtsies. Instead of exchanging a few words with the ladies attending the King's mistress, Marie-Antoinette turned straight to the latter and said to her prettily: 'What a crowd there is today at Versailles!' It was a commonplace remark, which might even be taken as having a *double entendre*, though the Dauphine did not mean it that way. The remark was repeated and Louis XV was pleased. To thank her for her effort, he loaded her with presents. The aunts were furious and accused their niece of having deserted to the enemy.

Things got a little better, but relations remained chilly. The court ladies were either for the Dauphine or for the Comtesse: 'They live like cats and dogs,' wrote Mme du Deffand.

Marie-Antoinette had not given up fighting. Lent came and, as usual, feasts and balls stopped. In the palace chapel, the Abbot of Beauvais, the King's almoner, preached with unusual strictness. The Dauphine was delighted: 'We have a very good preacher,' she wrote to her mother. 'He preaches the good Gospel morals three times a week. He tells simple truths to everyone.' The King was in high spirits; those home truths did not trouble him.

'Tell me, Richelieu,' he once said to the incorrigible Marshal, 'it seems that this preacher has thrown a good many stones into your garden.'

'Yes, Your Majesty,' answered the Marshal-Duke. 'Some of them fell so heavily that they rebounded and landed in the park of Versailles.'

Louis XV smiled and went to his mistress.

With alternating pleasantness and frigidity, both women fought hard until the King's death. Then, in the name of outraged respectability, Marie-Antoinette revenged herself in a contemptible way by having Mme du Barry sent to a convent.

### A COURTIER IN THE AGE OF ENLIGHTENMENT

Among all those intrigues, courtiers felt uncomfortable. What was the court like at the end of Louis XV's reign? A man of taste who lived there for many years described it with as much clarity as cleverness.

The Duc de Nivernais was one of Mme de Pompadour's friends. He gave up his post as an ambassador when his protectress died, and retired into his beautiful mansion in the Rue de Touron, in Paris. Here gathered the wittiest people in the capital, and he only went to court to discharge the duties of his rank. He observed what took place round him and deplored the violent rivalries.

To warn his son, or any nobleman anxious to make a career, against the snares that awaited him, he amused himself by writing letters on the profession of courtier: they give a lively picture of the habits of the time, and some of them are very bold. His position gave him a right to state his opinion without mincing his words. 'There are people who have to live at court. Yet it is not an obligation. One must go there, but not live there permanently.'

'This duty must not be neglected,' the Duke added at once. 'An honest field-marshal, a zealous intendant, a stern magistrate, who never left his command, his province or his court of justice would be a bad courtier. Under Louis XV, a courtier has to frequent the palace galleries to know about events, to repeat the news and eventually discuss them with ministers. The consideration they bestow is in proportion to one's standing with the Prince.' The Duc de Nivernais was a little bitter about this. Here is a little scene which he described with plenty of irony.

'A mere clerk is much more likely to find a minister's door open to him than a man who has high birth and long service, but is unknown at court. The minister receives him at once. He signs a few letters in front of him without interrupting his conversation, which is gay and light like that of a man who meets a friend. He then tells him a few scraps of news of no importance. He tries to catch some idea of what was said or done the day before in the King's circle. He speaks in a very low voice, so that people in the ante-chamber will think it is a matter of great confidentiality. Finally, he escorts the courtier out and mutters something into his ear with the door ajar, so that everyone can see it and draw conclusions, for he knows few people are clever enough just to laugh and take no notice.'

Credulity and naiveté were among the distinctive characteristics of courtiers. Nivernais also gives much wise advice about behaviour towards the King's mistress. He knew all about it. He was thinking about the Marquise de Pompadour when he wrote:

'This woman, who is not a minister, is greater than any of them, for she holds the department of graces. One must avoid treating her lightly. Women who dabble in State affairs want to be taken seriously as the most serious of statesmen.'

A light and gallant tone was quite out of place when talking with them on some important subjects.

'When a woman has become a minister, when she deals out good and evil at court, she loses all her natural rights to be flattered, because that would merge on baseness. But it is permissible to please her and to make oneself pleasant.'

If a courtier fell from favour, he must take a dignified attitude:

'If he has kept his honour whole, his reputation intact, his own conscience clear, then he may withdraw discreetly. He must give the impression that he is happy to leave his chains, however gilded they might have been. It is gratifying to leave court with as much honour as when one entered it and, consequently, with more merit. But at the same time it is wise enough to shut that feeling away in one's heart. It is as stupid to boast of disgrace as to wail

188

over it. A wise and honest courtier must keep a religious silence about the faults and whims of the King, especially if they have something to do with himself.'

When writing these words, the Duke was thinking of a recent event and alluding to the totally different attitude taken by Choiseul when he was dismissed. Instead of departing serenely, the minister made plenty of noise before going to his Touraine estate. For twenty-four hours, all the streets leading to his mansion in the Rue Grange-Batelière were blocked with the coaches of men and women of quality coming to pity him and assure him of their friendship. Versailles had been deserted. Courtiers believed that Choiseul would one day return to power and they were thus preparing for the future. As soon as he was settled at Chanteloup, he drew the whole opposition around him, and even invited the most noteworthy people to join him. The court of Chanteloup was face to face with that of Versailles. The Duc de Nivernais was too clever and too refined to approve such a fuss. His advice, 'which blended the nobleness of the old court with the philosophy of the new one', was both wise and delicate.

### THE KING'S DEATH

Versailles was speculating about the King's death. Yet he had taken a new lease of life at his mistress' side. He was working longer with his ministers, pressing radical reforms which might have saved the monarchy, had they been maintained. But in the palace, everyone was certain that with the King's death everything would change and a new spirit would enter into court life.

Louis was sixty-four. His physical strength was unimpaired. He hunted for several hours without apparent fatigue and showed no sign of illness.

On April 27, 1774, he was with Mme du Barry in the Little Trianon which he had had built eleven years earlier for the Marquise de Pompadour. He woke up shivering and aching. He thought it was nothing worse than a slight attack of influenza, the fashionable illness. He got up and hunted as planned, in his coach. He returned late in the afternoon, feeling more tired than in the morning. During the night, he was ill. The first doctor, Lemonnier was summoned and could not find any serious symptom, yet the pain did not go. The first surgeon also arrived, examined his royal patient and bluntly told the King: 'Sir, it is at Versailles you must be ill.'

'Back to the castle,' ordered Louis, 'and in haste!'

A few moments later, the Royal coach galloped back to Versailles, bringing the King home. He went to bed, and was bled again and again, without improvement. He spoke in a hoarse, harsh voice. By ten at night his face was covered with pustules and there could no longer be any doubt: this was small-pox of the most virulent kind.

This terrible disease was less deadly after Jenner discovered inoculation, but Louis XV had always refused to be inoculated. The new cure was just getting known and doctors were rather reserved about it. Later, Louis XVI set an example: he was inoculated in 1774, a few months after his grandfather's death.

It was possible to recover from small-pox when one was young, but at Louis' age it was hopeless. Courtiers were rushing about like maddened flies. The Dauphin and Dauphine had been sent away, to shield them from infection. With a quiet courage, the King's daughters came to their father's bedside, in spite of the suffocating atmosphere of the room, with all the windows tightly shut. At night, Mme du Barry replaced them.

For a few days it was possible to hide from the King the seriousness of his illness. The various parties were at loggerheads. Was this going to be 'the second act of the Metz affair', as Mme de Pampadour had written after the assassination attempt by Damiens? The Archbishop of Paris had presented himself and had been sent away.

In the afternoon of May 4th, looking at his hands, the King realised the truth. He at once asked for a mirror, and looked at his face.

'But this is small-pox!' he exclaimed.

'Yes, Your Majesty,' the doctor answered.

That very evening, at midnight, as Mme du Barry was softly passing her hand over his brow, he said: 'Now that I know what is wrong with me, the scandal of Metz must not be repeated. Had I known earlier, you would not have entered the room. Now, I owe myself to God and my people. You must go tomorrow. Tell d'Aiguillon to come to me tomorrow at ten.'

The Prime Minister came and the King had a long talk with him.

At four in the afternoon, Mme du Barry entered the Duchesse d'Aiguillon's coach which took her to Rueil.

Three days passed; the court waited. All daily rites had stopped and the gentlemen of the household walked around aimlessly. The King's latest remarks were repeated. He was suffering more and more. A pestilential odour filled the King's room.

On May 7th, at seven in the morning, the Holy Sacrament was carried into the chapel. The King had great difficulty in taking the Eucharist. A few minutes later, the Grand Almoner, His Eminence the Cardinal de la Roche-Aymon, declared in a loud voice to the courtiers who were massing in the doorway: 'Gentlemen, the King asked me to tell you that he requests God's forgiveness for his trespasses and for the offence he has given his people.'

'I wish I had the strength to say it myself,' muttered the King.

On May 10th, early in the afternoon, the wavering candle on the window-sill of his room, which told the courtiers that the King was still alive, suddenly went out.

In the Queen's former apartment, where they were living, the Dauphin and Marie-Antoinette were kneeling and praying. 'Suddenly', wrote a witness, 'a frightful sound was heard, exactly like thunder.' The crowd of courtiers was racing across the Great Gallery. The First Gentleman of the Bed-Chamber opened the door.

'The King is dead. Long live the King!'

A second King had died in Versailles. He would be the last.

# CHAPTER THIRTEEN

# THE DECLINE OF ETIQUETTE

The courtiers breathed more freely. Louis XV was dead and Mme du Barry had gone. Reformers followed. The new King was generous, sensitive and popular. Hope was reborn.

The obsequies had been scamped. The monks and priests, who by all the rules should have watched over the corpse, had taken refuge in the Council Room, giving as a pretext that the air of the bed-chamber was unbreathable. During the night of the 11th to the 12th, the royal coach drove to St Denis, escorted by only forty Life Guards and thirty-six pages of the Grande and Petite Écurie. Only a few loafers watched the meagre procession off. In the taverns beside the road people shouted: 'Tally-ho! Tally-ho!,' and wafer-sellers cried out as they peddled their wares and the procession went by: 'Here is pleasure for you, Ladies!'[1]

The court was in mourning, but everyone was happy, hoping that this young King and the lovely, charming Queen would bring new ways of living into the palace. It was said that Louis XVI and Marie-Antoinette would change all the rules of precedence—all those minute gestures which stultified the courtier's mind and deprived him of everything natural. It was rumoured that the King had ordered from M. d'Estissac, the Master of the Robes, eight suits of simple rateen, and that he had been seen in the park, seated on a bench with his sisters-in-law, like anyone else enjoying the fresh air. Here lay the promise of better times.

### THE QUEEN AND ETIQUETTE

Marie-Antoinette tried hard to throw off the rules of etiquette. While she was only a young Dauphine, she had already brushed tradition aside. Young and gay, disappointed by a husband who did not provide her with what a woman might expect, she tried hard to forget her troubles. She escaped from Versailles as much

[1] There is a pun here. Wafers are *plaisir* in French.

as she could. She was seen at the Opera with her brother-in-law Artois. A few months before Louis XV's death, she welcomed Glück, her former music master. She forced his works on the Paris public and *Iphigénie* was a triumph, in spite of Mme du Barry's contempt for Glück's music. A great quarrel between Glückists and Puccinists shook the palace for several weeks. The Dauphine attended the first performance with her husband, the Comte and Comtesse de Provence, the Duchesse de Bourbon, the Duchesse de Chartres and the Princesse de Lamballe. A few people protested that it was scandalous. Marie-Antoinette applauded the performance throughout, and the public clapped 'to please Mme la Dauphine'.

Grimm wrote: 'One thinks or dreams of nothing but music. It is the subject of all our quarrels, all our talks and all our suppers.'

A Dauphine could do things which were impossible for a Queen of France. Marie-Antoinette should have bowed to the habits of Versailles: instead, she had decided to make her will and independence clear. A first incident happened at the beginning of the period of mourning. Austerely dressed in black, with coiffs, stockings, gloves and fans to match, all court ladies came to curtsey to Marie-Antoinette. It was a very long procession. A few old-fashioned dresses promoted laughter and the Queen could not hide her air of raillery. Some Duchesses were offended and swore they would not set foot again in 'that little girl's court'. An oath which would not take them very far. Could they exist without Versailles?

The Queen breezily declared: 'They are old-fashioned hags, living in the last century. All those old frumps may go, if they wish.' And again: 'When they are over thirty, I can't understand how they dare to appear at court.'

Her tactless remarks were repeated and, the next day, everyone was humming:

> *Petite reine de vingt ans,*
> *Vous qui traitez si mal les gens,*
> *Vous repasserez la barrière . . .*[1]

But there was also something of greater consequence: the Queen tried conscientiously to conform to the tradition of the Grand and Petit Lever. She had been taught the gestures she was to carry out

[1] 'Little Queen of twenty, who treat people so badly, you will be driven back across the frontier. . . .'

as the various entrances took place—for the Dukes, Duchesses and Gentlemen of the Bed-chamber, a mere bow of the head. For a Prince or Princess of the Blood, the Queen, sitting in her armchair while her women combed or powdered her hair, would press her hands to the arms of her chair as if to rise, and yet remain seated.

Such an insignificant rigmarole was just tolerable, though it was out of date. The dressing ceremony made her furious, and this was that sort of intimate ballet she was to try and suppress, after having been exasperated beyond belief by the absurdities of precedence. Mme Campan's comments are famous:

'The Queen's dressing was a masterpiece of etiquette. Everything was regulated. The lady-in-waiting or the lady of the bed-chamber, or both if they happened to be there together, with the first woman in attendance and two ordinary women, would do the greater part of the work, but there were differences between them. The lady of the bed-chamber would pass over the petticoat and the dress; the lady-in-waiting poured out the water for washing hands and handed the Queen her chemise. When a Princess of the Royal Family was present, the lady-in-waiting would yield to her the latter function, but not directly to a Princess of the Blood. She would then give the chemise to the first woman who would hand it to the Princess. Each of those ladies strictly respected those habits as a matter of right.

'On a winter day it happened that the Queen, quite undressed, was about to slip on her chemise. I was holding it unfolded. The lady-in-waiting entered, hastened to remove her gloves and took the chemise. Someone scratched at the door which was opened; it was the Duchesse de Chartres. She had removed her gloves, came to take the chemise, but the lady-in-waiting handed it, not to her, but to me. I gave it to the Princess. Someone else scratched at the door: it was the Comtesse de Provence; the Duchesse de Chartres passed her the chemise. The Queen had folded her arms over her bosom and looked cold. Madame saw her strained attitude, just dropped her handkerchief, kept her gloves and while passing the chemise over the Queen's head, ruffled her hair. The Queen started laughing to hide her exasperation, but grumbled several times between her teeth: "It is unbearable! What importunity!" '

She decided she would tolerate it no longer. In future, the first lady in the room would hand her her chemise. There was a great hub-bub of protest. Marie-Antoinette just ignored the permanent rights of hierarchy. Further, she suppressed, or rather simplified, the ceremony of the *lever*. As soon as her hair was done, she left the ladies who were standing in great court dress around her, dismissed them with a charming smile and retired into her private rooms to finish dressing with her own women. Mme Campan wrote: 'Those habits were respected because they were right. The maintenance of precedence is a form of vanity.' The Queen hurt the ladies of the court at their most sensitive point.

She attacked other aspects of etiquette with the audacity of a young woman who fears nothing. She had hundreds of servants, yet she was the worst served woman in France. Each office-holder had one definite task to fulfil and stuck to it strictly, less from lack of helpfulness than to avoid conflicts. Once the Queen noticed there was dust under her bed. She summoned the servants of the bed-chamber, who refused to do a thing. 'When Her Majesty was not in bed, the bed was a piece of furniture. Dust sweeping was then a duty of the chamber valet. The Queen was thirsty, but no woman had the right to give her a glass of water; that duty should be discharged by the lady-in-waiting or the first lady of the bed-chamber. If they were absent, the Queen could not drink.'

Marie-Antoinette decided to drink and pay no more attention to those time-honoured privileges. Until then, Queens of France could only appear in public surrounded by women, and servants of the other sex had to draw away. This tradition dated back to Anne of Brittany, who had organized the ladies-in-waiting service at court. Marie-Antoinette broke the tradition. Men would have the right to serve her directly, and she was accompanied by a single valet or two footmen if passing through the palace when her women were not at hand.

The older courtiers grew more and more hostile. The Mistress of the Household reminded her respectfully of what Marie Leczinska did or did not do. She was given the following curt response: 'Madam, you will do as you wish, but please do not think that a Queen who was born an Archduchess of Austria is as interested—or not interested—as a Polish Princess who became Queen of France.'

In order to receive her hairdresser quietly—Léonard, who called himself a *physionomist,* or Rose Bertin—she got the Superintendent of Buildings to alter her own apartment. Mique made the plans and the Rousseau brothers carried out the decoration.

The public knew about these expensive alterations. The court discussed them and made comments. The young people were delighted with the new fashion, while older courtiers regretted the old décor to which they were accustomed.

### THE KING'S HABITS

Louis XVI agreed with the latter, but he could never refuse the Queen anything and he gave way to her whims. For his own part, he was content with little. He had serious tastes. His grandfather's card room, on the first floor, became his library. On the other three floors and even on the fourth, in the garrets reached by four little staircases, he organized all his study-rooms: he was an expert locksmith and clock-maker, and was interested in physics and geography. They were really laboratories where, with the help of specialists, he often studied new inventions.

The King has often been depicted as a mere locksmith, fascinated by machinery, and delighting in forging, with the celebrated Gamain, keys, steel boxes, padlocks and other things which he gave his friends. In fact, those laboratories were put to many other uses. The King was interested in applied sciences and was very deft with his fingers. One can see how silly was the remark Marie-Antoinette is supposed to have made: 'I have married a Vulcan whose Venus I don't want to be.' But did she really say these words?

Pierre Verlet has made a list of Louis XVI's activities. When he studied new weapons, compared the models of ships, or made small-scale engines work, it must be admitted that this was not merely amusement, but serious work.

Historians have been hard on this King. He had neither Louis XIV's grandeur nor Louis XV's refined elegance, but he was industrious and full of good-will. According to some writers, after his official *lever* and a solid breakfast of mutton-chops, ham and eggs, which had little in common with Louis XIV's breakfast of herb tea, he would spend most of the morning in his smithy, or, with his eyes glued to binoculars would stand on the roof and look at people moving towards the chateau. In fact, he presided over the council meetings several times a week, listened to his ministers, weighed their varied advice, and then took his own decision.

He was conscientious, sometimes hesitant and full of doubt. He had no illusion as to the merits of those who surrounded him.

This lover of nature, who had had the park of Versailles replanted and had given it the shape we now know, wanted as badly as his grandfather to escape the public life prescribed by etiquette. But he accepted the situation without complaint, while Marie-Antoinette did not.

He was precise and meticulous to a degree. In 1787, Constant de la Motte, the King's geographer, drew up a new coloured map of the castle, the park and the town of Versailles. He submitted the original to the King before sending it to the printer. Louis XVI examined it carefully and, in his small, precise handwriting, noted in pencil a few errors he had detected: 'Gardens between the Rue de Maurepas and the park are not right. The pond is too large. A fallow field has been forgotten.'

Such details delighted the King. He was slightly shocked by the way in which Marie-Antoinette rebelled against the rules of precedence, and he kept up the great customary ceremonies. The Queen had to come back from Trianon on Tuesday to attend the reception of ambassadors, as that was the day set aside for them. The smallest details of etiquette were still respected. When an audience was given to the Comte du Nord (the Russian Empress' son), the Duc de Croÿ gravely noted that just one side of the King's chamber door was open, as the Czarewitch was travelling incognito.

However, Louis had introduced a certain degree of *bonhomie* in contrast with his grandfather's elegance and Louis XV's carefully measured gestures. He was gay and often gave vent to heavy guffaws that resounded through the bed-chamber during the Grand Lever. He was amused by anything. He threatened an old valet to have him tickled by a page; the old man dreaded that sort of joke so much that he fled in terror. When another page succeeded in stealing a certain Laroche's wig, he was the first to be delighted by the joke. Laroche was the *concierge* of the Ménagerie. 'Covered with rings and diamonds like a financier, he was dirtier than his inmates. Never did a boar in its lair waft such a repulsive smell,' wrote the Comte d'Hézecques. The King would argue with him and contradict him. Though he was a respectful courtier, the old man would answer back, start an argument and commit a few blunders that delighted the audience; then he agreed to drop the subject, and at that very moment his wig flew to the tester of the King's bed.

## THE OLD AND THE NEW COURT

Members of the old court were horrified by such easy-going ways. Some of them were deeply shocked. The Prince de Montbarey, Minister and Secretary of State, who observed Versailles during the first years of the reign, commented acutely on Marie-Antoinette's attitude.

'The Queen's youth and her craving for pleasure led her to find the rules of etiquette too troublesome, and she regarded those who still held to them as silly creatures who must be got rid of. This Princess, who otherwise had so many rare qualities and whose only defects were those of her years, did not remark, or allow herself to be told, that at court appearances are more important than reality.'

The Prince was lenient and his last remark was very wise. What becomes of a court when the gestures which justify its existence are performed no longer? There is no court without its etiquette. Sovereigns in exile understood it so well that, without power or money, they still maintained the time-honoured rules. Charles X and even 'Henri V' (his grandson) kept a number of rules revived from the Tuileries period. Montbarey continued:

'Without a plan or a preconceived idea, out of mere childishness, the Queen completely disorganized the court. During the first years of Louis XVI's reign, she was completely dominated by her craving for festivities, even though her husband put in an appearance only to please her. Those frequent entertainments gave birth to a desire to invite people of a class who were strangers to the court but who had a reputation for their talents. Little by little the mixing of classes became considerable.'

Louis XV had created a scandal by bringing a *bourgeoise* to court, but Mme de Pompadour was his mistress. Now one would meet in the galleries people who, in the reign of the *Bien-Aimé*, would never have been seen at court except as awe-struck spectators. Such people were now among the Queen's intimate friends!

It is understandable that some elderly persons preferred to retire. The Maréchale de Mouchy, a lady-in-waiting, resigned. Marie-Antoinette, who had often thought she was unpleasant, did not regret her. She replaced her by the Princesse de Chimay, who was given an apartment of twelve rooms in the south wing, which

198

vanished when the Grande Gallerie des Batailles was built in the nineteenth century. 'A model of sweetness, she never raised any difficulties to the innovations which the younger members of the court wished to organize, and she endured them without approving of them.' The Prince de Montbarey concluded:

'This inner disorganization of the court created an easiness in relations which soon led to familiarity and, confusing everything, destroyed the respect and veneration which Louis XIV, knowing the national temper well, thought necessary to his own person.'

Montbarey belonged to the old school. According to him, after all those changes the most wary people appeared at court only when 'duty and decency compelled them to do so'.

Such a statement calls for examination. Voluntary departures were few. Marie-Antoinette's alterations did not lead courtiers to abandon offices they had by hereditary rights that had lasted for more than a century. There were a few crises, a few pieces of gossip. The two courts regarded each other askance for a while, then eventually blended into one.

It happened one evening during the Queen's first pregnancy. Though very happy about an event she had hoped for during eight years, the Queen was slightly exasperated at not being able to attend a masked ball at Carnival time, because of her condition. To comfort her, the King decided to take to her apartments a whole procession of masked people in fancy dress. At its head was old Maurepas, back in office after twenty years in exile, dressed as Cupid, and leading his wife as Venus. It was a decidedly comic sight, since Maurepas was seventy-seven, his impotence having been celebrated at Versailles by twenty malicious couplets like these:

> *Maurepas était impuissant:*
> *Le roi l'a rendu puissant;*
> *Le ministre reconnaissant*
> *Dit: 'Pour vous, Sire,*
> *Ce que je désire,*
> *C'est d'en faire autant!*[1]

Eventually, Louis XVI fulfilled his minister's wish! Further guests followed: Marshal de Richelieu as Titan and old Marshal de

[1] 'Maurepas was impotent; the King made him powerful. The grateful Minister said: 'What I wish you, Sir, is that I could do as much for you.'

Mirepoix's wife as the Dawn; the Marshal de Brissac (seventy-eight years old) appeared as a dervish and the Princesse d'Hénin, who had one of the wickedest tempers at court, was a fairy! Younger couples followed, half-mocking, half-amused. After having bowed to the Queen, the Duc de Richelieu and the Marshal de Mirepoix's wife danced a minuet, as if they had been twenty. 'And now,' said the Duc, gallantly kissing his partner's hand, 'let the young do better . . . if they can!'

After this, those who were for tradition and those who were for the new way mixed more freely. Marie-Antoinette had succeeded in breaking down the barriers. Yet etiquette survived and, if intrigues centred round her or her brothers-in-law, and if a youthful air and a sense of careless gaiety hovered over Versailles, appearances were preserved in the way that Prince de Montbarey desired.

## THE NUMBERLESS SERVANTS

The palace was always a huge, inarticulate caravanserai. Never had the offices been so numerous, so varied and so pointless. 'Here everyone glories in his office and thinks he is connected with the Crown if he so much as touches the King's boot.'

The King's household, the Queen's, and those of the other members of the Royal Family, teemed with servants. The *Almanach Royal* limited itself to the names of the holders of the highest offices. Since the beginning of the reign, Blaizot, the royal bookseller, published an *Almanach de Versailles*, in which everyone was mentioned, down to the least cook's assistant. This endless list filled 165 pages in small type. It is interesting to pick out the names of a few picturesque offices.

The King's Music, attached to the chapel, consisted of some sixty musicians—a very reasonable figure (there were only twenty violinists and ten 'cellists), but there were also those whose only duty was in coming each morning to ask the King when he would hear mass. There were two organists (Couperin and Paulin) but three organ builders (Cliquot, Chiquelier and Pascal). Brière's only duty was to carry the musicians' instruments.

Victualling officers were more numerous than under Louis XIV. In the butlers' section, there were two wine carriers and two 'leaders of the hocks'. Men specializing in making soup, providing vegetables, mending the spits or mere assistant cooks had increased in number. Most of them had nothing to do, or were occupied for only a few moments each day or each week.

The King's bed-chamber was equally well provided: first gentlemen of the bed-chamber, first valets, valets (forty of them), all on quarterly duty. There were four clock-makers, and one of them simply wound the King's watch every morning. The room servants were only eight and they were in fact the only ones who really did anything useful. The last, M. Antoine, had retired, but according to the directory had 'kept his honours' and also his profits. And then there were the fire-makers, and the commode-carriers who had nothing to do after the English water-closets had been built, together with bathrooms, in most apartments of the palace. And what about the captain of the mule team (there were actually no mules left in Versailles) and the gentleman whose job it was to hand the *Gazette Royale* to the King, the Queen and the Royal Family? This distributor of the official bulletin had appointed a representative close to the King and therefore enjoyed a pleasant sinecure.

One could go on like this for a long time, listing all the offices attached to the Menus-Plaisirs—M. Papillon, for instance, who looked after the silver—or to the Queen's household, with twenty chamber-maids, and Mme Campan as one of the most outstanding personalities, or the two admirable Hautier brothers—called Léonard—the Queen's hairdressers.

The military household of the King, Queen and Princes had not been deprived of a single unit, in spite of some vague efforts to diminish these bodies, which were more decorative than really useful to the sovereign's safety. A cohort of guards followed Marie-Antoinette wherever she went. The Abbé de Vermont, her reader, could not refrain from mocking her. He asked her one day: 'What is the meaning of this army of warriors I found in the courtyard? Is some general about to inspect his army?' Until the dawn of the Revolution, Versailles was a gilded prison, out of which no one really wanted to escape.

### IMPOSSIBLE ECONOMIES

One day Louis XVI said to M. de Coigny: 'I mean to carry out some essential cuts at court. Those who object will be broken like glass.' The King assumed a tone of authority in using these words, and the Grand Equerry remained sceptical. He knew that the sovereign spoke in vain. It was not enough to be full of good intentions; they had to be translated into concrete deeds. But Louis XVI was weak and was influenced by anyone. He kept careful accounts, but he soon discovered that, apart from altering the whole structure of the palace, the economies he recommended were insignificant.

The fault was Louis XIV's. Versailles had been planned on too grand a scale. Abuses were innumerable. According to Pierre Verlet, 'everyone was accustomed to live at the King's expense', and the King's weakness merely encouraged them. Since Louis XIV the expenses had increased continuously, and even when taking into account the general inflation, their rise was incredible. Here are some figures taken from the King's accounts. Louis XVI drank little, and yet his wine cost 6,567 *livres* in 1785, 16,640 in 1787, and 60,899 in 1789. The cost had increased tenfold in four years. Of course, it is true that intermediaries, among whom was the Marquis de Vaudreuil, took a heavy commission.

As soon as they were born and handed over to the governess, the children of France were a heavy burden on the Treasury. Their wardrobe was renewed each year and swallowed a fortune: that of Mme Royale, the King's daughter, cost 299,000 *livres* in 1779; the figure doubled after the Dauphin's birth. It became so fantastic at this point that, when their governess, Mme de Marsan, was sent away, some dared to accuse her of having managed badly the money allowed her. The court's tradesmen took unfair advantage of the situation, everyone agreed, but to take a strong line with them seemed an impossible task. There was a danger of toppling the whole edifice.

Next to expenses, there was waste. Any innovation immediately became a tradition or a permanent right. Marie Leczinska's dentist once received a present of six dozen handkerchiefs; after that and until the fall of the monarchy he punctually received his six dozen every year. The Queen's tall footmen had to carry Her Majesty's parasol; they were given a tip, and after that, each year, they demanded their 'parasol tax'.

According to an age-old rule, the candles in the Queen's Little Apartments were always put out as soon as the Queen left them, and were immediately replaced by new ones, even if they had burned for only a few minutes. Still whole, they were resold by privileged people, according to an invariable order. Those of the ante-chamber, great cabinet and corridors went to the valets; those of the card-room and bedroom to the Queen's women. If the candles had not been lit the privilege holders were paid a daily 'candle tax' of eighty *livres*. It has been estimated that Marie-Antoinette's chambermaids thus received a yearly profit of 50,000 *livres*.

Everything could be sold or re-sold. Tipping had become a right. The resale of food and articles that had been scarcely touched was no longer limited to the *serdeau* officers. Everyone tried to 'grab something', to use the words of the Duc de Croÿ.

These peculiar habits were known to the furthest ends of the kingdom. High court ladies, to make some money, never hesitated to sell clothes which had been given them for some special occasion and for which they had no further use. When the court went into mourning, the Royal Family paid for their servants' black garments. As soon as mourning was over, they hurried to sell them at a fair price. In 1783, it was rumoured that the Duchesse d'Angoulême would soon die.[1] Immediately, a friend of one of the Comtesse d'Artois' maids wrote from Pont-à-Mousson: 'Mama asks that when mourning is over, you should buy one for her and, as she is not in a hurry, to wait until they are sold for almost nothing.' Second-hand clothes were sold at the palace, as well as by the local rag-men!

Office holders were no less stingy. Honest Papillon de la Ferté, who directed the Menus-Plaisirs, confessed that for a performance of *Athalie* he had had shepherds' wands and farm hats made which had not been used! He also admitted that his expenses were not without profit, since he was associating with the contractors of the Menus-Plaisirs. To this candid confession, he added a remark which was almost cynical: 'I would never end if I tried to go into all the details of the useless expenditure I see every day, subalterns following the examples of their chiefs without ever being supervised.'

'Following the example of their chiefs!' The remark applied to the whole court. Yet meritorious efforts were made by the King. In 1787 he decided to reduce the costs of the Stables which had climbed to fantastic figures; four million for the Grande Écurie and 3,400,000 for the Petite Écurie. He simply suppressed the

---

[1] The lady is unidentifiable.

latter with a stroke of the pen. The number of horses fell from 2,400 to 1,125 and several servants were dismissed.

But what could such economies mean when the Queen set an example of endless extravagance?

## MARIE-ANTOINETTE

One would like to be lenient towards Marie-Antoinette and to find excuses for her. She was a victim of her surroundings, a young court in which the members were all under thirty. To her face there was no end of adulation and all her whims were thought delightful. Those who did not belong to her coterie harshly criticized her.

She should have had a firm husband, but Louis XVI was also very young. In 1780, he had already reigned six years and he was barely twenty-six! Towards the Queen, for several years, he felt vaguely guilty and never refused her anything. Later, he would sometimes try to stand by his decisions, forbid some expenses one day and give way the next.

Marie-Antoinette had that supreme charm which allowed her to bewitch with her smile all those who served her. All were intent to please her. She was carried away in a bustle of games, balls and fashionable distractions. 'She is hare-brained,' said her brother, the Emperor Joseph II.

She loved acquiring jewels. At the end of 1775 she bought a pair of diamond ear-rings for 200,000 francs, and before the end of the year she was tempted by some bracelets costing 250,000 *livres*. The Empress Maria-Thérèsa could not refrain from scolding her darling Antonia, who answered: 'I could not imagine one would have bothered my dear Mamma's goodness with such trifles!'

Louis XVI tried to resist. During that very year, 1775, the jeweller Böhmer brought to the Queen a pair of magnificent ear-rings costing 300,000 *livres*. She was tempted! The King demurred. So she paid an instalment to the jeweller, kept the jewels—and asked her husband to pay the rest, which he did out of his private purse. The payments went on until 1782.

'I really must amuse myself and can only do it by increasing the number of my pastimes.' This remark, made by the Queen, explains her passion for games—all sorts of games. She had a passion for billiards, which was shared by Louis XVI. So billiard tables were put into all the palace rooms, so that they could indulge in their favourite game. But Marie-Antoinette liked cards even better. Card games were played at Versailles every night she was not attending a ball or a spectacle, and stakes were very high. Heaps of *louis* were piled on the tables and card tables overflowed everywhere. The Queen's example was followed by her servants. There were tables in the rooms of the King's table waiters, in the Queen's ante-chamber, in the Little Apartments and on every floor. According to Pierre Verlet, the Queen's partners were not always of the best nobility and their honesty was sometimes questionable. Louis XVI, who had no wish to gamble away the kingdom's money, also refused to play and eventually forbade faro, which swallowed enormous stakes. The Queen sulked and the King gave way, allowing faro, 'but just for one evening'.

The game began at ten o'clock. A Paris banker was summoned, who was impressed by the crowd of gamblers he met. The game began. The Queen left by 4 a.m., having lost but ninety *louis,* while the Comte d'Artois had won 450. Interrupted at the end of the morning, the game began again in the Princesse de Lamballe's apartments and went on until the end of the afternoon. Louis XVI was displeased. The Queen quieted him with a joke: 'You allowed the game, but you didn't say for how long. So we had the right to make it last for thirty-six hours!'

The King laughed heartily and a few days later allowed another game of faro. By the end of the year, the Queen discovered with surprise that she was 487,272 *livres* out of pocket. She mentioned it to the Austrian Ambassador and things were settled. When Joseph II came to Versailles as Count Falkenstein, his sister managed to hide her follies. Yet he scolded her and she promised to mend her ways . . . after he had gone.

She was not forbidden to busy herself with her dresses. Each morning she locked herself up with Rose Bertin in her private rooms, for the great dressmaker was not allowed access into the Queen's bed-chamber. It was the Duchesse de Chartres who had introduced this great artist in couture, just a few months after Louis XV's death. The dressmaker, surrounded by a few young girls, would open the boxes she had brought with her. Marie-Antoinette would look at materials and discuss colours. One day, Louis XVI happened to be present. He looked at some brownish taffetas which Rose Bertin had just displayed for a dress which was to be called *Composition honnête.* 'It is puce-coloured,' remarked the King, who did not lack sense.

His remark was a success. Puce became fashionable at once, in various shades. There were dresses of all tinges, old puce, young puce, thigh puce, back puce and stomach puce. All the dresses worn that year at Versailles were puce-coloured. As the Queen dreaded nothing so much as the commonplace, she soon abandoned puce for an ash-blonde colour, which matched her hair. It was a new craze. Courtiers were sent to Lyons with a lock of the Queen's hair, to get silk-weavers to reproduce the colour exactly. On an average the Queen ordered some 150 dresses a year and spent 200,000 *livres* on them.

The *physionomist* shared with the dressmaker the Queen's favour and expenses. Léonard Hautier, the divine Léonard, created for her fantastic head-dresses, the height of which was a delight to cartoonists. One drawing represented the hairdresser arriving at Versailles with a ladder under his arm. It consisted of several layers of hair brushed up and creped. There was the greatest rivalry among the court ladies to find who was wearing the tallest or most original head-dress. Hair was set *à la belle poule,* with feathers, ribbons and accessories reproducing the rigging of the illustrious frigate of that name. The Duchesse de Lauzun had a great success with a sort of landscape in relief, with a huntsman shooting at ducks near a pond, and a miller's wife flirting with a gallant abbé while her husband rode discreetly away on a donkey. Some of those contraptions, thanks to a spring cleverly hidden in the chignon, could be raised or lowered at will. If some glum-looking lady of the old court came into the salon, the hair was lowered, but it rose again when she left.

Marie-Antoinette had too much taste to wear such contraptions. She was satisfied with what Léonard designed for her, naming his head-dresses *Eurydice* or *Iphigénie* on account of her liking for Glück's operas. He also decorated her hair with tall feathers, for she revelled in them. One evening she had ten of them in her hair. Maria-Thérèsa scolded her daughter once again. The portrait she had been sent had not pleased her: 'I did not find in it the portrait of a Queen of France, but that of an actress,' and she added these words in conclusion: 'A young and pretty Queen, very pleasant to look at, has no need of all those fripperies.' They were expensive fripperies, harshly criticised at court by courtiers, most of whom did not belong to the Queen's coterie—her celebrated coterie which was now screening the Queen from the rest of the court.

## THE QUEEN'S SURROUNDINGS

This was a serious mistake in the daily life of the chateau. Of course, from the days when Versailles had risen from the marshes, plots and intrigues had flourished. Neither Louis XIV's reign nor Louis XV's had been free from them. But until now the King had always tried to keep above politics. We have seen how Louis XV warned Mme du Barry against the interested advice of her friends.

Marie-Antoinette had allowed herself to be surrounded by real coteries which had erected for her, inside the palace itself, a private realm where nobody had access but the privileged. Her first favourite was Mme de Lamballe, the Duc de Penthièvre's daughter-in-law, widowed when she was eighteen. The Princesse and Marie-Antoinette were for several years united by the closest friendship. The Princess was made a Superintendent of the Queen's household and was given the apartment where her father-in-law had lived at the end of the south wing. With time, their affection cooled and other women replaced the Princess.

Then there was Mme de Polignac. The Comte Jules de Polignac's wife was very lovely and modest; she was made a Duchess in 1782. She seldom appeared at court, as the couple was not rich. Marie-Antoinette conceived a fervid passion for her, and gave her friend's husband the inheritable office of the Queen's First Equerry. But she wanted to have her dear Yolande constantly at her side. In 1782 the Rohan bankruptcy gave the Queen an opportunity to get her own way. Since the days of Louis XIV, the office of governess to the Children of France belonged to that illustrious family. Marie-Antoinette broke with tradition abruptly and gave the office to Mme de Polignac, who moved into the first floor of the old wing, between the Royal Courtyard and the Prince's Courtyard. Marie-Antoinette could then enter her favourite's apartment, merely by crossing Mme de Maintenon's former suite. It was apparently the finest suite in Versailles. Later she moved into the governess' apartment which was completely renovated for her benefit, and at the Crown's expense.

Mme de Polignac was not greedy, but her friends were and she could not refuse them anything. Marie-Antoinette eventually grew weary of their constant begging. Among those friends was Vaudreuil. He had a great influence over the Queen until the day when she discovered the part played by the Polignac group. Then Vaudreuil's star declined. There was Besenval, lieutenant-colonel of the Swiss. He was fifty-three and looked an old man among all those young people. He amused the Queen by telling her the daily gossip, and the most high-coloured stories which he told with consummate art, 'risking insolent remarks which suited him well'. He knew exactly how far he could go. When his tone became too vivid, the Queen stopped him with a tap of her fan.

Louis XVI did not like this sort of conversation, which did not fit his solemn, formal temper. Risqué subjects were discussed only after he had left. He always retired at eleven sharp. One night one of the guests secretly pushed forward the hands of the clock—and boasted of it the next day! The whole court commented on that daring move. The old courtiers thought it was in very bad taste and Marie-Antoinette only laughed.

Such tricks were sometimes dangerous. The Empress' daughter still held a high idea of the respect due to her and did not tolerate certain familiarities. One day Lauzun discovered this to his cost. This vain Gascon had been flattered to see the Queen wearing a white heron feather he had given her, and therefore thought he could show more tender feelings. He begged for an audience and the Queen granted it, 'as she would have done to any other courtier of equally high rank', wrote Mme Campan, who recorded the scene. 'I was in the room next to the one in which he was received. Shortly after his arrival, the Queen opened the door and in a high and furious voice said, "Get out, Monsieur!" M. de Lauzun bowed very low and disappeared. The Queen was very agitated and she told me: "Never shall this man enter my apartments again!" '

Lauzun gave a completely different account of the incident. The Queen henceforth refused to receive him and ignored him when he was in her presence. Then the incorrigible courtier dressed as a footman. One day, when Marie-Antoinette was driving back from Trianon and was about to alight from her coach, 'he knelt so that she could step on one of his knees, instead of using the velvet-covered steps. Her Majesty pretended not to recognize him and called a page, saying: "Please, have this man dismissed. He does not even know how to open the door of a coach". This time, Lauzun did not insist and left the court.'

13. Versailles, the Park

14. Versailles, the Galerie des Glaces

Everyone knew of Marie-Antoinette's irresponsible actions. Rather cruel songs were written about them. She was blamed for her passing fancies for this or that person; above all, she was blamed for keeping all her graces and favours for her coterie of young people who amused her and abused her light-heartedness. Some of the nobility left Versailles. The old servants of the monarchy were back in their Paris mansions or their ancestral chateaux. Those great noblemen who had been domesticated by Louis XIV and kept in Versailles by Louis XV's skill, were now back on their lands. Sometimes the palace would be almost empty. Just one part of the palace remained alive, according to Pierre Verlet: the corner where Marie-Antoinette lived privately with her friends. She felt bored in this huge and pompous framework, so she took her group to her beloved Trianon.

### THE TRIANON SHEPHERDESS

The first stone of the Petit Trianon was laid in 1763. This pavilion, Gabriel's delightful, harmonious masterpiece, was intended for the Marquise de Pompadour. Jeanne-Antoinette hardly saw its foundations rise. It was completed in 1768 and was given to Mme du Barry. When the King died, Marie-Antoinette asked the new King to give her this country house.

'Madam,' Louis XVI is said to have answered, 'that lovely place has always been the favourite's abode. It ought, therefore, to be yours.'

The King's will was done. In the Petit Trianon, Marie-Antoinette was at home, free to do as she liked and to see whom she wanted. Even the King had to be invited. Things went so far that Marie-Antoinette had her boudoir furnished with a clever contrivance of mirrors which covered the windows and completely hid the room from the outside. Of course, people asked why she wanted such seclusion. But the gossip was without foundation. It is true that Thetis' Cave had been dug in such a way that it was possible to detect visitors from afar and escape through a secret passage if they were unpleasant. But this was only a pretext for more gossip.

Marie-Antoinette could not suffer bores. She took refuge in the Hamlet. Those light and charming buildings, designed by Mique, stood above a lake and gave the illusion of the rural life made fashionable by Jean-Jacques Rousseau: country life and wholesome nature! The Queen was not the first to rave about such structures. The hamlet built at Chantilly, on the Condé estate, was older than the one at Versailles. But Mique had reached the acmé of refinement. It was a farm in miniature. There was a genuine farmer, in charge of the unpleasant tasks. His name was Vally Bussard. He looked after the cowsheds, where quiet and beribboned cows, calves and goats lived, and even a kind white ram, imported from Switzerland.

The mill had a genuine wheel, but it never ground corn. The bailiff pronounced no sentences in his little dwelling. The Queen's house, with its billiard room, dining room, boudoir and bedrooms, was used only for ordinary amusements.

At Trianon the Queen thought she was 'a hundred leagues from court'. That was said by the Prince de Ligne. She indulged in her ordinary amusements, cards and play-acting. The most delightful theatre in the world had been contrived for her. It had cost 50,000 *livres*: an effort had been made to avoid spending too much. Sculptures were done in pasteboard, and there was more copper than gold in the decorations.

Marie-Antoinette was delighted to have her own theatre. Just like Mme de Pompadour, she loved acting. She created a 'company of lords' with her brothers-in-law and their friends. The public was limited to the Royal Family and its intimate friends. The Comtesse de Provence had refused to appear, under the pretext that it was all beneath her. They played comedies and fashionable light operas: *L'Anglaise à Bordeaux* by Favart, *Rose et Colas* and *La gageure imprévue* by Sedaine, Rousseau's *Devin du village*. The Comte d'Adhémar, who acted Colas, wobbled as he sang and the Queen had great difficulty in keeping a straight face.

Otherwise, they would play billiards or backgammon, or gather round the piano to listen to the song of the moment. The ladies went back to their tapestry frames. Towards midnight, the King would withdraw—when he had been invited. He never slept in the Queen's house.

A few splendid feasts brought a large number of courtiers to Trianon: for instance, when Joseph II came for the second time in 1781. Invitation cards were required for admittance to the gardens. There were other brilliant receptions, in 1782 for the future Czar Paul I, or for Gustav of Sweden in 1784. Those were exceptional days. Usually, Marie-Antoinette tried to preserve her privacy.

This determination increased the anger of those who were not admitted to the Queen's company. Little by little, she put aside all those who were taken up with the King's personal service. And yet she did not lack warnings: 'A big court must be accessible to many people,' the Austrian Ambassador told her. 'Otherwise hatred and jealousy stir people up and cause complaints and disgust.'

She understood and decided she would stop being only the Trianon Queen. She held her Grand Couvert again and received people at Versailles three times a week.

In spite of all these upheavals, etiquette and ceremonial were still supreme. 'The big machine was still working, but its wheels were creaking a bit,' said André Castelot.

# CHAPTER FOURTEEN

# THE TWILIGHT

Receptions for ambassadors had lost nothing of their intricate etiquette, yet one of them was a little different. The event explains its surprising features.

## A QUIET AMERICAN

March 20, 1778: the park was shaking off its dull winter garb and waking up to the rays of a still timid sun. The weather was fine but chilly. Marie Antoinette could have said: 'There are a lot of people at Versailles today!'

Courtiers repaired there from the morning onwards and the galleries were overcrowded, as during the greatest days of Louis XIV's reign; noblemen, prelates and diplomats were there with the Princes of the Blood, the dukes and the ministers. Ladies were numerous and in full court dress.

Versailles was awaiting the arrival of Mr Franklin, Envoy Extraordinary and Plenipotentiary of the young Republic of the Thirteen United States of America to his Most Christian Majesty.

A treaty had been signed between the two countries a month earlier. M. de Vergennes, in the name of France, had pledged himself to help the new allies to gain their independence. The King could therefore receive Mr Franklin officially.

The latter had not changed his dress for the reception. His steel-framed spectacles perched on his protruding nose, he wore a brown velvet suit and heavy buckled shoes. On his head he wore no wig! Never had an ambassador come before the King dressed in this fashion. But it had to be accepted: no wig was large enough to cover the broad head of the inventor of the lightning conductor. When he appeared, the crowd exclaimed: 'He is dressed like a Quaker!'

So great was Franklin's prestige that those mocking, blasé courtiers never thought of chaffing him. They were delighted. It seemed that a wind of liberty and simplicity, with portents of reform, was blowing over the palace.

With his companions, Franklin went first to M. de Vergennes. Then the Minister took him up the big staircase, while the drums of the French guards in the courtyard rolled slowly and the troops presented arms. The major of the Swiss guards had the doors of the King's apartments opened, announcing: 'The Ambassador of the Thirteen United States!'

Franklin was choking with emotion and Vergennes had almost to hold him up. A double row of courtiers filled the passage. Louis XVI took his visitor's hand and in a loud voice said: 'Gentlemen, I wish you to assure the Congress of my good will. Please let them know that I am greatly pleased by your conduct during your stay in my kingdom.'

In a faltering voice, Franklin thanked him soberly. The delegation bowed and walked towards the Great Gallery. The Ambassador could hear the 'murmur of adoration' of the young noblemen and the ladies who greeted him as the Patriarch of Liberty. They admired his wisdom and his genius.

M. de Vergennes had asked them to dinner. As soon as the crowd which was gathered near the castle saw Franklin, they shouted with joy. After a sumptuous meal, the Ambassador of the United Provinces was taken to the Queen's apartments and admitted while she was playing cards. She received him with 'marked benevolence and kindness'. At the end of the day, the philosopher drove back to the little house in Passy where he had been living for some months.

That night Versailles dreamt a beautiful dream: 'The alliance between the oldest Monarchy in Europe and the youngest Republic had been sealed,' to quote Alain Decaux.

### THE INN OF EUROPE

Franklin could have found lodgings near the palace. The town was still growing. New streets had been opened up: the Boulevard du Roi and the Boulevard de la Reine. At the outskirts, the village of Montreuil had been swallowed. The royal city had now almost fifty thousand inhabitants.

Most of them made their living out of the court. The best trade was innkeeping still. Versailles had become the inn of Europe.

Just as today, if one wants to succeed in any undertaking one has to go to Paris and kick one's heels in the ministries or administrations, or in big business enterprises, in Louis XVI's day one had to go to Versailles to contact the all-powerful businessmen and other important persons. There was a large number of inns and hotels all over the city: over 200 in fact. From the modest house where two or three people were crammed into the same room, to the hotel provided with every desirable comfort, with dressing-rooms and water-closets, the variety was enormous. This explains why, in 1789, Versailles was selected as the place to which to summon the States General: it was usual to group them round the King, but the King could move. Former assemblies had been held in the provinces, in the Loire valley. Now the housing capacity of Versailles enabled the city to accommodate a thousand deputies.

One of the most famous hotels was the *Juste,* in the rue du Vieux-Versailles. It belonged to Jacques-Pierre Delcroc and his son-in-law Etienne Touchet. In May, 1777, the Austrian Emperor Joseph II, Marie-Antoinette's brother, who travelled incognito under the name of Comte Falkenstein, stayed at the *Juste.* The crown had furnished the two big rooms which had been put at the Emperor's disposal. Courtiers wishing to see him, journalists, hoping to collect news, rushed to the hotel, which thereby acquired a high reputation. Comte Falkenstein returned to Versailles in 1781 and again stayed at the *Juste,* but curiosity had cooled a great deal.

There were other princely visitors, including the Grand-Duke Paul of Russia, the Empress Catherine's son, and his wife. They assumed the names of Comte and Comtesse du Nord, but were officially received at the palace in May 1782. The Versailles inns were at once invaded and filled for several days by a brilliant and rather mixed crowd: side by side with comtes and marquises were opera singers and dancers who had come for a gala performance on the stage of the royal theatre. At the Hôtel des Ambassadeurs in the rue de la Chancellerie the Baroness of Oberkirch, the Comtesse du Nord's close friend, the well-known dancer Guimard passed along the corridors wearing the most outrageous dress; also M. de Montyon, the Comte d'Artois' chancellor, who in that very year (1782) founded the *prix de vertu* which still bears his name.

The inns provided very good meals; the Versailles cuisine was highly reputed, less for its refinement than for its abundance. At table, the heartiest appetites grabbed the best seats and 'armed with tireless jaws, they would start masticating at once . . . Woe to the man who chews slowly! Placed between these swift, greedy cormorants, he will fast throughout the meal. Everything will have been cleared before he is served.'

An amusing English cartoon illustrates this picturesque description by Sebastien Mercier. A valet, staggering under the weight of a dish of roast meat and vegetables, approaches a table where guests, their purple noses in their plates, gobble at top speed. A kitten vainly tries to find something to eat in the dishes on the floor, and the number of overturned tin jugs is clear evidence of the fact that the guests have relished the wines of Burgundy or the Ile de France.

Less hearty travellers could be served in their rooms or, if they stayed in Versailles long enough to rent furnished flats, ask the innkeeper to bring their meals to their dwellings. This is what the Chevaliere d'Eon did; she had moved into a little pavilion in the rue de Noailles. She had been obliged by the King to put on a woman's garment. One evening she invited a few friends there, and this is the list of dishes brought by the innkeeper Lolandre to Mlle d'Eon:

A melon;
Stewed eels and a carp;
Two chickens *à l'Italienne*;
Roast veal with sorrel;
Four boiled pigeons;
A rabbit *à la poulette*;
A larded levret on the spit;
Three larded partridges on the spit;
A custard tart;
French beans;
Fried artichokes;
Whipped cream;
Pears and peaches;
Two pails of fresh walnuts;
Echaudes.

The bill came to fifty six *livres* twelve *sols* without the wine, which is reasonable. But it should be noted that there was just one roast, poultry and game, and several vegetables. The most expensive dishes were the eels and carp (nine *livres*), the partridges (five *livres*) and the whipped cream (five *livres*).

On the whole, people complained of the price of food. Already, in the reign of Louis XV, the innkeepers asked too much and people complained. Rooms in the most unattractive inns and dirty garrets were terribly expensive. In 1764, Mozart and his father, when they were received at the palace, stayed at a modest hotel, the *Cormier*, rue des Bons-Enfants. Leopold Mozart was fleeced by the proprietor, who demanded twelve *louis* for sixteen days pension.

Yet all the innkeepers did not make fortunes; some of them were rooked in their turn. Some trusted well-dressed customers. Once the proprietor of the *Croix Blanche*, Simonnet, reaped bitter fruit as a result of his benevolence. He had taken into his hotel a man who stayed two days, grandly treated three guests to supper, and disappeared with the silver cutlery. How could Simonnet have suspected anything? The man was dressed in a well-cut grey suit, and had sent his servant in advance to book his room. There was nothing to do but complain to the bailiff.

An even stranger incident happened to Bouquiet, who ran the *Image St Claude* in the avenue de Paris. He found in his stables ten horses nobody knew anything about. He told the police, who made enquiries and discovered that this suspicious troop had been left behind by a band of highwaymen for whom all the police of France were looking. The troop had spent a quiet week at the *Image St Claude*, feeding at Bouquiet's expense, and had had to run away in haste after an incident. The poor innkeeper could not even recoup himself by selling the horses. They were seized by the law.

It is understandable that the bailiff, after 1780, compelled all the hotel and innkeepers or other people who let furnished rooms to keep a register which all travellers had to sign. Versailles was not only the rendezvous of all Europe: the palace attracted all sorts of thieves and shady people in search of high profits.

### THE FALSE AND THE TRUE COMTESSES DE LA MOTTE

One had to live! At court many noblemen were still living on their wits. Others strove to obtain office. To the latter obligingly came some go-between who pretended to have very influential friends at court, even in the Queen's most intimate circles. It is strange to note that such people always succeeded in finding victims.

The Comtesse de Walburg-Frohberg, better known as the Comtesse de la Motte, was one of those clever women who shamelessly pursued her little trade at Versailles. Born in Swabia, she had married a certain Stanislas du Pont de la Motte, a sub-director of ordnance. The couple lived a perfect life, he in Paris and she in Versailles.

The Comtesse lived at the Hôtel de Fortisson, rue des Bons-Enfants, in a little furnished flat. And she 'did business', trying to find dupes and dazzling them with her alleged high position at court. She pretended to know everybody, including the Queen. People agreed to lend her money in the hope of securing a favour, the passing on of a petition or some intervention. She had such assurance that she took in several persons of quality.

It was this assurance that eventually ruined her. In order to secure even greater favour at court she did not hesitate in 1782 to slip into the file of court coaches which escorted the King and Queen to Paris. The city of Paris was receiving them to celebrate the Dauphin's birth, but Mme de la Motte had no right to be in the procession. As ill luck would have it, she was recognized. The police lieutenant was warned, made enquiries and had no difficulty in convincing the King of the Countess' doubtful dealings. A few days later the lieutenant of the Provost's guards searched her flat, seized her correspondence and, furnished with a *lettre de cachet* signed by the King, requested Mme de la Motte to follow him to the Versailles gaol.

Her correspondence was edifying—too edifying! There were letters from Vergennes, the Minister for Foreign Affairs, the Duc de Bouillon, the Prince de Polignac, the Duc de Brissac, the Marquis de la Châtre . . . and even from M. Lenoir, a lieutenant of the police. They all assured the Comtesse of their desire to please her.

That is exactly what she declared with perfect simplicity to the Provost's lieutenant-general when questioned: 'I helped friends by using the prestige of princes, princesses and other noble people who were kind to me. But I always did it for nothing, just to oblige.'

What a good soul! She did not add that she used her credit to avoid paying her tradesmen, who soon appeared with bills in their hands. She also forgot to say that for handing in a petition from the Vicomte de Roquefeuille she asked the insignificant sum of six *louis*. This was proof that she made a practice of obtaining money under false pretence, for the petition had not been delivered. Other victims preferred to keep silent.

The police merely expelled her. She knew too much and had known too many people. She returned to Germany. We have only brought this rather sordid episode to light in order to give an example of the miserable intrigues so frequent between courtiers longing for honours, and clever thieves—so often female—who only regarded them as prey. It enables us to understand the extraordinary success of another Comtesse de la Motte Valois, this time the one who conceived the whole Diamond Necklace affair.

In March, 1782, Jeanne de la Motte came to Versailles and lodged in a furnished room near the Hôtel de la Belle Image. That year, she was content to have herself presented to the Comte and Comtesse d'Artois in the palace chapel. A year later she took lodgings in the hotel. The *Belle Image* had a reputation as the lair of petitioners, journalists, penniless officers and a whole mob of interlopers in search of profit, among whom the Comtesse did not fail to mention her exalted connections and display her fine dresses.

The various partners met at the *Belle Image*, and later in the Hôtel de Jouy, into which she moved. Jeanne had succeeded in making herself known at the chateau and, by feigning illness, she attracted the attention of Madame Elisabeth. The King granted her a pension of 1,500 *livres*. It was easy for her to make the Cardinal de Rohan believe that she was a member of the Queen's circle. It should be added that the Queen admitted into her circle persons of doubtful repute, whose real identity she sometimes did not know.

In fact, during the night of August 10–11th, when the well-known meeting took place, all the members of the party had registered at Gobert's hotel under false names. How many shady characters did the same thing when they came to Versailles!

It is not necessary to tell again the story of the necklace, which was the one topic discussed for a whole year, to the point that it began to shake the throne. Jeanne de Valois' intrigues, the silliness of a vain cardinal, hurt because the Queen scorned him, and no influence on daily life. There is no reason to be shocked because, one summer night, in one of the park bowers, a pretty wench, well-dressed and groomed by the Comtesse herself, tried to be taken for Marie-Antoinette and performed a reconciliation scene with the Cardinal. Everyone at the palace knew that the Queen loved to gather a few friends and at nightfall desport herself with them away from interference. It is not impossible that the Queen, told of the secret meeting, was a witness of it, hidden among the bushes, seeking a laugh at the Cardinal's expense.

This was her one mistake. The plot was on foot, but she knew nothing of it. She did not know that the Comtesse de la Motte had suggested to Rohan that, as a proof of his reconciliation with Marie-Antoinette, he should act as go-between to purchase the fabulous necklace Louis XVI had refused to buy.

It is surprising to see how easily the Cardinal was swindled. The Queen's promissory letters were signed 'Marie-Antoinette de France' and Rohan did not know she never signed in that fashion! This courtier, who had frequented Versailles for so many years, had not the faintest idea how the Queen checked the numberless papers submitted to her. The lowest clerk of any ministry could have uncovered the trick.

The next episode took place at the *Belle Image*. On February 1, 1785, the Cardinal received the necklace from the jeweller Auguste Bohmer. Mme de la Motte was present. The Queen's messenger was announced; Rohan hid in the Comtesse's alcove and vaguely saw the man to whom she respectfully handed the casket. This man was her accomplice, Retaux de Vilette. A few days later, the necklace was taken to pieces and the diamonds sold in England.

The scandal broke on August 15, 1785. A few days earlier, the jeweller Bohmer, as the Queen passed by, handed her his bill and showed her the alleged commitment. In this incident we can see one more surprising detail, that it was now possible to talk freely to the Queen in the galleries of Versailles. The Queen was aghast. She told Louis XVI at once, and the Baron de Breteuil, Minister of the King's Household, in charge of the police. Breteuil detested Rohan and this was an opportunity to destroy his enemy. He convinced the King of the Cardinal's complicity. It would have been wise to silence the whole affair or to handle it with the greatest discretion, but the contrary advice prevailed. While the Cardinal was about to celebrate the Assumption and was already in full sacerdotal dress on his way to the chapel, two guards approached him. They asked him to go to the King's room, where Louis XVI was waiting for him. The explanation took place in the presence of the Queen.

'I can see that I have been cruelly deceived,' muttered Rohan.

'You may go, Sir,' the King replied.

Rohan left with M de Breteuil. Courtiers, who had already heard of the incident, were crowding into the Great Gallery and the Oeil-de-Bœuf. Then a voice was heard 'which startled everybody': 'Arrest the Cardinal!' That very evening, Rohan slept in the Bastille.

Now the incident was public and its repercussions were enormous. The Rohans, who were numerous and powerful, reacted. The whole aristocracy sided with them, and there were few people to defend the Queen. Parliament was only too happy to oppose the King. The thieves were condemned and the Cardinal acquitted; it was a terrible insult to the Queen. She was in tears and poured out her sorrow in a letter to the Duchesse de Polignac: 'This judgment is a fearful insult. I am bathed in tears of sorrow and despair.' But the authenticity of the note is questionable.

The pamphleteers scribbled to their hearts' content. There were even some pamphlets in which the Queen was reputed to be with child by the Cardinal:

> Pour certain cardinal elle entre en passion,
> Rohan, tout glorieux d'une aussi belle flamme,
> Fait avec ses catins bientôt diversion,
> Ne quitte plus la cour, a le bonheur de plaire,
> Obtient une entrevue, a chez la reine accès,
> Enfin couche avec elle et la rend bientot mère.
> Ce pauvre cardinal n'eut pas un long succès:
> Toinon s'était donnée, elle voulut se vendre.[1]

It was no use for Marie-Antoinette to become more sober, to abandon her crazy life, and to be seen with her children more often.

---

[1] 'She conceived a passion for a certain cardinal; Rohan, proud of such a noble flame, made a change from her former lovers; he did not move from court, was lucky enough to please, was granted an interview, admitted to the Queen's apartments, finally went to bed with her and gave her a child. The poor cardinal was not happy for long. Toinon had given herself and now she wanted her reward.'

The evil was done. The affair of the diamond necklace rang the death knell of the monarchy.

## THE QUEEN AND HER PAGE

The lesson had been so hard that the Queen tried to reform even the conduct of her servants. She sought the company of wise and careful people, listened to the advice of her sisters-in-law and scolded her pages. The latter were so surprised by the sudden change that they looked elsewhere for the amusements that were no longer to be found at Versailles. She had them summoned and she admonished them.

The Comte de Tilly, in his *Memoires*, wrote about the new attitude. He had begged for an audience. One of his country cousins was looking for an office and Tilly had agreed to hand his request to the Queen. She received the page in her Little Apartments. As he entered, she launched at once into an attack:

'Good afternoon. Where have you dined?'

'At Mme de Beauvillier's, Madam.'

'My Mme de Beauvillier?'

'No, Madame. Madame Adélaïde's.'

'Does she often entertain at dinner?'

'Yes, **Madame**. At least, she does for me, as she knew me when I was a child and she doesn't stand upon ceremony with me.'

'Had M. de Champcenetz been at Versailles, you would have dined with him. A pretty company!'

'Madame, he has some wit and is very amusing.'

'How charming! That will take him a long way!'

M. de Champcenetz was reputed to be one of the court rakes and he was reproached for his debauched life. Marie-Antoinette returned to the attack at once.

'Well, what do you want?'

'Madame, a gentleman has arrived here . . . a sort of magistrate, with whom my parents and I are very friendly; he would like an office in Alençon: it is vacant. Here it is, on that bit of paper . . . It depends on M. de Miromesnil. My gentleman is a very good sort and I would be delighted if he could secure that employment. If the Queen would say a word to the Keeper of the Seals, it is obvious . . .' Tilly did not end his sentence.

'Well? It is obvious . . .'

'Yes, Madame; he could not say no.'

'I will write. Give me that paper and come back tomorrow at half-past three. The letter will be ready. Goodbye.'

'I don't know how to express my gratitude to the Queen.'

'By behaving well.'

The ease of that dialogue is surprising. This was how a mere page addressed the Queen of France at the end of the eighteenth century! Of course, Tilly came from an excellent family; nevertheless he was only a page. Yet he spoke in a playful, almost impertinent tone: '. . . a gentleman, a kind of magistrate . . .' He did not know quite what his friend was seeking and he had put it down 'on a scrap of paper' which he handed the Queen. She promised the letter of recommendation the next day. A century earlier the highest nobleman in the kingdom would have lost face and stammered at meeting Louis XIV. The old court had gone. Etiquette itself was disappearing.

Yet Marie-Antoinette insisted that her pages were well turned out; Mme Elisabeth and the Comtesse d'Artois also watched over their servants' lives. The letters of a chambermaid give us unpublished evidence of this.

## A PROVINCIAL GIRL AT COURT

Rose de Mamiel, the daughter of a widow with three children, a native of Pont-à-Mousson, had been lucky enough to secure the post of a chambermaid to the Comtesse d'Artois. She was scarcely twenty when she left home to take up service at court. Her mother, rather worried to see her go away and dreading the dangers which threatened a pretty girl, sent her plenty of good advice. To this provincial lady the royal palace seemed a den of vice.

'Never go out without being escorted by a valet, or in a sedan chair. Do not fail in your duty to your adorable mistress . . . and above all be very careful. Think, my dear child, that you are going to be watched by everybody, that your conduct will be constantly observed, and that the slightest fault, however trivial, may deprive you of your post and rob you of the Princess' kindness, strike me dead and dishonour you and your family.'

She added: 'Never be intimate with a man and beware of women. It is as a friend and not as a mother that I give you this advice.' She was in fact a good mother, who knew all about the intrigues of the lesser servants as well as the servants of the great. Mme de Mamiel, who was rather hard up, dreaded that Rose would fail to please. She often returned to the subject in later letters: 'My daughter, you are now in your duty week. Tell me if everything is still all right and if people are nice to you.' 'People' was the Comtesse d'Artois, reckoned as 'adorable' at Pont-à-Mousson. In fact, Marie-Thérèse de Savoie was plain and dull, but through her civil income she was able to pay her chambermaids properly, so she was 'adorable'.

Mlle de Mamiel soon discovered all the means used at court to make extra money. Advised by her mother, she thought of exchanging her silver buckles for fashionable necklaces. Life was expensive. A chambermaid had to dress herself according to etiquette and change frequently. The problem of new clothes was often mentioned in her correspondence:

'It seems you are only allowed to wear court mourning. If that is so, my dear, do inform yourself and buy a little dress of some inexpensive material which need not be lined, or one of those little taffetas which are lined and can be worn also in winter. One dress will be enough, as you will not be in service more than three times this season.'

There was talk of going with the court to Fontainebleau. Rose de Mamiel was to accompany her mistress. At once, her mother wrote to her to be even more careful:

'I am delighted, my dear child, that you will make the journey to Fontainebleau. First, it will certainly provide you with some amusement, and I hope it will help you to get to know your adorable mistress better, as you will be closer to her. My dear daughter, I pray you to be more careful, more reserved, more attentive, more helpful, more polite than ever, and to avoid any absentmindedness. Do partake of the pleasures, but with every possible decency. Above all, make not the slightest indiscretion, for all eyes will be on you; your most trivial action will be discussed, controlled and may possibly make people jealous . . . Above all, do not get too familiar with gentlemen who may say nice things to you . . . See that you are respected without being haughty.'

On the journey everything went well. 'I am glad to hear you are very much liked. You were right to avoid M. Graibe. Continue that way and avoid all dangerous company: that is what ruins young people . . .'

Rolse had avoided M. Graibe, who pursued her. Eventully, she fell in love with one of the Comte d'Artois' life guards, M. de Maret d'Abancourt, whom she married in July 1784. The young couple remained in the Comte and Comtesse's service until the Revolution. They had been given a pension. It seemed that they were happy. They had two children. The chambermaid had not been caught in the snares of Versailles.

### A NEW KIND OF SPECTACLE

Rose de Mamiel may have seen one of the first aerostatic experiments in the world. It took place a few months after her arrival at the palace, in September 1783.

Etienne de Montgolfier had been allowed by the King to show his invention at Versailles. As Louis XVI was fascinated by all new inventions, he promised to be present when the balloon was launched. It had been brought into the ministers' courtyard. On Friday, September 19th, the crowd began to gather by 7 a.m. and it was so dense that a line of French guards had to be called in to keep it back. Journalists reckoned that 120,000 spectators were present.

As the Comte de Duras had suggested, Montgolfier had given the King a short note explaining the nature of the experiment. The whole Royal Family was present. The first to arrive was the Comte d'Artois, who prided himself in his love for novelties; with him was a large group of friends. Then came the Comte and Comtesse de Provence with Mme Elisabeth. Finally, to a roll of drums the King and the Queen arrived, preceded by a detachment of French and Swiss guards. They were followed by the usual courtiers. The sovereigns talked for a while with the inventor, who gave them information. They examined the way in which the balloon was inflated, after which, the rules of daily life being always strict, they returned to the palace to hear mass. Montgolfier took this opportunity to hurry the preparations for his ascent.

Coming out of the chapel, Marie-Antoinette, 'with all that the court reckoned most brilliant', went on the terrace of the south aisle, where a large tent had been erected, while Louis XVI was in the big bed-chamber balcony to watch the take-off. Three animals had been put into the gondola, a sheep, a cock and a duck. In conquering the air man worked carefully, and our lesser brethren paid the cost of the early attempts.

15. Petit Trianon, the Hamlet

Louis XVI, by Callet

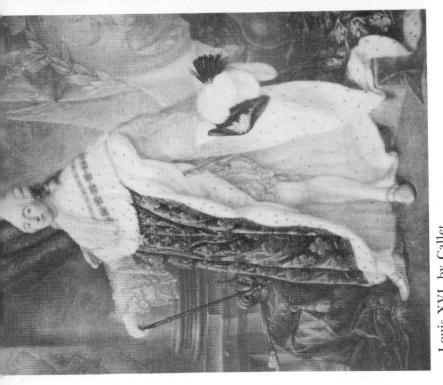

16. Marie Antoinette, by Callet

At 12.45 the King gave the signal. A first cannon shot announced that the inflation of the sphere was beginning. The crowd fell silent. A second shot, seven minutes later, announced that it was complete. At last, following a third shot, the men who had been holding the ropes let go and the *montgolfier* rose majestically into the air. Tremendous applause greeted the flight.

The balloon took a north-easterly direction. It did not go very far and Louis XVI could follow its course with his telescope. It returned to earth in the woods of Vaucresson, at the Font-Maréchal cross-roads, three kilometres from the Place d'Armes. Two keepers rushed to find it. They found the sheep calmly grazing in its cage. The cock had fought with it a little. The sheep was given an honourable resting place in the King's menagerie.

At the palace that day the flight was the main topic of conversation. After dinner, Montgolfier went to see Mme d'Ossun, the new lady-in-waiting, who had just succeeded Mme de Polignac in the Queen's favour. He has left an interesting description of his reception:

'I was admitted into a lovely apartment under the roof. In the second room, in a pleasant half-light, sat a charming row of some twenty to thirty ladies, who might have served as models for painters who worked to depict the Olympian gathering. They were rehearsing a new opera by Sacchini.[1] Mme d'Ossun said the most flattering things to me and made me sit to listen to the music.'

Montgolfier found it difficult to get away, for the King was awaiting details concerning the state of the machine. Montgolfier then thought he was free to go back to his friends, but someone followed him with the request: 'The Queen wants to see you.' He returned to the castle, and was met by the Maréchal de Duras: 'I sent them to find you: you have kept the Queen waiting!' Marie-Antoinette came out of her apartments and listened 'with kindness' to the inventor's story.

As everything in the palace 'ends with a song', someone at once composed *L'ariette de la nouvelle sphere aerostatique* or *Le globe volant lancé à Versailles*:

> Tout Paris court, ou dérobe
> Au devoir le plus urgent,

1 *Chimène*, which was performed at Fontainebleau in November.

*Pour voir ses rois et le globe*
*Le nouveau globe volant.*[1]

## THE END OF A WORLD

This was life at court. France was growing restless and about to erupt. M Necker published the nation's accounts and denounced without ambiguity the waste and extravagance of a régime which could not restrain itself. Louis XVI listened anxiously. Marie-Antoinette sought solace at Trianon with Fersen. Courtiers and office holders changed none of their ways. In 1787 the Vicomte de Chateaubriand was admitted to the honours of court; after the usual presentations he was lucky enough to be invited to the hunt and put on the proper uniform—a grey habit, red jacket and breeches, top-boots, a hunting knife at the belt, and a three-cornered hat with a gold band. He was present at the King's departure. Etiquette was still the same: 'Drums rolled, weapons clattered, orders were shouted, and a voice cried "The King". He came out and climbed into his coach. We climbed into other coaches behind him.'

The hunt took place in the forest of St Germain. Chateaubriand admired this brilliant, colourful scene, but could not hide from himself the fact that it was rather out-of-date.

'The coaches halted in the forest; the guards, the groups of men and women, the packs controlled with difficulty by the grooms, dogs barking, horses whinnying, horns sounding, created a very lively scene. Our King's hunt recalled the old and the new habit of the monarchy at the same time, the rough pastimes of Clodion, Chilperic or Dabobert and the gallantry of François I, Henri IV and Louis XIII.'

Back in the palace, Louis XVI was feeling gay and happy, and began to relate the incidents of the day. There was nothing new about this: there were incidents every day, and Louis XVI contrived them in order to vary this daily routine. Chateaubriand was bored and refused to take part in the ceremony of removing the King's boots. 'Instead of changing my clothes to take part in the

[1] 'All Paris seems to neglect its most urgent duty, in order to see its sovereigns and the new flying globe.'

*debotte*, the time of triumph and favour, I threw myself into my coach and returned to Paris, glad at last to be rid of my honours and my worries.'

These hurried journeys through the rooms in order, to meet and greet, in a strict order of precedence, the first gentlemen, the princes, the ladies-in-waiting and the princesses, who alone could take the newcomer to their masters or mistresses, this stiff decorum and aimless business had wearied René. He went back to Brittany, certain he had witnessed the vain turmoil of a dying world.

In fact the crisis was deepening. Finally, the King summoned the States General to meet at Versailles on May 4, 1789.

The opening ceremony, according to Pierre Verlet, was the last great spectacle of the *Ancien Régime*. On May 3rd, the King-at-Arms and the heralds proclaimed at the cross-roads that the general procession and the mass of the Holy Ghost would take place the next day.

The deputies from the three orders met in the church of Notre-Dame. The King arrived at ten in the morning, surrounded by the Princes of the Blood. Marie-Antoinette arrived shortly afterwards and was met by the Princesses of the Blood. The procession set out: first the clergy of the Versailles parishes, surrounded by guards, then the deputies (those of the Third Order were in black breeches, black silk cloaks, white muslin cravats and bands, while the aristocracy was dressed in the most sumptuous of court costumes). The clergy walked before the King and the high Crown officers. The Queen was on the left, with white plumes in her hair. The canopy was carried by the Counts of Artois, Provence, Angoulème and Berry. The holy sacrament was carried by the Archbishop of Paris. The procession wound slowly from Notre-Dame to Saint-Louis. The streets were lined by a huge crowd which murmured or was silent when the Queen passed, but cheered the Duc d'Orléans.

At St Louis, in his sermon, the Bishop of Nancy dared to make a public attack on court luxury and the prodigality of its members. On returning to her apartments, Marie-Antoinette, who had controlled herself so far, broke down and sobbed. It was very difficult to comfort her.

The opening of the States took place in the Menus-Plaisirs. Thereafter things developed quickly, though they effected little change in royal routine. Late in the evening, when the Bastille was taken, the Grand Master of the Robes, the Duc de la

Rochefoucauld-Liancourt, created a great sensation when he decided he would wake the King to tell him what had happened. Wake the King in the middle of the night? Such a sacrilege was unprecedented at Versailles! The Duke succeeded in forcing his way into the King's room, and this famous dialogue took place:

'So there is a rebellion?'

'No, Sire, it is a revolution.'

This revolution was to carry the court of Versailles into oblivion. Several noblemen were already emigrating: the Comte d'Artois, the Prince d'Hénin, the Marquis de Vaudreuil, all the Condés, the Duras, the Mortemarts, the Harcourts. The wind of rebellion was blowing through some of the men of the military household. As they had gone over to the people in July, the French guards were no longer on duty at the castle. On the other hand, the Life Guards and the Swiss were still completely loyal.

October 5th and 6th followed. The Paris mob was inflamed by uncontrolled rumours. The tricolour cockade had been trampled on at a banquet given by the Life Guards in the Versailles Opera to the officers of the Flanders Regiment, which had arrived as reinforcement. The King had refused to sanction the Declaration of the Rights of Man; the bakeries were short of bread. The mob decided to march upon Versailles. Several thousands of armed men and shouting women made for the palace.

In the chateau uncertainty reigned. The gates had been carefully locked. Several ministers advised the King to retire to Rambouillet, but Necker was against this. A delegation of women was received by the King and was overcome by his kindness. Courtiers and servants gathered fearfully in the Great Gallery. By 10 p.m. La Fayette arrived, heralded by the sound of cannon rolling over the Versailles pavement. He ascended the stairs, traversed the drawing-rooms, and as he passed a courtier observed:

'Here comes Cromwell.'

'Cromwell would not have entered alone,' answered La Fayette.

He assured the King that he could keep order. His men were exhausted by seven hours marching in the rain, so he decided to replace them by French guards who had accompanied the people of Paris, and with the King's permission were allowed to resume their duties at Versailles. They were on guard during the night. At 5.30 in the morning, according to an invariable rule, they opened the gates. For although rebellion threatened at the gates, the castle service continued as usual. Orders were carried out: the Marble Courtyard gate was opened at the prescribed time.

What happened next is well-known. The rioters rushed across the courtyard and raced up the staircase to the apartments of the Queen. Half-dressed, Marie-Antoinette was just able to flee. The Life Guards who tried to stop the invasion were killed or wounded. La Fayette returned. He had slept at the Noailles mansion of his parents-in-law. The King and the Queen came out on to the balcony, and the King gave orders to get the coaches ready to drive to Paris. These scenes have nothing to do with the daily life of the court of Versailles: they merely mark its end.

The procession left at 1.30 in the afternoon. There had been no mass in the chapel that day.

\*　　\*　　\*

Versailles was deserted. During the days which followed the Royal Family's departure everyone fled. Yet for some of them the return to the Tuileries might have seemed only temporary. At the Superintendence of Buildings, as if nothing had happened, alterations that were to be carried out during the following years were still being planned, but Louis XVI himself, it seemed, had no illusions.

'You are the master here,' he had said to La Tour du Pin, the War Minister. 'Try and save my poor Versailles.'

The monarchy had already withdrawn from the chateau.

The curtain had fallen on the great daily performance that had lasted for over a century in a scene created by Louis XIV, maintained and embellished by his successors. The stage was to remain empty. The actors who moved under our eyes have gone for ever and they only survive as those ghosts that are evoked by Alfred de Musset:

> Dites-nous, marches gracieuses,
> Les rois, les princes, les prélats
> Et les belles ambitieuses
> Dont vous avez marqué les pas ...[1]

---

[1] 'Tell us, Oh graceful stairs! about the kings, the princes, the prelates and the ambitious beauties whose steps you have counted' (Musset, *Sur trois marches de marbre rose*).

# SOURCES AND BIBLIOGRAPHY

An inventory of sources and a full bibliography of books about the court of Versailles would require dozens of pages. We did not think it necessary to list them, but only to give the main sources, archives, chronicles or memoirs, and the main books we have consulted.

The *Série E* of the Seine-et-Oise Archives and especially the *Série B* provided us with most of the unpublished documents we have used in this book.

We have arranged the authors in accordance with the plan of the book itself: the period before the court moved into Versailles; the courts of Louis XIV, Louis XV and XVI. For each of these reigns there are two paragraphs, the first for the chronicles and memoirs and the second for modern works, and of these only the most recent.

A first section is devoted to general works. We have avoided giving a full bibliography of all that has been written about the palace. Pierre Verlet's book, which provides everything necessary, is the result of thirty years of research. It would discourage anyone from writing about Versailles, except that some inexhaustible subjects can always produce something new, when drawn from a different angle. Hence, this book.

# INDEX